FROM SEASON TO SEASON

Sports as American Religion

Edited by Joseph L. Price

Mercer University Press

ISBN 0-86554-694-0
MUP/H513

© 2001 Mercer University Press
6316 Peake Road
Macon, Georgia 31210-3960
All rights reserved.
Printed in the United States.

First Edition.

Book and jacket design by Burt&Burt Studio.

∞The paper used in this publication meets the minimum
requirements of American National Standard for Information
Sciences—Permanence of Paper for Printed Library Materials,
ANSI Z39.48-1992.

CIP data are available from the Library of Congress

Table of Contents

Introduction

Sports and Religion in America

Baseball

Football

Basketball

Hockey and Wrestling

Conclusion

Contributors

Charles S. Adams is associate professor of English at Whittier College. His principal field is American literature, especially the nineteenth century, with a particular interest in the genre of autobiography. However, much of his recent work is in areas of contemporary popular culture, particularly sports. A longtime Mariners' and Seahawks' fan, he is currently working on a book on the presence of baseball in American literary culture.

Lois Daly, a native Hoosier and consequently a basketball junkie, is a professor of religious studies at Siena College. An avid fan of the college game and the WNBA, she connects to her sports interest regularly in her role as a "soccer mom," having also served as the manager of the under-ten girls team for her daughter. Currently, she is pursuing interests in religion and popular culture, particularly the religious dimensions of science fiction literature and episodes of the Star Trek series.

Tom Faulkner is professor of comparative religion at Dalhousie University in Halifax, Nova Scotia. In a grudge match in 1967 in Varsity Arena, he scored his team's only goal against the reigning Canadian University Hockey Champions. His joy was delivered a high stick by the fact that the camps scored 37 goals. Subsequently, he resumed his earlier career as a fan.

Paul Christopher Johnson is assistant professor in the Department of Religious Studies and adjunct professor in anthropology at the University of Missouri, Columbia. His fascination with sports began with the short story "The Most Dangerous Game," and ever since he has figured sports are the sublimated, "civilized" form of the war and the hunt.

Lonnie D. Kliever is professor of religious studies at Southern Methodist University. His interest in sports has personal and professional dimensions. A sports fan all his life, he has studied the play element in culture as it has intersected contemporary theology and sports ethics, and he has written about it in his book *The Shattered Spectrum*. He also served as SMU's Faculty Athletic Representative to the NCAA, leading the investigation of reports of violations that led to the "death penalty" for SMU's football program in 1987.

James Mathisen is professor of sociology at Wheaton College (Illinois). At some point after an undistinguished career as a middle distance runner in high school and college, he began teaching sociology of religion and sociology of sport in the 1970s. Having first written about sports and religion in 1986, he co-authored *Muscular Christianity: Evangelical Protestants and the Development of American Sports* in 1999. As a life-long Cubs' and Packers' fan, he continues to attend, according to his wife Sharon, far too many games.

Bonnie Miller-McLemore is professor of pastoral theology and counseling at Vanderbilt University. Author of *Also a Mother: Work and Family as Theological Dilemma* and co-author of *From Culture Wars to Common Ground: Religion and the American Family Debate*, she grew up in a household with two sports-loving brothers and a father who was a sports physician. Now she regularly stands on the sidelines watching three active sons compete in various games.

Joseph L. Price is professor of religious studies at Whittier College. Co-editor of two theological handbooks, he devotes much of his scholarly attention to the spiritual significance of secular artifacts, texts, and rituals in popular culture. As the son of a Baptist minister and a life-long fan of most sports other than auto racing, he most often connects his appreciation of ritual studies with sports by performing the national anthem at Major League Baseball games.

Peter Williams is College English Professor at the College of Morris (New Jersey). Son of the golden-era sportswriter Joe Williams, who was also one of the honorary pallbearers at the funeral of Babe Ruth, Peter is editor of *The Joe Williams Baseball Reader* and author of *When the Giants Were Giants* and *The Sports Immortals*.

Acknowledgments

The publication of this collection of essays culminates two decades of invigorating conversations with friends and colleagues, especially the authors who have contributed to this volume. Several of the essays were written initially for presentation at various scholarly meetings of the Society for the Scientific Study of Religion, the Network for the Study of Implicit Religion, and the Popular Culture Association. My firts essay on sports and religion was conceived during a 1983 Dodgers-Phillies game at Dodger Stadium, where our transcendent perch in the fifth deck behing home plate prompted Glenn Yocum and me to muse about the similarities between the pitcher's mound and myths connected with the sacred mountain. I am indebted to Glenn, a historian of South Asian religious traditions, for his exemplary departmental mentorship and colleagiality during the last two decades, throughout which he has consistently nurtured my work on sports and religion. My own work has been stimulated by students in my course "Sport, Play, and Ritual." The stimulus for developing the interdisciplinary course was a prolonged discussion that began during graduate study at the University of Chicago with compassionate friend and creative theologian James R. Price III. Throughout early stages of course development, my good colleague Hilmi Ibrahim, a sociologist of sport and recreation, was persistent and expansive in his support of my exploration of the religious significance of play and sports. In more recent years, literary scholar Charles Adams, whose dramatic reading of WWF wrestling appears in this volume, has provided consistent encouragement and criticism as he has attended numerous presentations that I have made. Philosopher David Paulsen has also rendered invaluable assistance in the growth of this project, as he sponsored a series of lectures at Brigham Young University that enabled me to develop substantial portions of the first and last chapters. The improvement of the volume can be credited to historian William Trent Foley, a long-time friend who offered detailed suggestions about essays and their organization. And Donald Musser, with whom I have collaborated on previous editorial projects and fishing expeditions, has been a silent partner in the shaping of this collection. Many of the provocative insights in this volume can be attributed to these fine friends.

Although several of the essays were conceived and written a decade ago, their imaginative perspectives and provocative perceptions reflect a growing scholarly sensitivity to the significance of sports in American culture. I am grateful to several authors, journals, and publishers for permission to reprint previously published works, versions of works, and portions of works.

"God and Games in Modern Culture," by Lonnie D. Kliever, originally appeared in *The World and I*, October 1988. Reprinted with permission of the author and publisher.

"The Super Bowl as Religious Festival," by Joseph L. Price, originally appeared in *The Christian Century*, 22 February 1984. Reprinted with permission of publisher.

"The Final Four as Final Judgment: The Cultural Significance of the NCAA Basketball Championship," by Joseph L. Price, originally appeared in the *Journal of Popular Culture*, spring 1991. Reprinted with permission of editor.

"A Puckish Reflection on Religion in Canada," by Tom Sinclair-Faulkner, originally appeared in *Religion and Culture in Canada*, ed. Peter Slater (Waterloo, Ontario: Wilfred Laurier University Press, 1977). Reprinted with permission of author and publisher.

"The Fetish and McGwire's Balls," by Paul C. Johnson, originally appeared in *The Journal of the American Academy of Religion*, vol. 68, June 2000. Reprinted with permission of editor.

"An American Apotheosis: Sports as Popular Religion," originally was published in Bruce David Forbes and Jeffrey H. Mahan, eds., *Religion and Popular Culture in America* (Berkeley: University of California Press, 2000). Reprinted with permission of publisher.

And portions of "American Sport as Folk Religion: Examining a Test of Its Strength," by James A. Mathisen, originally appeared in his essay "From Civil Religion to Folk Religion: The Case of American Sport," in *Sport and Religion*, ed. Shirl Hoffman (Champaign IL: Human Kinetics, 1992). Reprinted with permission of editor.

I am particularly appreciative for the support that Andy Manis, Marc Jolley, and Mercer University Press have offered in the publication of this volume. Without their assistance, this volume would not have come to fruition. And finally, the enthusiastic encouragement and patient support offered by my wife Bonnie and two sons, Jared and David, have been invaluable. They have tolerated my passionate devotion to favorite teams like the Bears. They have consoled me in times of agonizing defeat, like the Yankees' playoff elimination by the Mariners. And they have celebrated with me as "my team" has won, as when Kentucky came back against Utah.

Joseph L. Price
Whittier College
January 2000

INTRODUCTION

FERVENT FAITH
SPORTS AS RELIGION IN AMERICA

Joseph L. Price

During the early summer of 1994, frenzy, fervor, and fanaticism were words often applied to sports fans. Soccer fans expressed their devotion to national teams seeking to win the World Cup. New York Rangers fans anxiously followed their team, which finally overcame a half-century jinx and won the Stanley Cup for the first time since World War II. Even commuters and television gawkers in Los Angeles crowded freeways and perched on overpasses to display signs encouraging sports hero O. J. Simpson in his slow-speed flight from police. In the pre-game telecast of fans' preparations for the Stanley Cup's final game, ESPN included a clip taken earlier that day in one of the Gothic New York cathedrals near Madison Square Garden, the site of the Stanley Cup final game. Amid the flickering candles was propped a hand-lettered card pleading for mercy and victory for the Rangers. Several hours later as the Rangers celebrated their victory over the Canucks, fans in Madison Square Garden held signs aloft that read "Now I can die in peace" and "All is forgiven." In all of these examples, the sports fans manifest a spiritual dimension in their sports allegiances.

One of the most telling indications of the religious significance of sports for contemporary American culture is the spirit that underlies a quip by Martin Marty, who suggests that the definition of an atheist is a person who does not care about the outcome in a football game between Notre Dame and SMU. Certainly, sports fans exhibit a kind of devotion that often is described in terms of religious dedication or intensity. For there seems to be a sense of ultimate devotion associated with the fanaticism of certain fans in their support for their teams. One example of the extreme devotion and obsession of fans is the tragic death of Andres Escobar, the Colombian soccer player who was assassinated upon returning to his home country for having errantly scored a goal for the opposing United States team in the World Cup competition during the summer of 1994. More commonly and acceptably, the intensity of fans' dedication and devotion is manifest in the size of wagers that they place on their favorite teams, in the extent to which they will go—the sacrifices that they will make—in order to make a pilgrimage of sorts to the site of an important game, and in the ludic masking that they often assume in order to establish full identity with their teams or the teams' mascots. And for the majority of fans who attend games vicariously through mediated means or who follow reports of games, there is often a sense of religious fervor attached to their devotion. Following the 1999 World Series, for example, owner George Steinbrenner of the victorious New York Yankees touched upon this dimension as he noted that "a lot of people depend on us [the Yankees] for their daily feelings. Our job is to make them happy."[1]

Given the range of historical, geographical, and cultural experiences and expressions of sport as reflecting religious rituals, myths, and spiritual exercises, it should not be too surprising that a number of scholars in various academic disciplines have begun to analyze contemporary American sports by exploring their connections to ritual and myth and by examining the spiritual dimensions of fan behavior. Throughout the past decade, in fact, such "religious" interpretations of sports activities and fans responses have gained increasing recognition and respect among scholars through presentations at various meetings of learned societies in religious studies and American studies (with papers on the Super Bowl having been read at meetings of the American Academy of Religion, with a session devoted to religion and sports at one of the annual meetings of the Society for the Scientific Study of Religion, and with papers regularly read at meetings of the American Culture Association). A willingness to explore various religious studies interpretations of sports has also increased with publication of several essays (a few of which are included in this volume) in journals and periodicals such as *The Christian Century*,[2] *Aethlon*, and *Journal of Popular Culture*. And in disciplinarily oriented textbooks and anthologies, sociologists of sport have led the way in addressing the convergence of sport and religion; exemplary among the efforts is the chapter on "The Religious Dimensions of Sport" by Eldon Snyder and Elmer Spreitzer in *Social Aspects of Sport*,[3] and the anthology of essays edited by D. Stanley Eitzen, *Sport in Contemporary Society*.[4] In more recent years sociologists of religion have also begun to pay attention to the religious function and impact of sports.[5] Finally, philosophers of sport have also issued collections of essays that consider specifically "Sport and the Religious,"[6] and at times they have dealt with fundamental issues that prompt religious interpretations, such as considering the topic of the metaphysics of sport.[7]

While a number of sociologists in the 1970s were beginning to explore conceptual and functional connections between sport and religion, several theologians, building upon the foundational work of Johan Huizinga (who had analyzed the character of play in terms of its liminality and its potentially transformative power),[8] began to develop theologies of play. First among these was Harvey Cox, whose *Feast of Fools*[9] bounced surprisingly like an overkicked ball into the schoolyard of theologians, prompting some of them to set off part of their theological turf as a playground—a liminal sort of space where other conceptual rules might apply, where traditional relationships could be shifted, and where new outcomes might be entertained. In the same year that Cox published his celebration of a festive reversal of traditional modes of thinking theologically, Robert Neale published *In Praise of Play*, which celebrates the possibility that theology can take account of the imaginative dimensions of the universal search for God.[10] A few years after the appearance of the works by Cox and Neale, Hugo Rahner produced *Men at Play*, which sought to reaffirm the ancient play spirit that had characterized classic Greek poets and early Christian believers.[11]

Although each of these works in some ways anticipates a more imaginative way of conceiving and construing theology than the predominantly neo-orthodox and neo-Thomist models that immediately preceded them, none of them moves to a point of affirming the distinctive character of humans as *homo ludens*—the person as player, as Huizinga had done in the mid-1950s. Such a celebration was forthcoming, however, in the incredibly joyful, lyrical, and playful celebration of sports that Michael Novak offered in 1976, *The Joy of Sports*.[12] Throughout the book Novak revels in various acts of sporting competition and in the admiration of sports heroes. His chapter on basketball, "The Black Myth: Basketball as Jazz," is so exuberant that it evokes images of Magic Johnson leading a Laker fast-break.[13] Novak's work often resembles the effusive field notes of an enthusiastic participant-observer who has experienced a spiritually transforming and enriching set of exercises. In short, *The Joy of Sports* is a spirituality of sports.

    In the same year that Novak published his celebration of sports, James Michener produced a 550-page treatise on the status of sports in America. Focusing on sports institutions and athletes in the United States, Michener examines the economics and ethics of sports, he comments upon the professionalization of sports even in the supposedly amateur realm of collegiate athletics, and he identifies, quite briefly, several possible points of convergence between religion and sport. In his few remarks on the significance of religion for American sports, Michener focuses on the invocation that the Reverend Richard J. Bailar offered on Monday, 2 December 1974 prior to a game between the Miami Dolphins and the Cincinnati Bengals. The controversy erupted around the address of God as "Creator God: Father and Mother of us all." Michener's evaluation of the religious connections with professional football is oriented toward the kinds of religious services that the Fellowship of Christian Athletes sponsored prior to games. In his comments on sports and religion, Michener does not celebrate, like Novak, the mysteries and miracles of sports accomplishments; rather, he remarks on traditional forms of piety as influencing players and fans in their preparation for games.[14]

    During the late 1970s two literary scholars began to interpret sporting events as texts, and therewith and therein they began to recognize the potential religious import of the games as spectacles. In his analysis in *The Big Game*, Edwin Cady examines the ways in which college games in particular provide a cultural spectacle for intensifying and celebrating rivalries. Yet Cady contends that the Big Game is not in itself fundamentally religious since it is not, as he perceives it, essentially sacramental. Nevertheless, he allows that the Big Game might *feel* sacramental in approximately the same way that good art does, and he identifies the Big Game as being "the most vitally folklorist event in our culture."[15]

    The other literary scholar who has attended to sports concerns about the concrescence of sports and religion in American culture is the Americanist Allen Guttmann, who in the past two decades has produced three distinct volumes that always implicitly, and occasionally explicitly, comment on the religious significance of American sporting events, especially for the fans. Guttmann's earliest work, *From Ritual to Record: The Nature of Modern Sports*, includes the trenchant observation that "one of the strangest turns in the long, devious route that leads from primitive ritual to the World Series and the *Fussballweltmeisterschaft* is the proclivity of modern sports to become a secular kind of faith."[16] In his subsequent works, Guttmann treats sports spectators in their fascination with and devotion to sports spectacles throughout history, particularly the American sporting phenomenon.[17] He traces myths and rituals to early Native American practices and identifies some of the modern reservations about the significance of sport with early Puritan attitudes.[18]

Even though a number of the works cited thus far consider some of the religious dimensions or phenomena associated with sports in America, none of them develops an extended analysis of the American sporting scene in terms of a religious studies orientation. Novak's work indeed celebrates the spiritual dimensions of experiences associated with several sports, but he does not undertake a thorough analysis of why or how the sports themselves might be interpreted as religion. Rather, he celebrates the mysteries of the games' rules or the wonder of certain sports accomplishments. A handful of works, however, have been devoted in their entirety to interpreting the convergence of sports and religion, a few focusing on how sports have been used as a means of Christian evangelism—thus "muscular Christianity,"[19] or "sportianity," as sports journalist Frank Deford has dubbed the phenomena. Notable among these recent works are Robert Higgs's trenchant history of the interplay between collegiate sports and religious ideals and discipline,[20] and the recent contribution by James Mathisen and Tony Ladd, *Muscular Christianity: Evangelical Protestants and the Development of American Sport*.[21] Taking a different approach to the "muscular Christianity" movement, Steve Hubbard provides samples of the testimonies and expressions of faith offered by athletes in *Faith in Sports: Athletes and Their Religion on and off the Field*.[22] By contrast, Shirl Hoffman's collection of essays *Sports and Religion*[23] is not concerned exclusively with the American scene, nor does it focus exclusively on the "sportianity" phenomena. Although most of the essays concentrate on the ways that sports serve as a manifestation of "muscular Christianity," several consider how sports function *as* religion. A few more essays comparing sports to religion or identifying sports fanaticism with religious faith appear in Charles Prebish's collection, *Religion and Sport: The Meeting of the Sacred and the Profane*.[24] For the most part, Prebish's volume is devoted to foundational considerations about about how sports can be understood as religious.

The orientation of the present volume is different from these earlier works in several respects, most significantly by focusing on specific sports and the ways in which they command or display distinct religious dimensions. In this collection the essays analyze and celebrate sports as religious in two ways, always considering sports *as* religious rather than looking at the impact of sports on ecclesiastical traditions or trying to decipher the ways in which a particular form of religious ethics is challenged or buttressed by sporting competition. Most of the essays included in this volume reflect and acknowledge a conceptual kinship with the perspective of Mircea Eliade, whose two works *The Sacred and the Profane* and *Cosmos and History: The Myth of the Eternal Return* repeatedly are cited by the various authors. The core of their arguments resides in Eliade's recognition that many forms of contemporary secular rituals manifest fundamental religious proclivities of human beings and reflect the sacred rites and myths of previous, religiously oriented cultures. A second way of construing the relation between sport and religion is one that emerges out of the sorts of analysis frequently undertaken by sociologists and historians in their discussion of civil religion. In this regard several of the essays direct attention to Catherine Albanese's discussion of sports as one manifestation of "Cultural Religion" in her imaginative survey of American religious history and experience.[25]

The essays in this volume begin with a survey of the history of sports' interaction with religion in America, and then turn to foundational studies that explore various ways of interpreting sports as religion: I provide an overview of how sports have begun to function as a popular religion in the latter half of the twentieth century, Lonnie Kliever proposes the analysis of sport as religion by focusing on the human need for play and games, and James Mathisen examines NFL football as a test case for interpreting sport as a civil religion. After analyzing sports seasons in terms of a ritual or secular liturgical calendar, the essays are clustered in terms of the seasons of various sports.

Baseball begins the cycle of seasons and introduces the sets of sports-specific essays because baseball is the season that begins in the New Year, providing a fresh start that coincides with the onset of spring. Initially, I look at baseball as a manifestation of cosmogonic myths and as an expression of public fascination and fanaticism, Paul Johnson analyzes the fetish character of some baseball relics, and Peter Williams examines the need for apotheosis in America's "national pastime," thus rendering it effectively the "national faith." Using Mircea Eliade's *Patterns in Comparative Religion*, as well as several others of his works, Bonnie Miller-McLemore concentrates on the transitional and transformative power of professional football. Also relying on Eliade, I offer a brief analysis of the Super Bowl by focusing on its rituals, not only those of the game itself but those of the celebration that now engulfs the game. In the first of two essays dealing with basketball, Lois Daly explores the religious complexities of perfectionism as expressed in the coaching style of Bob Knight. Then, following the approach of Novak, I fathom the spiritual significance of the NCAA basketball championship tournament, comparing it to the obsession with singular supremacy that monotheistic values germinate and cultivate. In order to interpret the national appeal of ice hockey, Tom Faulkner applies the insights of Thomas Luckmann to Canadians' fascination with the sport. Next, Charles Adams, turning again to Eliade, interprets the ritual drama played out in professional wrestling as an index of the racist attitudes structuring much of American culture. Finally, I provide a concluding analysis of various ways in which sports function as a popular religion in America. The essays in this volume explore and expound the mythic, ritualistic, and cultic character of sports in contemporary America.

Throughout history, sports contests have been liminal occasions that operate in ritually defined space. They have transpired in a kind of time that is more akin to *kairos* than chronos. They have often commanded the dedication (often seemingly ultimate) of athletes and fans, and they have inspired the adulation of successful players and contestants. They have frequently appealed to the human interest for hope and renewal. And as sportswriter Frank Deford suggested in the last decades of the twentieth century, sports have now become the opiate of American masses. Indeed in North America at the start of the twenty-first century, sports have become "a secular kind of faith."

---

[1] Quoted in George Vecsey, "A Mighty Team with a Mortal Touch," *New York Times*, October 29, 1999, D1.

[2] One of the earliest essays to appear in religious studies publications is still one of the best: Cornish Rogers, "Sports, Religion, and Politics: The Renewal of an Alliance," *The Christian Century* (April 5, 1972): 392-94.

[3] Eldon E. Snyder and Elmer A. Spreitzer, *Social Aspects of Sport*, 2nd edition (Englewood Cliffs NJ: Prentice-Hall, 1983) 262-78. Cf. Hilmi Ibrahim, *Sport and Society: An Introduction to Sociology of Sport* (Long Beach CA: Hwong Publishing Co., 1975), especially chap. 4 on "Sport, Kinship, and Religion."

[4] D. Stanley Eitzen, *Sport in Contemporary Society: An Anthology*, 3rd edition (New York: St. Martin's Press, 1989) 269-98.

[5] See Gregory Baum and John Coleman, *Sport*, vol. 205 of *Concilium* (Edinburgh: T & T Clark, 1989).

[6] See, especially, David L. Vanderwerken and Spencer K. Wertz, *Sport Inside Out: Readings in Philosophy and Literature* (Fort Worth: Texas Christian University Press, 1985) 293-375.

[7] See, for example, Paul Weiss, *Sport: A Philosophic Inquiry* (Carbondale: Southern Illinois University Press, 1969). For philosophers of sport, a more frequent concern than that of the metaphysics of sport tends to be one of ethics; but in most cases the discussions of ethics focus on the behavior expected of athletes and observers rather than on some kind of ethical challenge or affirmation issued by the sport itself.

[8] Johan Huizinga, *Homo Ludens: A Study of the Play-Element in Culture* (Boston: Beacon Press, 1955).

[9] Harvey Cox, *Feast of Fools* (New York: Harper and Row, Colophon Books, 1969).

[10] Robert E. Neale, *In Praise of Play* (New York: Harper and Row, 1969).

[11] Hugo Rahner, *Man at Play* (New York: Herder and Herder, 1972). In the same year, fellow German theologian Jürgen Moltmann issued his *Theology of Play* (New York: Harper and Row, 1972), which provides a rationale for liberating the theological enterprise from its previous strictures—thus suggesting that theology itself play. A succinct summary, analysis, and critique of the various theologies of play identified here can be found in Lonnie Kliever's impressive survey of modern theology, *The Shattered Spectrum* (Atlanta: John Knox Press, 1981) 124-52. Among other insights, Kliever points out that the argument that Rahner constructs, for instance, pays (plays?) only passing reference to the work of Huizinga, marshaling instead a vast array of data on religious significance of play from ancient Greek and early Christian sources.

[12] Michael Novak, *The Joy of Sports: End Zones, Bases, Baskets, Balls, and the Consecration of the American Spirit* (New York: Basic Books, Inc., Publishers, 1976).

[13] For a variant reading of the spirituality of basketball, cf. Jeff Wagenheim, "The Tao of Hoops," *New Age Journal* (November-December 1992): 76-79.

[14] James Michener, *Sports in America* (New York: Random House, 1976) 476.

[15] Edwin Cady, *The Big Game: College Sports and American Life* (Knoxville: University of Tennessee Press, 1978) 78.

[16] Allen Guttmann, *From Ritual to Record: The Nature of Modern Sports* (New York: Columbia University Press, 1978) chap. 2.

[17] Allen Guttmann, *Sport Spectators* (New York: Columbia University Press, 1986).

[18] Allen Guttmann, *A Whole New Ball Game: An Interpretation of American Sports* (Chapel Hill: University of North Carolina Press, 1988). See especially chaps. 2, 5, and 6 in which Guttmann treats "The Sacred and Secular" in Native American games, "The National Game" (thus implying some sort of national identity associated with baseball), and "Muscular Christianity."

[19] See, especially, Robert Higgs, "Muscular Christianity, Holy Play, and Spiritual Exercises: Confusion about Christ in Sports and Religion," in Shirl J. Hoffman, ed., *Sport and Religion* (Champaign IL: Human Kinetics Books, 1992) 89-103. Cf. James A. Mathisen, "From Muscular Christians to Jocks for Jesus," *The Christian Century* 109 (1-8 January 1992): 11-15.

[20] Robert J. Higgs, *God in the Stadium: Sports and Religion in America* (Lexington: University of Kentucky Press, 1995).

[21] Tony Ladd and James A. Mathisen, *Muscular Christianity: Evangelical Protestants and the Development of American Sport* (Grand Rapids: Baker Books, 1999).

[22] Steve Hubbard, *Faith in Sports: Athletes and Their Religion on and off the Field* (New York: Doubleday, 1998).

[23] Hoffmann, *Sport and Religion*.

[24] Charles S. Prebish, *Religion and Sport: The Meeting of the Sacred and the Profane* (Westport CT: Greenwood Press, 1993).

[25] Catherine Albanese, *America: Religions and Religion*, 2nd edition (Belmont CA: Wadsworth, 1992) 463-500.

SPORTS AND RELIGION IN AMERICA

FROM SABBATH PROSCRIPTIONS TO SUPER SUNDAY CELEBRATIONS
SPORTS AND RELIGION IN AMERICA

Joseph L. Price

Introduction

Throughout the twentieth century, American religious leaders often wrestled with the ways in which faith and sports can be related, frequently focusing on how sports might challenge faith and considering how faith might conscript sports in its own service. Yet the attention given to sports fascination by faithful believers is not new in American experience, for since the earliest days of Puritan settlement in New England ministers and theologians have expressed concern about the distractions that leisure and sports afford. On Christmas day in 1621, for instance, Governor William Bradford of the Plymouth Colony reprimanded young boys and men whom he found "in the street at play, openly; some pitching the bar, and some at stool-ball and such like sports."[1] Leisure itself was often considered the devil's playground by Puritans, and playing sports on Sundays or religious holidays, like Christmas, was particularly regarded as sinful.

The twentieth century, however, brought about a number of changes in Christians' attitudes toward sports engagement, ranging from the sponsorship of sports teams by religiously affiliated colleges and the coordination of church leagues for basketball and softball, to the acceptance of professional competition on Sundays and the celebration of sporting events with invocations. "The story of the changes in the attitudes held by most older Protestant denominations," Ralph Slovenko and James Knight concluded shortly after mid-century, "is largely one of grudging but accelerating accommodation, a contrast indeed to the nineteenth-century practice of attaching the label 'sinful' to each new sports innovation, as well as to the dance, the theatre, the opera, the saloon, and the novel."[2]

Indeed, there is abundant evidence of the convergence and confusion that have emerged between sports and religion in America in the late twentieth century. The blending has become enmeshed in everyday consciousness as the testimonies, rituals, and affiliations of players and fans have been portrayed in popular media, religious publications, and scholarly tomes. The perceived infiltration of sports into religion is so pervasive that movies get titles mixing angels with ballplayers—*Angels in the Outfield*—and a championship university athletic team is known commonly by its dubious, perhaps Dantéan, mascot—a Blue Devil.

Certainly, perceptions of, impressions about, and responses to sports and religion have fused in various media in modern America—from comics to literature to film—in part because sports and spirituality have been so thoroughly blended in the lives of athletes and fans. During the postseason play of Major League Baseball in early October 1997, for instance, there were several distinct examples of athletes' testimonies affirming their faith or attributing sports success to divine intervention. Following his defeat in game 1 of the World Series, Orel Hershiser remarked on his manner of praying before games: "People are surprised, I suppose, because I really haven't had a bad outing in the postseason. But when I pray before a game and think about the game, it's not that I'm supposed to win or do well because it's the postseason, but it's that I'm thankful I'm here and able to pitch, and hopeful I do my best."[3] In contrast, Cleveland players Bip Roberts and Tony Fernandez credited the Indians' extra-inning, pennant winning victory to divine intervention—that Roberts, who had been scheduled to start in, as he put it, "the biggest game of my life,"[4] was scratched from the line-up after getting injured during pre-game warm-ups. His replacement, Tony Fernandez, hit a solo home run for the game's only run and credited God with helping him to see the pitch well.

The contemporary tendency to connect athletic success and divine favor—or simply to blend the spirit of sporting competition with the fervor of evangelical piety—suggests that the convergence of sports and religion involves a kind of denigration of one or both, the profanation of the sacred or the diminution of sporting competition. However, the process of their modern mixing perhaps represents a reintegration of two sorts of ritual rather than a profanation of sacred rites. In several respects the fusion of sports and religion, especially during the latter portion of the twentieth century, represents the restoration of metaphysical and mystical impulses that generated or characterized early forms of play.

According to the historian of American culture Allen Guttmann, the activities that we now classify as sports first claimed the participation of humans "primarily in conjunction with some form of religious significance."[5] In other words, sports activities fulfilled some sort of ritual function, whether as pleasing or humoring the gods (as with the ancient Olympic games in Athens), supplicating their intervention (as with the Oglala Sioux's rite of throwing the ball), or rehearsing their roles in creation and continuation of the world (as with the Mayan game of ball). Since the earliest days of the full fusion of sporting activity with spiritual significance, sport and spirituality have become divorced, with sport having been warped, as Shirl Hoffman observes, "by converging forces of specialization, rationalization, bureaucratization, and quantification, so warped in fact, that contemporary societies find it difficult to imagine any substantive commonalties between it and the practice of religion."[6]

In contrast to the integration and holistic fusion that characterized the combination of sports and religion in pre-modern days, the convergence between sports and religion has taken many popular forms in modern times. As we can see from evidence in current media and experience, the mixtures of sport and religion, of disciplined faith and fervent fanaticism, are often different in their modern manifestions. Consequently, a major challenge in dealing with the phenomena of sports and religion is to understand their plural relationships in American experience, from the conflict and prohibition of sports by early Puritans to the featured spectacles of sports by religious institutions in recent decades and the present day.

Sports Conflicting with Religion

Before 1850 most Protestant groups condemned sports because sports diverted attention and consumed energy that could have been spent in the exercise of faith. Protestants often denounced specific sports because they presented distinct temptations; for example, horse-racing was thought to promote gambling, and football, prizefighting, cockfighting, and even town-ball (the forerunner of baseball) were considered to be brutal. Boating and fishing were also thought to lead to vice, and "the sports pages" of newspapers similarly were thought to generate unhealthy appetites for non-spiritual concerns. Even croquet, that "civilized" sport satirized by Scottie Pippen in television commercials, was considered to pose moral problems: "When young Christians should be reading the Bible, meditating, conversing about religious matters, praying or attending to some important religious duty, they are often found playing croquet," a Christian advocate wrote following the Civil War. "We have in our mind the history of two interesting young ladies who were in the habit of playing croquet by moonlight, frequently until past twelve and even until two o'clock. The result of their dissipation was consumption from cold, a very sad and untimely death, without that preparation which consists in holiness, without which no one shall see the Lord."[7]

Throughout the nineteenth century sports and leisure were often suspect since they deflected attention away from possible service to God or the study of God's word. And toward the end of the nineteenth century, one Texas minister wrote: "Sport, fun, and frolic, have no chapter in youth's Book of Life in our day; *learning* and *doing* fill up the entire volume."[8] Yet the emergence of Christian liberal arts colleges during the nineteenth century coincides with and supports in several ways the rise of American-style football. In his history of the emergence and rise of "muscular Christianity" in colleges, Robert Higgs avers: "The early history of American college sports generally follows the paths of the Congregationalists and Presbyterians, especially in the case of football, ...the sport most frequently linked with education and religion, and also war."[9]

Although football was the dominant sport on college campuses during the last three decades of the nineteenth century, the popularity of professional baseball began to expand and gained the attention of religious institutions and their leaders. Throughout the country, thousands of amateur teams and leagues were formed to accommodate the burgeoning interest in baseball. "Churchly opposition to professionalism in the sport gradually subsided except in the South, where the attack shifted to a denunciation based on the rowdy nature of the spectator crowds and on the unquestioned fact that both professionals and amateurs played on Sunday."[10] Although denominations differed in the degree of their proscription against baseball on weekdays, they uniformly endorsed the Sabbath ban. Professional baseball, for instance, continued to be banned on Sundays in Philadelphia until the trauma of the Great Depression prompted the repeal of blue laws. During the late nineteenth century, however, "the profanation of the Sabbath became a symbol of the evil the early churches sought to confront, and frontier sports and rough amusements figured prominently in such profanation, along with drunkenness, which had reached epidemic proportions."[11] Even in the North, the issue of Sabbath observance was a concern for sports-minded evangelists who sought, nonetheless, to spread the word to the "unchurched" who would not darken the doors of God's house on a Sunday. In the view of Billy Sunday, a professional baseball player turned evangelist, the schedules and demands of professional sport and religion could not be reconciled, "especially if baseball persisted in breaking the Sabbath commandment." Yet before he gave up the basepaths in Pittsburgh for the sawdust trail of evangelists, Billy Sunday participated in "Athletic Sundays," whose goal was to reach "unchurched" men in the Northeast. With other notable athletes and coaches, he spoke about the manliness of Christianity while denouncing the evils associated with Sunday sports competition, drinking alcohol, and gambling. Along with evangelist Dwight L. Moody, Billy Sunday helped to shift the emphasis in muscular Christianity toward triumphalism, toward winning big, toward registering large numbers of conversions rather than cultivating a disciplined form of faith among fervent believers.[12]

Meanwhile, many Southern Protestants feared, as one member of the Disciples of Christ put it, that any and all "base ball playing is apt to lead to Sunday base ball playing," and the editor of the Arkansas Baptist paper in the early 1890s decried that baseball players often would "execute more deviltry, use more profanity, and make idiots of themselves in more ways" than other men. Similarly, a decade later, the editor of the Mississippi Baptist paper castigated baseball fans because the "murderous" game is, as he put it, "more brutal than a bull-fight, more reprehensible than a prize-fight, and more deadly than modern warfare."[13] Underlying most of the accusations about baseball's violence were assumptions that leisure and play themselves were inherently tempting players to exercise evil, permitting if not cultivating the lack of moral character that threatened the model of Victorian piety to which many of the religious leaders then aspired.

Less than a century later, however, a more violent game would be so celebrated on Sundays that its championship event would even change the name of the day on which it is played. "Super Sunday," which is the name for the climactic winter festival of professional football, suggests the degree of resignation and accommodation afforded by religious institutions as the sporting event has grown in international popularity. Certain adaptations have been made by several religious groups to meet the desires of their faithful attendees. On Super Bowl Sunday in the late 1960s, for instance, the Tabernacle Baptist Church in Richmond, Virginia, like several of the other progressive churches in that city, shifted the time of its evening services to a vespers hour—an unusually "Catholic" timing for an evangelical congregation—in order to facilitate the football spectatorship that many of its deacons enjoyed. As a further accommodation to the prominence of the sporting event, a number of churches in subsequent years featured a noon-time fellowship meal as "*Souper* Sunday" on Super Bowl Sunday. In this way the First Friends Meeting at Whittier sought to increase attendance at its morning worship service, which was followed by the meal and party to watch the game on a large screen television. One cannot help but notice the irony of this congregation, connected as it is to a strong pacifist tradition, gathering to watch a game so physically violent as professional football.

Although accommodations have been routinely made to reduce the apparent time conflicts between the Super Bowl and Sunday worship services, some religious groups have sought to heighten the conflict between the demands of their religious traditions and the sports devotion by distributing evangelistic tracts at the site of the Super Bowl stadium and by advertising Christian supremacy. At various Super Bowl sites, one evangelistic group repeatedly has distributed tracts, which nonetheless feature sporting images and metaphors, about Christ as the real champion, and a group of Methodist churches in Miami contracted a single-engine airplane to tow a huge banner over Joe Robbie Stadium, as it was then called, that read "JESUS IS THE REAL SUPER BOWL HERO."

In other sports as well, evidence of the conflict between religious devotion and sporting participation and allegiance has continued throughout the period of accommodation. On a personal level, for instance, Sandy Koufax refused to pitch in particular games of the 1965 World Series because of his celebration of Jewish High Holy days, and Ken Holtzman subsequently adhered to his faith in a similar way as the Yankees pursued a pennant in the late 1970s. At that time Holtzman's refusal to pitch so mired him in manager Billy Martin's disfavor that his career never recovered the luster that it had enjoyed only a short while earlier. In professional basketball, too, the conflict about Sabbath play became apparent as the Utah Jazz made the NBA Finals for the first time in 1997. Larry Miller, their Mormon owner, missed their Sunday games during the playoffs in order to devote the time to his faith and his family. Also following his religious convictions, pitcher Al Worthington manifested incredible ethical resolve when he once refused to pitch for the White Sox because they were reputed to have a scout in the scoreboard who, using binoculars, stole signs from the opposing team.[14]

Sports Commingling with Religion

The confusing American interplay between sports and faith did not begin when the Super Bowl began to challenge Sunday worship services nor when evangelistic groups began to use sporting language and images to attract and orient prospective devotees. At the turn of the twentieth century many Southern Protestants compared baseball to other evils such as the sinful "social dance." While they were voicing final protests against baseball before accepting it as the lesser of two evils, some Northern and Midwestern Christian institutions began to blend evangelical forms of piety into sports in an effort to provide a strong, male-oriented paradigm for Christian faith. These foundations for a muscular Christianity gained strength as two Springfield graduates—Amos Alonzo Stagg and James Naismith—combined sports competition and Christian discipline. As a young man, Stagg had planned to pursue a vocation in Christian ministry, but he also exhibited a passion for sports. Between these two apparently conflicting lures, Stagg found a common ground or goal that enabled him to play ball and express his faith at the same time. He began to use sports—its discipline and its celebration of winning—as a tool for religious evangelization by requiring players to exercise traditional forms of piety (such as praying and attending worship services) and by focusing on the goal of the game—victory—which resembled, at least in a rudimentary way, the Christian belief in the victory of Christ over death. Yet his innovations in the game of football often challenged the decorum, if not the ethics of fair play, which many thought Christians should exercise in competition. While he was head coach of the YMCA Christians at Springfield, Stagg "introduced the game's first hidden ball play," which he called the "dead man play," in the game against Harvard. To his delight, the play worked effectively, although some labeled the deceptive tactic "most unchristian." The famous Notre Dame shift which was attributed to Knute Rockne's predecessor had actually come from Stagg, who, according to the Notre Dame coach Jesse Harper, had gotten it from God. Others of Stagg's innovations include the use of a tackling dummy, the creation of the Statue of Liberty play, the development of the T-formation, the introduction of place kicking, and the design of several uniform and equipment advances.[15] In the administration of the game off the field, he also engaged in a number of practices that raise questions about "fair play." In a university setting he demanded full autonomy as athletic director, and a secret budget; he developed a physical education curriculum to appeal to potential athletes; he emphasized winning; he devoted special attention and favors for athletes; and occasionally he used ineligible players. When Stagg was asked to recommend someone for the position of athletic director at Kansas who could, like himself, lead both athletics programs and prayers, he wired succinctly: "Recommend James Naismith, inventor of basketball, medical doctor, Presbyterian minister, teetotaler, all-around athlete, non-smoker, and owner of vocabulary without cuss words."[16]

While Stagg was establishing the football prowess of the University of Chicago and Naismith was introducing his new game of "basket ball," many northern colleges and universities began to affirm the model of "muscular Jesus," fusing faith and athletics in an educational environment. Student Christian groups began to align with the YMCA and its advocacy of exercise, competition, and faith, as was the case at the University of Michigan. There, the athletic programs became highly successful under the leadership of the football coach, Fielding "Hurry-Up" Yost, who introduced the idea that "Winning is the only thing." In four years his teams amassed 2,271 points while giving up only 42 to opponents, averaging a score of 65-2 per game in eight-game seasons, and he cited the success as the result of sportsmanship derived from the "Golden Rule in Action." Although his teams often devastated the opposition during his years as coach, he is remembered by some university historians more for his inculcation of Christian values among students than for his demand for victory on the football field.[17]

As Americans began to grapple with ways to deal with the public fascination with sports and their spectacles, the Boston *Congregationalist* undertook the study of football in an effort to find its possible redeeming qualities. The study noted that football helped young men to develop "self-control and readiness in the tremendous emergencies which men must meet in the busy, struggling life of these times," and it lauded the sport for cultivating a form of "mental discipline" that was as significant as the study of mathematics.[18] Following World War I, church-sponsored sports leagues—especially for baseball—began to organize in order to capture the attention of the unchurched and to provide social outlets for men of faith.

During the 1920s in Paducah, Kentucky, some ministers even formed the BPBL—the Baptist Preachers Bowling League. On the eve of the Great Depression, the *Christian Advocate* advised Methodist leaders to seek opportunities directing play and competition: "Don't fail to capture some of the summer athletics for your church. We need to keep play wholesome, clean and Christian, just as much as we need to keep civic or industrial life Christian."[19]

Especially among religiously sponsored colleges and universities, sports provided opportunities for engaging in fair competition and for expressing the faith of players. At Mars Hill College in North Carolina, for example, the football and basketball players organized a special Sunday school class for which they then took the efficiency prize, and they carried Bibles with them on their athletic trips. The *Baptist Student* magazine that reported their success, and a witness concluded that "the athletes of Mars Hill College therefore challenge athletes of all other colleges to fear nothing in playing the game fair, to be up and doing in the Master's work."[20]

Throughout the latter half of the twentieth century, missionary opportunities for sports teams expanded. As the Liberty University Eagles moved to NCAA Division I football, evangelist Jerry Falwell, who also served as the university's president, expressed a somewhat different "outreach" goal for the university's team. He most wanted the Eagles to "knock the bejabbers out of Notre Dame," as he put it, all "in the name of the Lord." Falwell not only desired to field competitive athletic teams; he also aspired to have the Liberty program conquer all others in order to promote fundamentalism. "After all," he reasoned, "look at the attention focused on the Mormon Church since Brigham Young University became a national football power."[21] At BYU a few years earlier it was reported that the Cougar's football coach could "move a Mormon student pep rally to tears with a talk about the power of prayer."[22]

Religion Conscripting Sports

One of the ways that sports and religion have cooperated with each other is through the use of sports by religion. In the Jewish and Christian traditions, the earliest records of such use are in scripture, where sports metaphors were employed for the purpose of explicating or clarifying aspects of faith. In his first letter to the Christians at Corinth, Paul used images and language drawn from track and boxing in offering advice to the faithful: "Do you not know that in a race, all the runners compete, but only one receives the prize? So run that you may obtain it" (9:24, RSV). In the Epistle to the Hebrews, there is an appreciation for the endurance of distance running, perhaps the marathon: "Let us lay aside every weight, and sin which clings so closely [to us], and let us run with perseverance the race that is set before us" (12:1, RSV). Then there is the pugilistic voice of Paul that implores the faithful in I Timothy "to fight the good fight of faith" (6:12) and that reflects on his own bout, perhaps with doubt, as he closes II Timothy: "I have fought the good fight, I have finished the race, I have kept the faith" (4:7, RSV).

More general and significant than these metaphors in the New Testament epistles, early Christians thought of themselves as being "athletes for Christ." For the roots of the Greek word for "ascetic" go back to the word for exercise. And in his first letter to Timothy, Paul writes: "...exercise thyself rather unto godliness. For bodily exercise profiteth little: but godliness is profitable unto all things" (I Tim 4:7-8, KJV).

Moving from the language about sports to the courts and fields themselves, we note in the nineteenth century the attempts of various colleges and universities to use sports for religious purposes, for exercising and training the body toward faith, for establishing discipline, even for expanding mission opportunities. One of the earliest American attempts specifically to use sports as a means for attracting potential converts to a gospel session was in the mid-nineteenth century announcement for services in a then frontier, now midwestern community:

> The reverend Mr. Blaney will preach next Sunday in Dempsey's Grove at ten A.M. and at four o'clock P.M., Providence permitting. Between services the preacher will run his sorrel mare, Julia, against any nag that can be trotted out in this region for a purse of five hundred dollars.

The report about the race notes that the purse was made and that Julia won the race. Not only did the congregation then stay for the afternoon service, but about 200 new members affiliated with the church that day.[23]

At the turn of the twentieth century professional baseball assumed apologetic dimensions for Mormons as it came to Utah for the first time. It also assumed ecumenical possibilities for the Mormons as it provided a point of common contact for them with men from other religious traditions in the Western states. "While baseball in other Western cities often served to legitimize claims to civic status and to give peaceful voice to regional rivalries," Jim Warnock observes, "in Utah the sport offered a vehicle to unite Mormons, members of a formerly radical and now accommodating religious sect, with their 'gentile' neighbors." At the time of the congressional hearing about the viability of seating a Mormon elected as a Senator from Utah, baseball essentially demonstrated to all Americans, and particularly those in states near Utah, the thorough American character of the Mormons because baseball transcended religious differences between Mormons and other Americans. It provided a common ground and afforded Mormons a chance to affirm "broader American values."[24] As the "Salt Lake City Mormons, Elders of Bishops" (perhaps the longest name of any sports franchise in modern history) joined the Pacific Northern League in 1903, the professional organization was welcomed by both the *Deseret News* and the *Salt Lake Tribune.*

In addition to the ways that religious institutions have used sports leagues and games to expand their evangelical outreach and to solicit acceptance by other groups, traditional religious spaces have also incorporated and celebrated sports events and activities. Sports events and accomplishments are vividly portrayed in the stained glass of New York's Cathedral of St. John the Divine, which boasts a sports window among its stained glass tributes to saints and scriptures. "The sports bay of St. John's suggests a vital connection between sports and religion stretching back to biblical authority, as seen in the final design of the chapel window with scenes of Jacob wrestling with the Angel, David conquering Goliath, and the commandment of St. Paul to 'run a good race.'"[25] At the time of its installation in the 1920s Bishop William T. Manning commented:

> Clean, wholesome, well-regulated sport is a most powerful agency for true and utmost living.... True sport and true religion should be in the closest touch and sympathy.
>
> Few things have done more harm than the idea that religion frowns upon sport or is out of sympathy with it. The notion gives men the wrong idea of religion and it puts religion out of touch with the life of the people. A well played game of polo or of touch football is in its own place and in its own way as pleasing to God as a beautiful service of worship in the Cathedral.[26]

Rituals in the cathedral have also brought sports under the aegis of faith. Certainly, more than a few prayers have been offered in the cathedral for victory by the home team, but perhaps none so dramatic as ones displayed in a church near Madison Square Garden during the early summer of 1994. On behalf of New York Rangers fans who were beseeching their team to overcome a half-century jinx and win the Stanley Cup for the first time since World War II, some fans left, amid the flickering candles, a hand-lettered card pleading for mercy and victory for the Rangers. Several hours later as the Rangers celebrated their victory over the Canucks, a few fans in Madison Square Garden held their confessional signs aloft: "Now I can die in peace" and "All is forgiven." Not only have pious fans prayed for their sports heroes and offered expressions of thanksgiving for victory, they have also written evangelical hymns and songs that combine spiritual goals with sports activities, perhaps none more pointed than "Drop Kick Me Jesus through the Goal Posts of Life."

In contrast to the incorporation of sports images and enthusiasm in religious spaces, sports fields and arenas have occasionally been transformed from their competitive orientations to specifically sacramental and spiritual functions. The use of the baseball diamond as a wedding chapel is one of the vivid scenes in "Bull Durham," as utility player Jimmy marries Millie at the pitcher's mound. More significant, however, than the cinematic scene of a wedding at a ballpark is the convergence of prayer life and sports facilities found in Baltimore. At the new Oriole Park at Camden Yards, Orthodox Jewish fans gather after the fifth inning of every home game—except the ones on Sabbaths—in a small, cluttered pantry near Major League baseball's first kosher food stand, which offers bagels and cream cheese, potato knishes, and, of course, the kosher version of ballpark specials, hot dogs. In the small room often thirty men or more, some wearing baseball caps over their yarmulkes, sway back and forth and chant prayers in Hebrew. The occasion is the afternoon prayer time known as *mincha*. Although the prayer at the ballpark is not consensually endorsed by Orthodox Jews, Saul Newman, a professor of political science who enjoys the chance to pray among the quorum of ten adult Jewish males, notes that the Talmud does not explicitly forbid prayer at ballparks. In this case, the ten-minute prayer session is coincidentally held at the ballpark, not offered as a petition for the Orioles.[27]

In a similar use of sports facilities for religious functions, New York City is replete with images and memories of the fusion of sports and religion. In terms of sporting sites, Yankee Stadium, or the "House that Ruth built," has found that its largest audiences have attended religious events. More than 90,000 people attended a mass held by Pope Paul VI on his first trip to North America in 1965. Almost a decade earlier at least 100,000 people attended the final service in Billy Graham's Manhattan Crusade even though more than 10,000 people were turned away. That crowd eclipsed the previous stadium record, which had been 88,150 for the championship bout between Joe Louis and Max Baer in 1935. But the largest crowd in Yankee Stadium history was a meeting of 123,000 Jehovah's Witnesses in the late 1950s.[28] Although a number of weddings have taken place at Yankee Stadium since it was made ready for play in 1923, the most spectacular wedding in New York's sports facilities' histories took place July 1, 1982, when more than 2000 couples were blessed by the Reverend Sun Myung Moon in a single ceremony at Madison Square Garden, the home of the Knicks, the Rangers, and championship boxing matches.[29] In late 1997, the Reverend Moon similarly rented RFK Stadium in Washington, DC for a ceremony of marital blessing for 28,000 couples, some of whom represented ecumenical outreach to mainstream Christian denominations.

In addition to these large celebrative services, Yankee Stadium has provided the site for a funeral, albeit a mock cortege led by devout Yankee fans in October 1996 to celebrate the demise of the Atlanta Braves before game 6 of the World Series. Yankee Stadium is even the site for memorials, in ways more personal than the venerated statues and plaques in center-field commemorating the great Yankees of bygone days. For at least one fervent Yankee fan, the stadium provided a final resting place. The ultimate, or at least final commitment to a team, involved a family effort on behalf of the late grandmother of Eddie Ellner, a California writer. An ardent Yankee fan who had even taught her pet parakeet to squawk "Go, Mickey. Go, Yankees," the woman had requested, as a dying wish shortly before her death at age eighty-two in 1990, that if the Yankees ever won the pennant again, she wanted Eddie to scatter her ashes across the field at Yankee Stadium. So Ellner flew across the country in late October 1996, and dusted her ashes on home plate, along the first base line, across the infield, and in the on-deck circle. Although Ellner would not confirm how he had gotten access to the field, he did remark: "It is serendipity. Somehow my grandmother arranged it," suggesting that even in death her spirit might prevail.[30]

The repetition of sacramental and memorial ceremonies at Yankee Stadium and Madison Square Garden resonates with the observation of Ray Kinsella, who, in *Shoeless Joe*, perceives that "a ballpark at night is more like a church than a church."[31] Because stadia often evoke an aura of otherness and frequently facilitate a communal or congregational unity of joy or mourning among spectators, Philip Lowry titled his celebration of 273 ballparks in the Major Leagues and former Negro Leagues as *Green Cathedrals*, a phrase that recognizes sports fields as sacred space. Invoking the potential spiritual significance of the action that takes place in ballparks, Lowry indicates that he had struggled to find the right title for his book. "The more I studied ballparks," he confesses, "the more they have begun to resemble mosques, or synagogues, or churches, or similar such places of reverent worship." In Philadelphia, for instance, he notes that the former site of "Shibe Cathedral," or Connie Mack Stadium, now features an evangelical church. Because baseball fans, like the fictive Ray Kinsella, often experience a spiritual sense of awe and wonder at ballparks, Lowry concludes that a green cathedral "holds treasured memories and serves as a sanctuary for the spirit, a haven where the ghosts of Babe Ruth, Josh Gibson, Lou Gehrig, Cool Papa Bell, [and] Cy Young…can continue to roam…[and] where the soul of the game of baseball resides."[32]

Not only has religion conscripted sports in using its language, directing its prayers, and, at least temporarily, transforming its spaces from places for play and competition to sanctuaries for religious rituals, religion has also used sports for evangelistic purposes. The conception and development of basketball at Springfield College was prompted in part by the need to have a game that could be exported with the missionaries on their journeys to foreign lands. Consequently, some of the constraints that directed the early development of the game involved small team size, minimal equipment, and simple rules. To reinforce the religious underpinnings of the game itself, the initial set of thirteen rules was issued in the form of "Ten Commandments" and in line with the Puritan heritage of the Protestant school, with physical contact constituting a foul.[33]

Although basketball was from the outset designed to enrich mission work, it has become much more common to see how the play of sports facilitates evangelistic witness for players. The football and basketball teams at Mars Hill College, as I have mentioned, used their games as means to share their testimonies with opponents and fans during the period between the world wars. At about the same time, a barnstorming Jewish baseball team, the House of David, was formed in part to provide young Jewish men with an opportunity to compete regularly at a professional level since they then suffered discrimination in the Major League system. The team also enabled the players to adhere to the rituals of their faith, including the avoidance of playing games on the Sabbath, and thus to manifest their faith by means of their play. More recently, it has become common for churches to form sports teams—particularly basketball because of its minimal equipment needs and because of the small team size—to go on mission tours. In the late 1990s, for example, the Second Baptist Church of Richmond, Virginia, organized a basketball team to provide talented and enthusiastic players with an opportunity to undertake a special mission project. According to the Reverend Ray Spence, the church's pastor and a former All-SEC defensive lineman, a number of men in the congregation had felt excluded from mission opportunities to share their testimonies. Before the basketball mission trip, the church's special mission projects had often utilized the skills of laborers (such as carpenters and computer technicians) or the talents of professionals (such as physicians and lawyers). The players on the Second Baptist team included a former collegiate star, but featured men who enjoyed playing the game for the fun of the game. During their ten-day summer tour of Slovakia, they played twice a day, often targeting younger teams as their opposition and audience. Following each game, the players would share their testimonies, emphasizing that one did not have to be a professional athlete to continue enjoying to play the team game and sharing the special character of their Christian experience.[34]

In addition to these team oriented expressions of witness, various professional sports stars have begun to offer tributes to God and testimonies of their faith as they have celebrated victories in championship contests; others have regularly displayed a prayerful demeanor as they have prepared to play or as they have celebrated success. Consider, for example, the kind of embodied prayer that is manifest in crossing oneself before going to plate, as did Roberto Clemente before each of his at-bats, or in Bob Cousy's preparation to shoot a free-throw. In a more expansive appeal with prayer, Evander Holyfield's entire staff posed with heads bowed, holding hands in sign of unity, as the champion boxer prepared for his final title defense with Mike Tyson. Visible petitions by football players also characterized the 1997 Playoffs in the NFL. In the waning minutes of Pittsburgh's victory over the New England Patriots, Steelers' linebacker Jason Gilden could be seen along the sidelines, kneeling in reclusion by a portable equipment locker, crossing himself, and mouthing words in a prayer minutes after his game-saving recovery of a fumble in Steelers' territory and moments before he and the defensive unit would be called upon to make one final stand against All-Pro quarterback Drew Bledsoe. Following the final, incomplete pass attempt by Randall Cunningham for the Minnesota Vikings in their playoff loss to the San Francisco 49ers in early January, 1998, 49ers Coach Steve Mariuchi was observed on the sideline crossing himself in a display of thankfulness.

Not all prayers by players and coaches, however, beseech special blessing on their play or express thanksgiving for their success. Following an injury to quarterback Steve Mitchell during the opening round of the NFL Playoffs in 1997, several players from both the Detroit Lions, who had witnessed a life-threatening injury to one of their teammates only weeks earlier, and the Tampa Bay Buccaneers knelt on the field and along the sidelines, praying for the health of the injured player. Despite defeat on the field, many of the players on the University of Tennessee's team knelt in prayer of unity at mid-field in the Orange Bowl following their loss to 1997's Co-National Champion Nebraska Cornhuskers. Similarly, Reggie White and a cohort of stunned Green Bay Packers joined with several jubilant 49ers at mid-field and knelt in prayer following the last second victory by the 49ers in the NFL playoffs in late 1998.

Athletes not only use prayer as a means of supplicating divine inspiration, protection, or support in times of grief; they also offer prayers and testimonies in celebrating success, either scoring a touchdown—exemplified by Dallas Cowboys' superstar Emmitt Smith kneeling in the end zone following one of his touchdown scampers—or winning the game itself. One of the more extensive team testimonies following a victory was presented by the Green Bay Packers following their Super Bowl victory in 1997. Several of the players offered testimonies during their post-game interviews on national television. While praising the support of the Antioch Bible Church, Eugene Robinson noted "how spiritual this team is" and how effectively God brought the players together. Reggie White, a minister as well as All-Pro defensive end for the Packers, began his comments by saying, "You know I want to say...God brought me here. I want to say 'Thank you, Jesus.'" Similarly, Antonio Freeman, who scored the game's first touchdown, said that he wanted to "thank God first." Wide-receiver André Rison likewise testified: "First thank Jesus Christ. I have to get on my knees and pray to God and thank him."

In addition to the testimonies that are occasioned by victories, it is also possible for players to extend their witness to their faith in other distinct ways, one of which has to do with their use of scripture references in signing autographs. Former World Series MVP John Wetteland, for instance, adds biblical citations to his signature, and former Oakland A's pitcher Mike Moore similarly often added to his autograph the abbreviation PTL (for "Praise the Lord") or a reference to Joshua 1:9 ("Be strong and of good courage; be not afraid, neither be thou dismayed: for the Lord thy God is with thee whithersoever thou goest").[35] One does not have to be a star player, however, to bear witness to scripture through sporting events. For familiar to television audiences of prominent sporting events, including World Series games, during the late 1980s and early 1990s was the rainbow-wigged man who held aloft signs simply stating, "John 3:16."

Sports Co-opting Religion

Although sports spaces have been utilized for religious rituals and often have taken on a spiritual character, another manifestation of the confusion concerning sports and religion has to do with the ways in which sports have co-opted religious functions in order to increase or gain competitive advantage. Former Redskin coach and sometime presidential consultant George Allen insisted on locker room worship services for his players on Sunday game days because the services did more, he thought, "to produce togetherness and mutual respect than anything else I've found in twenty-one years of coaching."[36] Following consecutive close-call victories over Michigan and Michigan State several years ago, Lou Holtz blended faith and the sporting spirit as he reflected on the deflected fourth quarter passes that had determined the Notre Dame victories. "I know that you are going to say God doesn't care who wins," Holtz quipped. "And I say that's true, but I believe his mother does." Obviously, that theological sense and joke plays best with Christian traditions that esteem the role of Mary. Yet if God really did care about who won and lost, Notre Dame theology department chairman observed, "What was going on during the Gerry Faust era? Was God on vacation?" Or consider the implications about divine favor in ambiguous outcomes: "What kind of God is it," suggests Martin Marty, "who could make up his mind during Notre Dame's 10-10 tie with Michigan State in 1966?" Marty continues: "People are responsible to the ways of a God who cares. We can never be specific as to say that God's care is applied to a specific event—even those events that are as serious, especially in some people's minds, as Notre Dame football."[37] Yet by getting the Irish football players to believe that God is on their side, Holtz invokes the ultimate intangible—faith—which indeed often generates the spirit, attitude, and outcome of victory.

For some time invocations were traditional for many professional football games, and they continue to provide a point of focus for many contests hosted by religious institutions. In the secular sphere of professional football prior to a game between the Atlanta Falcons and the Miami Dolphins in 1970, Miami's Catholic Archbishop Coleman F. Carroll prayed: "Your son is our quarterback and you are our coach.... We sometimes get blitzed by heavy sorrow or red-dogged by Satan.... Teach us to run the right patterns in our life so that we will truly make a touchdown one day through the heavenly gates, as the angels and saints cheer us on from the sidelines." In reporting this invocation, the *National Catholic Reporter* added: "And when that final gun goes off, dear Lord, lead us out of the parking lot of life, through the interchange of Purgatory onto the freeway into Heaven, with our fenders undented, our spirits undaunted, and our metaphors untangled. Amen."[38]

Football, however, is not the only sport that provides the opportunities for co-opting religious orientations by using prayer to sanction contests and games. Before the 1976 World Hockey Association All-Star Game, for instance, Father Edward Rupp offered an invocation whose purpose seemed more to impress the audience with sports knowledge than to implore God for safe and fair play, and good sportsmanship. "Heavenly Father, Divine Goalie," he began,

> we come before You this evening to seek Your blessing.... We are, thanks to You, All-Stars. We pray tonight for Your guidance. Keep us free from actions that would put us in the Sin Bin of Hell. Inspire us to avoid the pitfalls of our profession. Help us to stay within the blue line of Your commandments and the red line of Your grace. Protect us from being injured by the puck of pride. May we be ever delivered from the high stick of dishonesty. May the wings of Your angels play at the right and left of our teammates. May You always be the Divine Center of our team, and when our summons comes for eternal retirement to the heavenly grandstand, may we find you ready to give us the everlasting bonus of a permanent seat in Your coliseum. Finally, grant us the courage to skate without tripping, to run without icing, and to score the goal that really counts—the one that makes each of us a winner, a champion, an All-Star in the hectic Hockey Game of Life. Amen.[39]

Perhaps there is more to the connection between games, players, and prayers than might initially be assumed, especially in light of Barry Bonds' assertion following the improbable pennant of the San Francisco Giants in

1997. "I'm just glad all those other teams gave up on the players we got. We're a throwback team," he declared in the interview following the championship game on the next-to-last day of the season. "Nobody thought we could do anything, but we played together and prayed together."[40] The path to success in recent professional American sports has seen the Bulls join together for a post-championship game recitation of the Lord's Prayer before they turned to the celebration of their NBA conquest with ritual champagne baptism. Recalling this event Coach Phil Jackson later commented on the Bulls' victory over the Sonics in the 1996 NBA championship:

> When some of the dust had cleared and we could retreat off the court to the privacy of our locker room, we entered our inner snactum [sic] and found it replete with a barrage of cameras. I went straight through the training room door, and we found a spot to join in our circle and say the Lord's Prayer: Our last time together doing a communal act that represented something that joined our spirits. I could look them individually in the eye as we joined hands and tell them I have never enjoyed a year as thoroughly as I did the year we had the Greatest Season Ever.[41]

Religious language has also been applied effectively to routine plays and distinct teams. In baseball, the identification of a bunt as a "sacrifice" or of a run-scoring fly ball as a "sacrifice fly" calls to mind the religious significance of the terms. And with respect to distinct teams, Notre Dame's stellar backfield during the Knute Rockne era was labeled "the Four Horsemen," obviously identifying the success of the team with the final judgment that they would wreak on opponents as the representatives of the onset of the apocalypse. Unrelated to biblical references as such, one of the more inventive verbal assimilations of spiritual language into the sports arena was offered by umpire Drew Coble. He described what he felt like after ejecting from a game Baltimore's nice guy and baseball's ironman Cal Ripken, Jr., who had recently broken baseball's seemingly unchallengeable record for consecutive game appearances. Inverting the reference to supremacy, Coble said, "That's like throwing God out of Sunday School."[42] More common than such singular metaphors, however, is the identification of religious images with major college teams—such as Holy Cross's Crusaders, Duke's Blue Devils, and Wake Forest's Demon Deacons. Sports language also utilizes theological terms to identify specific football plays: the "Hail Mary" pass, which is such a desperation play that it requires that prayers be answered in order to complete the pass and score a touchdown; or "the immaculate reception," which refers to Franco Harris's miraculous reception of the deflected pass in Pittsburgh's championship victory over Oakland, a play that was such "a delivery from above" that it has now become well known by that miraculous name.

The use of the language of prayer and testimony is one of the distinct ways that sports begin to co-opt religious practices and expressions. Like religious language employed for sports gods, visual images also get appropriated by sports in ways that retain, at the very least, echoes and shadows of their religious referents. Visually, few religious images are as prominent as the multi-storied mural of Jesus, arms up-stretched, on the library at the University of Notre Dame. The mural is intended to identify the spiritual center of the university. But its position directly behind the goal posts at the north end of Notre Dame's football stadium makes it appear that Jesus is the ultimate referee, signaling that the Fighting Irish have entered their opponent's end zone or that their field goal attempt is "good." Although university officials deny that the mural was designed to exert influence on officials in Notre Dame's games, the portrait is commonly known by the name "Touchdown Jesus," and it is understood by many that the giant mural of Jesus watches over the shoulder of the coaches, players, and officials, thus providing Notre Dame with a number of miraculous victories.

Sports Supplanting Religion

One of the threats for religious institutions as they embrace sports wholeheartedly is that of maintaining the playful and creative character of sports. It is possible, as we have seen from several of our earliest examples of the fusion of sports and religion, for sports to co-opt the allegiance elicited by religion and to become, in effect, a religion as such. *Sports Illustrated* journalist Frank Deford was among the first to identify the kind of religious power that sports exerts on modern Americans. Adapting the critique of Karl Marx, Deford suggested that, if Marx had lived at the end of the twentieth century in the United States rather than in Victorian England, he would have declared that sports is the opiate of the people, anesthetizing them to the struggles of the classes and focusing their hopes on events that project fulfillment through a vicarious form of participation and through an often delayed form of gratification.

In the last decades of the twentieth century, scholars from various academic disciplines—history, sociology, anthropology, and theology, to name a few—have analyzed sports as being religious. In 1972 Cornish Rogers, then one of the editors of the *Christian Century*, asserted that "Sports are rapidly becoming the dominant ritualistic expression of the reification of established religion in the United States."[43] The following year sociologist Harry Edwards similarly averred that "If there is a universal popular religion in America, it is to be found within the institution of sport."[44] Such scholarly observation about the character of American sports firmly entered popular consciousness a decade later as the popularity of Monday Night Football was featured in matchbook advertisements for the Church of Monday Night Football. In the late 1990s, the *Atlanta Constitution* ran a full-page ad for an internet sports venture that proclaimed "Baseball is our religion. The stadium's our temple. The beer and peanuts, our sacrament."[45] The ad goes on to say that the lines are spoken like a true fan, a true believer in baseball. In these specific ways, popular attention has been heightened about the religious potential of sports.

In her survey of religion and religions in America, Catherine Albanese locates the power of sports to assume religious significance in the ritual dimensions of sports activities and in the devotion of fans to various games and teams. Combining emphases from Johan Huizinga, a theoretician of play, and Mircea Eliade, historian of American religion Albanese points out that both play and ritual are "satisfying" for their own sake, "for each is an activity in which people may engage because of the pleasure it gives in itself."[46] She also draws upon Bellah's trenchant analysis of civil religion as a national, politically oriented form of "faith." Recognizing that other popular forms of religion develop in ways akin to those of civil religion, Albanese clarifies the idea of "cultural religion," which represents the apolitical cultural creeds and codes of a community that get enacted or dramatized in cultic ritual. In this regard, then, she compares sports and religions: "Sports and deliberate religious rituals, through their performances, create an 'other' world of meaning, complete with its own rules and boundaries, dangers and successes." In other words, both sports and religious rituals establish a sense of order by creating a "world." "By setting up boundaries and defining the space of the game, sports have helped Americans fit a grid to their own experience in order to define it and give it structure," Albanese continues. "Hence, it is not surprising that our public games have given people a code of conduct for everyday living. If the ball field is a miniature rehearsal for the game of life, it tells us that life is a struggle between contesting forces in which there is a winning and losing side." It also teaches that "success [or winning] depends on teamwork" and that in competition "loyalty, fair play, and being a 'good sport' in losing" are virtues.[47]

Specific lists of corresponding characteristics between sports and religion have been elaborated by sociologist Harry Edwards and theologian Michael Novak. Among the characteristics common to both religion and sports, Edwards identifies issues, ideas, and images related to deity, authority, tradition, beliefs, faithful followers, ritual sites, and material elements.[48] With his set of correlations, Edwards prompts further reflections on how aspects of sports indeed correspond to elements of religions. But most of Edwards's connections are drawn from a comparison of sports with theistic, scriptural religious traditions. In that regard, his suggestion that the superstar athletes somehow correspond to gods diminishes the power of his set of similarities because the sports heroes as living, physical actors belie most theistic understandings of deities as transcendent and invisible. In addition, one could ask about the distinction between saints and gods, other than the fact that one is apparently living and active (the superstar athletes as gods) while the other is deceased and inactive (the saints). Perhaps it is this shortfall concerning transcendence that prompts Edwards to conclude that "sport is essentially a secular, quasi-religious institution. It does not, however, constitute an alternative to or substitute for formal sacred religious involvement."[49]

Although the sociologist Edwards refrains from defining late twentieth-century American sports as a religion, theologians (like Michael Novak) and historians of religion (like Charles Prebish and Catherine Albanese) recognize that institutionalized sports have become such a dominant religious force in America that they indeed constitute a religion, secular or profane though it might be. No longer is the fusion of the sporting and the spiritual merely one of personal experience, wherein a devout believer might enjoy a peak experience or sense of "flow" in the celebration of a sports accomplishment or victory.[50] For institutionalized sports at the beginning of the twenty-first century have once again begun to exert the force of faith for fans and players by providing them with a centrifugal orientation to contests and heroes, to sporting victories and defeats.

[1] William Bradford, *Of Plimouth Plantation*, ed. Samuel Eliot Morrison (New York: Alfred A. Knopf, 1952) 97.

[2] Ralph Slovenko and James Knight, eds., *Motivations in Play, Games and Sports* (Springfield IL: Charles C. Thomas, Publisher, 1967) 119.

[3] Ross Newhan, "Hershiser Isn't Overly Perturbed by Defeat," *Los Angeles Times*, October 19, 1997, C14.

[4] Comments by Bip Roberts and Tony Fernandez telecast on ESPN Sportscenter, October 15, 1997.

[5] Guttmann, *From Ritual to Record, The Nature of Modern Sports* (New York: Columbia University Press, 1978) 19.

[6] Shirl J. Hoffman, "Recovering a Sense of the Sacred in Sport," in *Sport and Religion*, ed. Shirl J. Hoffman (Champaign IL: Human Kinetics Books, 1992) 153.

[7] J. R. Headington, "Base-ball—croquet—dancing, etc." *Cincinnati American Christian Review*, October 19, 1875. Quoted in William R. Hogan, "Sin and Sports," in Slovenko and Knight, eds., *Motivations in Play, Games, and Sports*, 127.

[8] H. A. Graves, *Andrew Jackson Potter: The Noted Parson of the Texan Frontier* (Nashville: Southern Methodist Publishing House, 1890) 448. Quoted in William R. Hogan, "Sin and Sports," in Slovenko and Knight, eds., *Motivations in Play, Games, and Sports*, 121.

[9] Robert J. Higgs, *God in the Stadium: Sports and Religion in America* (Lexington: University Press of Kentucky, 1995) 37.

[10] Hogan, "Sin and Sports," 129.

[11] Higgs, *God in the Stadium*, 55.

[12] Higgs, *God in the Stadium*, 255.

[13] Quoted in Hogan, "Sin and Sports," 129.

[14] Jerry Crowe, "At Falwell's College, They Stress Fundamentals," *Los Angeles Times*, December 19, 1985, CC/III:15.

[15] Higgs, *God in the Stadium*, 191-93.

[16] Quoted in Higgs, *God in the Stadium*, 193.

[17] Higgs, *God in the Stadium*, 196.

[18] Quoted in Hogan, "Sin and Sports," 134.

[19] Quoted in Hogan, "Sin and Sports," 135.

[20] Quoted in Hogan, "Sin and Sports," 137.

[21] Crowe, "At Falwell's College, They Stress Fundamentals," 1.

[22] Hogan, "Sin and Sports," 143.

[23] Higgs, *God in the Stadium*, 68.

[24] Jim Warnock, "The Mormon Game: The Religious Uses of Baseball in Early Utah," *Nine: A Journal of Baseball History and Social Policy Perspectives* 6/1 (Fall 1997): 1, 2.

[25] Higgs, *God in the Stadium*, 236.

[26] Frederick W. Cozens and Florence Scovil Stumpf, *Sports in American Life* (Chicago: University of Chicago Press, 1953) 104.

[27] Peter Maass, "A Gathering Place for Faithful Fans," *Washington Post*, May 16, 1996, B1, B5.

[28] Telephone interview with Michael Vassallo, Media Relations, New York Yankees, June 4, 1997.

[29] George D. Chryssides, *The Advent of Sun Myung Moon: The Origins, Beliefs, and Practices of the Unification Church* (New York: St. Martin's Press, 1991) plate 16.

[30] "Morning Briefing," *Los Angeles Times*, November 4, 1996, C2.

[31] W. P. Kinsella, *Shoeless Joe* (New York: Ballantine Books, 1983) 135.

[32] Philip J. Lowry, *Green Cathedrals: The Ultimate Celebration of All 273 Major League and Negro League Ballparks Past and Present,* rev. ed. (Reading MA: Addison-Wesley Publishing Co., 1992) 1-2.

[33] Michael Novak, *The Joy of Sports: End Zones, Bases, Baskets, Balls, and the Consecration of the American Spirit* (New York: Basic Books, 1976) 101-102.

[34] Interview with Raymond Spence, pastor, Second Baptist Church, Richmond, Virginia, October 15, 1997.

[35] Cf., Higgs, *God in the Stadium*, 12.

[36] Quoted in Hoffman, "Recovering the Sacred in Sport," 156.

[37] Quoted in Ed Sherman, "Holtz's Logic on God's Role More Holey than Holy," *Chicago Tribune*, September 27, 1990, 4:1.

[38] "Cry Pax! A Column without Rules," *National Catholic Reporter*, October 2, 1970, 7.

[39] Quoted in Frank Deford, "The Word According to Tom," *Sports Illustrated (*April 26, 1976): 65.

[40] Ross Newhan, "San Francisco Gets to Heart of Matter by Clinching First Title since 1989," *Los Angeles Times*, Sunday, September 28, 1997, C1. This statement about the connection between teamwork and spirituality might seem unlikely, coming from one of the premier individualists in professional sports. Bonds, you perhaps recall, had sulked about wanting to be highest paid player following several free-agent signings, contract extensions, and renegotiated agreements with several other stars.

[41] Phil Jackson and Hugh Delehanty, *Sacred Hoops: Spiritual Lessons of a Hardwood Warrior* (New York: Hyperion, 1995 [copyright for hardcover edition, new final chapter added about 1996 for this paper edition, although the publication date for this edition remains the same as the earlier edition in 1995]) 222.

[42] Reported in "Washington Whispers," *US News & World Report* (August 4, 1997): 18.

[43] Cornish Rogers, "Sports, Religion, and Politics," *Christian Century* (April 5, 1972): 394.

[44] *Sociology of Sport* (Homewood IL: Dorsey Press, 1973) 90.

[45] Advertisement for Fastball.Com, *Atlanta Constitution*, July 4, 1997, C7.

[46] Catherine Albanese, *America: Religions and Religion* (Belmont CA: Wadsworth, 1982) 322.

[47] Albanese, *America: Religions and Religion*, 321-22.

[48] For an enumeration and brief analysis of this list, see the concluding chapter in this book, "An American Apotheosis," especially fn 15.

[49] Harry Edwards, *Sociology of Sport* (Homewood IL: Dorsey Press, 1973) 90.

[50] For elaboration on the concept of peak experience as a religious experience, see Abraham Maslow, *Religions, Values, and Peak-Experiences* (New York: Viking Press, 1970), especially appendix A. For exploration of the concept of "flow" as a religious experience, see Mihalyi Csikzentmihalyi, *Flow: The Psychology of Optimal Experience*(New York: Harper and Row, 1990). For an application of these two concepts of personal spirituality to sports, see my essay on "The Spirituality of Naturalistic Recreations" in Peter H. Van Ness, *Secular Spirituality* (New York: Crossroad, 1995) 414-44.

GOD AND GAMES
IN MODERN CULTURE

Lonnie D. Kliever

Our culture seems bent on becoming one gigantic playground. Play in all its forms has a high priority in the lives of most North Americans. How else can we explain the spectacle of the Winter Olympics, the fervor of contract bridge, the wealth of movie stars? How else can we explain the energy and enthusiasm, the resources and ingenuity invested in the leisure-time activities of sports, games, and entertainment? We are becoming, in the words of Michael Novak's parody of the US Pledge of Allegiance, "one nation under play, with sports and games and entertainment for all."[1]

Commentators on the North American scene are divided over what to make of this preoccupation with play. Some pundits see today's culture at play as the decisive sign of our moral and spiritual decay. For them, the old ideals of thrift and work have disappeared in a land grown fat with indolence and abundance. Other commentators see our unrelenting pursuit of play as a necessary "safety valve" for handling the drudgery and boredom of living in a super-industrialized and super-urbanized society. Like the "bread and circuses" of imperial Rome, our leisure time distractions help compensate for the regimented labor and life we must otherwise endure. Still other interpreters take an even more positive view. They contend that play has its own place alongside of work in a life rightly ordered. Indeed, they believe that play has a crucial place in every era and area of human life—from infancy to old age, from religion to recreation.

My sympathies lie with those who see a close connection between human well-being and play, including those forms of play we call professional and amateur sports. Those who regard play at worst as a distortion or at best as a distraction from the serious business of living have little appreciation for the significance of play in human affairs. Scholarly studies in a variety of fields have shown that the play of children and of adults must be taken seriously because these experiences have a vital place in personal and social life.[2] Not only have these scholars studied play itself, but they have also applied the insights derived from studying play to other areas of thought and life with impressive results. Everything from the stock market to funeral rites is seen in a new way when viewed from the standpoint of play. Indeed, the increasing use of "game" and "play" metaphors by a variety of original thinkers suggests that a whole new understanding of human beings may be emerging. We may be neither *Homo sapiens* ("humankind the thinker"), nor *Homo faber* ("humankind the maker"), but *Homo ludens* ("humankind the player"). In short, the "play element" looms large in all human experience, though how that element is analyzed and related to other human activities is variously portrayed in recent scholarship.[3]

No encompassing "phenomenology of play" has yet emerged to correct and correlate all these different scholarly analyses. That achievement may be long in coming, because contemporary studies of play are deeply divided over important theoretical and practical issues. These disagreements are partly due to the different questions and procedures that prevail among the various academic disciplines. Scholars are sharply divided over contrasting definitions of play and over how play relates to questions of utility, rationality, and reality. Many scholars define play in opposition to all three—play is an "economically useless" activity of "make believe" that transports us from an "ordinary" to an "extraordinary" realm. Other scholars take exception to one or another of these definitional characteristics by tying play more closely to human productivity, problem-solving, or reality definition. But these disagreements need not concern us here. Regardless of how we define play, the power of play is obvious if we concentrate on the simple question "Why do people play?" Virtually all serious scholars on play agree on at least three crucial purposes of human play.

The educational significance of play is beyond question. Not only are children socialized through the games they play, but such activity is at the heart of all thinking. In play, the child takes on and acts out roles that exist in the wider world. In the process, the child learns to assume the perspective of others, thus developing those reflective and cooperative abilities that are the essence of human learning and discovery. Games of skill, games of strategy, and games of chance are the training grounds for both the scientific and the moral imagination. Human beings relive the past, envision the future. and construct the present by playfully creating and enacting model situations. The playing child and the thinking adult are doing essentially the same thing. They are trying out alternative ways of seeing the world and of being in the world.

Human social structures are held together by integrating norms and shared meanings. In order to integrate persons fully into society, the society must provide ways and means for such socialization. Human play, particularly when that play is governed by rules and focused on roles, has an indispensable place in the socialization process. Human play builds character by nurturing such social values as leadership, cooperation, loyalty, and courage. Human play also controls behavior by channeling and releasing such aggressive feelings as competition, anger, resentment and envy. Play helps hold human groups together by providing socially approved occasions for achievement and socially sanctioned outlets for aggression.

Both the cognitive development and the social integration functions of play sound terribly utilitarian. Viewed in this light, we play in order to become sound thinkers and good citizens. But there is always a further goal of play beyond such individual and social utility. Put simply, human beings play for the sheer fun of it. There is a personal expressive function that play affords that cannot be reduced to human learning and mastery of skills. Beyond the practice and perfection of hereditary and social skills, there is the joy of playing for the sake of the game. The pleasure that comes from the physical and mental exertion of play is an end in itself, like all intuitions of truth, goodness, and beauty. Play even more than work affords repeated experiences of self-satisfaction and self-fulfillment that provide and require no other justification than those feelings of satisfaction and fulfillment.

Beyond these widely shared views on the purposes of play is a growing consensus among scholars on the recurrent forms of play. Games of skill, games of strategy, and games of chance operate on very different assumptions and fulfill very different functions in human experience. The play of infants, the play of children, and the play of adults occur on very different levels of awareness and make very different demands on human capabilities. But more important for our purposes are the efforts to understand the changing patterns of play in the course of human history. Both the social attitudes toward and the institutional forms of play have undergone dramatic changes in the transition from traditional to modern cultural order.

Throughout most of human history, religion has been the primary vehicle for human forms of play. This statement may sound outrageous for one of two reasons. On the one hand, Christian cultures have typically valued work above play, sometimes to the point of regarding play as "the work of the devil." When play is considered less valuable than work we cannot imagine why religion has any connection with such frivolity. On the other hand, modern cultures have typically separated play from religion, even to the point of regarding play as an alternative to religion. When play is valued for its psychological and sociological benefits, we cannot imagine why play has any need of religious sanctions. Such Christian denigration and modern approval of play reinforce each other in separating religion and play in our time. But in traditional cultures, even in those shaped and sustained by Christian sensibilities, religion has been the primary vehicle of human play.

This intimate relation between religion and the forms of play in traditional cultures has to do with the power of play noted above. The common denominator of all forms of play is the experience of transcendence. Play takes us out of the limitations and obligations of the everyday world. In play, we are able to break out of the normal patterns of our social arrangements and psychic states. Seen in this light, play has enormous potential for either creativity or destructiveness. Play can open the door either to genius or to madness. The sheer power of play to create alternative views of reality and states of consciousness is why play always occurred under religious control in traditional societies. In the past, religion was the primary vehicle for wit and humor, for song and dance, and for games and sports to channel and control such ecstatic experiences. Religion thereby directed play's manifold expressions of transcendence into socially acceptable and personally beneficial channels.

In modernized societies both East and West, play in its many different forms has left the patronage of religion. To be sure, there are elements of play remaining in mainline religious belief and practice. The cultivation of mystical states of consciousness and the celebration of the great festivals of the religious year are survivals of the play element in modern religion. Moreover, religion still effectively sponsors and sanctions play in certain ways. Positively, the provision of recreation programs in large metropolitan churches and, negatively, the religious suppression of questionable forms of play are evidences that play has not been completely separated from religion. But for the most part, secular institutions have replaced religious institutions in providing and regulating the forms of play in modern societies.

This modern-day autonomy of play is hardly surprising. Religion has lost effective control over vast areas of cultural life that were once conducted under its watchful eye. Religion's monopoly on reality definition and personality formation in traditional cultures has been broken up by far-reaching changes in modern thought and life that can be summed up in the umbrella term "secularization." The process of secularization has redistributed the sources of human meaning and obligation among a variety of institutions and outlooks, some religious and some not. Religion has lost its control over play in the same way and for the same reasons that it has lost its control over the sciences and the arts, over politics and economics, over health care and social welfare. Like these other segmented areas of human life, play operates under its own rules and pursues its own ends.

This separation of religion and play has been anything but beneficial to religion. Religion deprived of the play element quickly hardens into sterile rituals and stagnant beliefs. A religion that loses its ability to transcend the given conditions of social and personal existence remains a religion in name only. There are signs that the spirit of play and the play of the spirit are making a return among the religions of our day, however. Serious Christian theologians are variously arguing for a recovery of faith's sense of honor, celebration, and adventure. A more visible and powerful recovery of the play element in today's religion can be seen in the charismatic movements that bring entertainment and ecstasy into the very heart of worship. While these revivals of playful religion remain on the fringes of respectable religion, they provide compelling evidence of the impossibility of totally suppressing play, even in life's most "serious" moments and matters.[4]

By contrast, play set free from religious controls and religious purposes seems to have thrived, just as politics, economics, science, and art have benefited from their secularization. The forms and occasions for play have been endlessly multiplied in a world with leisure time and financial resources to spare. The spontaneous and unstructured play of childhood has been extended into adult life in ways that previous centuries could never have imagined. All the typical forms of play—music and literature, drama and dance, games and sports—have become increasingly available to "professionals" and "amateurs" alike. No longer is adult play left in the hands of specialists who devote their lives to mastering its skills and strategies. While the "specialization" of play has never been more widespread, neither has the "democratization" of play. Everything from ballet to basketball, from chess to cards, has become the playground of young and old, rich and poor, male and female alike. We are, after all, "one nation under play, with sports and games and entertainment for all."

But not all is well in the world of play. With the expanding prospects of play have come increasing perils. These perils can be seen in every form of human play, but they are perhaps most visible in those forms that we call "sports." That sports is a problem area in modern society is obvious to rednecked devotees and cultured despisers of athletics alike. The sports world has been knocked off its pedestal by well-publicized stories of drug abuse, point shaving, rule violations, and crass mendacity. Thoughtful commentators see these problems as symptomatic of far-reaching distortions of the place of sports in human affairs. These distortions are usually traced to three problems: the displacement of the amateur athlete by the professional athlete, the replacement of the sports participant with the sports spectator, and the placement of competitive values ahead of noncompetitive values. This three-fold indictment was clearly evident in the faculty response to my own university's well-publicized football scandal. Many of Southern Methodist University's faculty called for an end to "quasi-professional" athletics, with its emphasis on filling the stadium and competing for the title, in favor of a benign amateur athletics, with less emphasis on competitive values and more emphasis on participative sports.

But the perils of play go much deeper than these familiar diagnoses of the sports establishment. There is nothing antithetical to play as such in earning a living as an athlete, in being a spectator at a sports event, or in striving to win in every sports competition. Why is it okay to pay ballet dancers but not basketball players? Why is it okay to watch a symphony orchestra but not a soccer match? Why is it okay to give Pulitzer Prizes to playwrights but not to all-American gymnasts? To be sure, the problems of play are most obvious in the world of professional sports, where unbridled competition and commercialized entertainment have become the name of the game. But the problems of play go deeper than any simple-minded dichotomy between professional versus amateur athletes, between spectator versus participant sports, between competitive versus noncompetitive values. These deeper problems have to do with the subversion of an *ethics of play* to an *ethics of work* in modern societies.

Both an ethics of play and an ethics of work center on competition. Both play and work are quests for success under the conditions of challenge. But competitive play and competitive work are worlds apart. Paradigmatically, competitive play means striving for two goals: seeking to win within the rules of the game and seeking to perform at the peak of one's abilities. By contrast, competitive work means pursuing for two very different goals: striving to succeed by whatever means are necessary and seeking to produce with the least expenditure of effort. In an ethics of play, competing to win does not mean that winning is everything. In play, the test is ultimately more important than the contest. But in an ethics of work competing to win does mean that winning is everything. In work, the outcome is always more important than the input.

We can see how the competitive values of work have subverted the competitive values of play at all the levels of athletic activity in modern societies. At the level of participation there are two kinds of rules governing how we play the game. There are *constitutive* rules, which create the game itself. Taking a baseball bat onto a football field is a rejection of the game of football, not a violation of the rules of football. To be sure, constitutive rules in a game can be broken without destroying the game, provided these violations are within the behavior allowed and sanctions are imposed for rule breakers within a game. There are also *strategic* rules, which govern competition within the game itself. Coaches and athletes are forever seeking ways to maximize their two-fold quest for victory and for excellence. Sportsmanship demands that these strategies fall within the constitutive rules of the game. But when coaches and athletes play only to win, these strategic rules of competition may turn the playground into the workplace—or even into the battlefield—where ruthlessness takes precedence over fairness. In that sports world, cheaters usually win and winners usually cheat.

But why do coaches and athletes play to win, even if their playing to win violates the rules of fair play? This question pushes us beyond the level of participation in sports to the level of motivation. At this level there are two kinds of rewards explaining why we play the game. There are intrinsic benefits for participant and spectator alike in athletic competition that can be realized whether we win or not. Competing in sports creates a sense of community, encourages respect for discipline, and develops pride in performance. But there are also extrinsic benefits in athletic competition, again for participants and spectators alike. Fame and fortune have always been accorded to those individuals and teams who play the game well. In a society where winning is everything, the rewards of fame and fortune are staggering for those who play to win. Small wonder that coaches and athletes are tempted to break the rules of fair play to win. The economic and political rewards for winning are so great in our society that it is a wonder that fair play maintains any grip at all over the sports world.

But why does our society revere and reward winners in athletics above virtually all other cultural heroes? This question pushes us beyond the levels of participation and motivation to the level of the validation of sports in our time. At this level, there are two conflicting value systems in our culture vying for control over how and why we "play the game." These rival value systems have their respective roots in conflicting traditions of individualism that reach back to the very beginnings of civilized life in the New World.[5] Some Europeans imagined the New World as a Lockean paradise where human beings could live together free of oppression and competition. Others pictured the New World as a Hobbesian wilderness where people survived only through bitter struggle and sacrifice. These rival mythic images of the New World were carried over into the developing social consciousness of colonial America. One tradition of American individualism drew on biblical and republican strands, which emphasized the creation of a community of persons in which a genuinely moral life could be lived. No person exemplifies this vision of republican individualism more clearly than Thomas Jefferson, who encapsulated his vision of private and public life in a single injunction: "Love your neighbor as yourself, and your country more than yourself." By contrast, another tradition of American individualism drew on Enlightenment and utilitarian strands, which emphasized the formation of a society of citizens focused on individual self-improvement. Benjamin Franklin championed this vision of utilitarian individualism, memorably summed up in his famous dictum "God helps those who help themselves."

These republican and utilitarian traditions are still very much a part of a North American sense of self and of society. Our history has been a continuing tug-of-war between the ideals of the covenant community and of the pluralistic society, as first one and then the other model of private and public life capture the national imagination. But over the centuries, the utilitarian morality of self-interest has become increasingly dominant. Indeed, a thinly disguised Social Darwinism heavily influences many of our cultural institutions—our educational system, military complex, market economy, and political order. Little wonder that the mentality of "the survival of the fittest" might spill over into other cultural institutions as well—into our homes and churches, into our entertainments and athletics.

Here finally are the roots of the problems that corrupt athletes and athletics in the modern world. Sports, whether amateur or professional are being subverted and suborned by the modern world's dominant ideology of progress. Indeed, the performance principle of modern sports is the idea of endless progress. On first glance, this emphasis on unlimited progress seems quite compatible with the experience of transcendence that lies at the heart of all play. Play always takes us beyond the limits of normal psychic states and social arrangements. But the idea of endless progress that animates modern sports is rooted in something other than such fantasy and festivity. The performance principle of modern sports is modeled on economic and technological assumptions about endless progress. This dependence on economics and technology goes deeper than the obvious fact that sports thrives on big money and new techniques. The athlete is regarded as a commodity. As such, sports are subject to the same market considerations as any other product in our consumer-oriented society—the struggle over scarce resources and the survival of the fittest. The athlete is treated like a machine and as such, is the object of the same refined engineering as any other product in our scientifically oriented society—the manipulative techniques of high-performance sports medicine and applied sports psychology.[6] The dynamic of modern sports is this promise of limitless performance aided and abetted by economic incentives and technological innovations.

Needless to say, these images of the athlete as commodity and the athlete as machine are in direct conflict with our basic ideas of what a human being should be. Herein lies the great danger of modern sports and the real peril of modern play. Sports and play are losing their humanizing influence—their power to broaden and deepen the finer sensibilities of the human spirit. Herein lies the great importance of amateur athletics—whether regulated, as in Olympic competition and intercollegiate athletics, or unregulated, as in fitness programs and personal recreation. By their very nature, amateur athletics are more resilient and resistant to the economic and technological perversions of play than are professional athletics. Living up to the ideal of limitless performance—reinforced by economic incentives and technological procedures—is less a problem for amateur than for professional athletics. Amateur athletics thereby keeps alive the ideal of playing not just to learn or to earn, but playing for the joy and fun of it.

In conclusion, play has always had a crucial role in all human pursuits. The power of play to transport us into another world beyond the ordinary world of fixed limits and set duties lies at the heart of the human imagination in all of its expressions. That power is the wellspring of human creativity as well as human perversity. The playful imagination can literally create a heaven or a hell on earth. Little wonder that primitive and traditional cultures kept these immense powers of play under the tutelage of religious institutions and functionaries. But religious control of play has long since disappeared in our modern world, and nothing we could ever do will reestablish religion's hegemony over play. The playful spirit has "free play" in all of the expressions of culture science and art, politics and economics, religion and recreation.

That there are dangers in uncontrolled and unchanneled play is beyond question. But the real danger in our time is not that we play too much but that we play too little. The legacy of a sports world built on the exchange values of the marketplace and the engineering techniques of the laboratory is the subordination of the values of play to the values of work. The sports world, which ought to be a glorious world of escape and ecstasy, is in danger of becoming a hideous world of bondage and utility. Small wonder that so many people in our society turn to the far more risky play of drugs and sex as a way of transcending their pointless and joyless lives. For all of our frantic devotion to sports and games, to entertainment and diversions, we need to rediscover the fun and grace of children at play. Perhaps this was what Jesus meant when he said: "Except you become as a little child, you will not see the Kingdom of God."

[1] Michael Novak, *The Joy of Sports* (New York: Basic Books, 1976) 1.

[2] For an excellent survey of the scholarship on play, see David L. Miller, *Gods and Games* (New York: Harper and Row, 1973) 17-117.

[3] The study of the "play element" in culture was pioneered by Johan Huizinga, *Homo Ludens* (Boston: Beacon Press, 1955).

[4] See my discussion on "theologies of play" in Lonnie D. Kliever, *The Shattered Spectrum* (Atlanta: John Knox Press, 1981) 124-52, 224-27.

[5] Vide Robert Bellah, et al., *Habits of the Heart: Individualism and Commitment in American Life* (Berkeley: University of California Press, 1985).

[6] John M. Hoberman, "Sport and the Technological Image of Man" (unpublished essay presented in the UT Ethics Lectures Series, University of Texas at Austin, April 25, 1986).

FROM SEASON TO SEASON
THE RHYTHM AND SIGNIFICANCE
OF AMERICA'S SPORTING CALENDAR

Joseph L. Price

While waiting in the wake of winter's frigid death and vacuous expanse for time to begin on Opening Day,[1] a sports fan celebrates the festivities of NCAA basketball's "The Final Four" only weeks after the National Football League's premier event, the Super Bowl. In early March, as in few other times of the year, Americans experience a phenomenon of convergence in the sports calendar: college basketball's season presses toward its climax while fans anticipate the imminent beginning of another season, the first in the cycle of new life of springtime—the start of Major League baseball.

Certainly, all sports seasons have definitive endings. College football crowns a national champion with its new bowl alliance that pits the top ranked teams against each other at the culmination of New Year's bowl games. The NFL's Super Bowl, initially conceived as a post-season game that would certify the NFL's preeminence following the merger of the NFL and AFL, has grown into a cultural event of unmatched proportions.[2] The NHL's Stanley Cup Playoffs, the NBA's Championship Series, and Major League Baseball's World Series can force the prevailing team to play seven games in a final "home and home series." Yet none of these periods of championship play at season's end occurs at a point during which another major sports season is dawning. The concurrence of seasons—their overlap—only indicates that they are not primarily chronometrical measures of time but somehow mythic separations of the rhythms of sports life that are cyclical.

During the unique splice of seasons that March and early April afford in the annual sports calendar, sports fans experience the arhythmic pulse and the mythic renewals afforded by the sports seasons. Before exploring some of the distinct rhythms and significance of the American Sports Calendar, however, I want to point out the significance of calendars, which will help to frame the concept of an American Sports Calendar.

Until the early twentieth century, probing analyses of calendars often described astral configurations or sequential enumerations of measure, thus signifying that the calendar was conceived as an abstract principle of time applied to human experience. But in more recent years, and coincidentally in concert with the development of professional sports seasons, calendars have begun to be analyzed in terms of the cultures of their origin. They have begun to be interpreted in the context of their culture's dominant myths, examining how they have been adapted or syncretized into the measures of a cycle that is oriented to astral configurations and the sequential differentiation of time into days, weeks, months, seasons.

One of the distinctions of a seasonal calendar is that it marks and measures mythic time, not history and its chronometric sequence. One of the characteristics of history is that it is often determined by unique events: "History is made up of single events that often never recur,"[3] as one liturgical guide puts it. By contrast, mythical time—or liturgical time—is qualitatively different from historical time because mythical time is characterized by cycles and seasons that infuse the very movement of history with regular periods of communal significance.[4] In addition, the pivotal events or transformative actions in history become occasions for narrative focus in the retelling of history. At such historical points, the specific time of history begins to generate a recreative time of myth—a time for retelling the story, for re-enacting the event, for ordering a culture's life.

In sports, incredible performances and feats become focal points of memory and celebration. Consider, for example, Bobby Thompson's dramatic homerun against the Dodgers and Ralph Branca, Mickey Owens's dropped third strike on the swing by Tommy Henrich, Willie Mays's sensational catch and cosmic whirl and throw against Vic Wertz, Kirk Gibson's crippled, pinch-hit World Series homerun against Cy Young reliever Dennis Eckersley with two on and two out in the bottom of the ninth, Secretariat's proletariat prance to the triple crown, Wilt the Stilt's hundred point game, Bobby Allison's bumper margin victory at Daytona, Darrel Waltrip's spectacular crash at Indianapolis, Bart Starr's frozen quarterback sneak against the Cowboys in the tundra at Green Bay, John

Elway's engineering and execution of "The Drive" against the Cleveland Browns, and Michael Jordan's final shot, an NBA championship buzzer-beating game winner. These unique performances in competition are certainly the source for memory, celebration, conversation, even consecration; but they can never be repeated. They are the mythic conquests or defeats that have arisen out of the history of seasons to give meaning to the past and hope for that which is unique to arrive in the seasons yet to come and their games.

The fusion of secular holidays and celebrations with several that have religious roots has produced what Catherine Albanese has called a sort of liturgical calendar for American culture. In her astute analysis of religious traditions, practices, and temperament in America, Albanese pays particular attention to the phenomena that she names "cultural religion," a rubric that designates non-ecclesial religiosity and incorporates elements of popular religion, mass religion, and folk religion. Whatever the particular shape that this odd beast now takes in America, she notes that it bears lines of continuity with public Protestantism and civil religion in the United States. The most obvious element of American cultural religion is what she calls "the American ritual calendar."[5] It features a variety of culturally accepted and adapted Christian holidays and festivals, such as Christmas, Easter, and Halloween, and it also highlights significant civil holidays like Memorial Day, July 4, and Thanksgiving. It is apparent that American culture indeed orients its pattern of rhythms—especially the economic and leisure ones, just witness the anticipation of seasons by Hallmark and the network television specials on each of the civic holidays—to the sequence and significance of these days.

In a similar way to the calendrical distinctions within the "American ritual calendar," the phenomenon of American Sports Religion also manifests the differentiation of seasons and celebration of holidays to form a liturgical calendar for American sports fans and even for American popular culture. The idea that sports seasons represent some kind of religious calendar of course presupposes that sports is, in American culture, a primary manifestation of a kind of civil religion or folk religion, as James Mathisen has argued in "From Civil Religion to Folk Religion: The Case of American Sport."[6]

For America's sporting faithful, the year is divided into seasons of sport, four of which dominate the calendar because of the length of their respective seasons, because of the quality and character of play at a professional (and near professional, i.e., collegiate) team level, and because of the increasing exposure of the sports on network and cable television. Obviously, the four major seasons are baseball, football, basketball, and hockey. Two of the four seasons—football and basketball—have clearly been subdivided into NCAA and professional seasons, even by the *Sporting News*, which for almost a century bore the subtitle of "Baseball's Bible," and now devotes regular, differentiated coverage to the sports' professional and collegiate seasons. In football and basketball, the professional and collegiate seasons begin at about the same time, but they conclude at separate championship events that occur months apart, with the professional seasons virtually doubling the length of the collegiate seasons. In recent years ESPN has generated increasing interest in college baseball, thus heightening American awareness and appreciation of the "sub-season" of collegiate baseball. Despite its rise in popularity, however, the collegiate world series (even in NCAA Division I) is not likely to challenge the dominant identification of baseball season with that of Major League play because of the association of baseball with summer and the expectations for the Major League World Series at harvest time. Nor has the international competition and the romantic attraction to children at play in the Little League World Series challenged the supremacy of the Major League championship.

In addition to its general orientation around professional team-sport seasons, the American Sports Calendar also features other sports festivals and holidays that offer contrast to the elongation of the team-sport seasons. Among the holidays and festivals are events that focus on individual play and performance: e.g., golf's series of major tournaments, highlighted by the Masters, the PGA, the US Open, and the British Open; tennis's grand slam of tournaments, with Forest Hills and Wimbledon accruing a temporary, sacrosanct character; auto racing's annual focus on the field of formula races, particularly the Indy 500 and the NASCAR circuit, featuring the Daytona 500; and the thoroughbred run for the roses in the Kentucky Derby, followed within the next four weeks by the Preakness and the Belmont Stakes, all of which constitute racing's Triple Crown. (With this metaphor, we can discern again the dominance of baseball as the paradigmatic season, since baseball metaphors are used to describe tennis's major championships—the Grand Slam—and horse racing's triad of prestigious races—The Triple Crown.)

In *The Sacred and the Profane*, Mircea Eliade repeatedly points to the various ways in which secular rituals and myths provide residual manifestations of the sorts of religious impulses that had generated and oriented rituals originally described as religious. For instance, New Year's eve parties and their festivities maintain a sort of residual contact with the origin of cosmic renewal festivals that have been common among many religious traditions. Similarly, the rather innocuous "down-home" celebration of a house warming party for persons moving into a new abode recalls, in at least rudimentary ways, the kinds of domestic consecration rituals that were (and are) enacted in many religious traditions wherein one's house or dwelling needs protection by particular deities or from certain cosmic forces. Because one of the primary purposes of religious rituals is that of purification, of restoration, of establishing and maintaining or legitimating the order of one's world, it is most often the case that residual rituals in secularity have to do also with some sort of renewal.[7]

In this regard it is not surprising that one of the most significant dates for the American Sports Calendar is that of its New Year, which might coincide with the start of the most significant—or most established—American sports season, baseball. Yet as Eliade remarks in *Cosmos and History: The Myth of the Eternal Return*, it is possible that several New Year's festivals would be celebrated in a single tradition. For where different cultivated grains and fruits required varied planting and harvest times, the host culture would likely celebrate several New Year's festivals to ensure the success of each of the crops. In each of these situations, Eliade avers, "the divisions of time are determined by the rituals…that guarantee the continuity of the life of the community in its entirety."[8] Similarly, with the varying cultivated sports in the American calendar, separate seasons require special inaugural ceremonies each year in order to legitimate the statistical results of the various sports. Nonetheless, the Opening Day of Major League Baseball is more celebrated as a national time of beginning again than the initial games of any of the other sports seasons in America for several reasons—functional, political, and mythical.

Functionally, Major League Baseball's season features twice as many games as the NBA, the second longest season in the calendar. More importantly, baseball has the most established tradition of opening day festivities among American professional sports. Because of its claim to be the national pastime, Major League Baseball is the only sport that regularly attracts the nation's president to toss out the first ball for the first game for one of the teams. In this way, there is a political and civic sanction accorded to baseball's season in a way that no other professional sport enjoys. By way of contrast, presidential consecration of other sports—particularly NFL football and NCAA basketball—comes after their final judgment, after the end of their seasons. Then the president calls the Super Bowl winner to congratulate the winning coach or invites the Final Four champion to the White House for a reception. Mythically, Opening Day of Major League Baseball is most important because of its timing in spring (the time of planting), a time that coincides with nature's new year and corresponding celebrations of fertility rites.

In terms of the new year's cycles that occur for all sports, Major League Baseball's Opening Day is certainly the most celebrated. For Opening Day, as Tom Boswell concludes, "is baseball's bandwagon. Pundits and politicians and every prose poet on the continent jump on board for a few days. But they're gone soon, off in search of some other windy event worthy of their attention. Then, once more, all those long, slow months of baseball are left to us. And our time can begin again."[9] In one sense, then, the significance of Opening Day is that it fuses history and myth, historical time and cosmic time. For baseball, like many team sports, is a sport that blends two kinds of games—the one on the field, which is bound by real time and contests and seasons, and the one in our minds. The interior game of baseball, as James Mote has noted,

> is played in the dreams of children and in the memories of old men and in the imagination of anyone who has ever wished, if only for a moment, that he or she could have been a big league baseball player. It is the mythical, magical game that transcends innings and outs and seasons—and lifetimes. It is the baseball we relive, reshape, and invent anew, and it is played—in winter as in spring—in fields as fertile as the human imagination.[10]

The mythic dimension of baseball, as for other sports, emerges out of seasons and transcends them, even orienting them. But it is to the seasons of the games on the grass, the hardwood, and the ice that Americans turn for ordering their quotidian interests and attention, for seeking escape from the boredom of work routines, and for thrilling with the vicarious conquest over stress. For with the games and in their fanatic observation, tension is created and resolved; and with the cycle of the seasons, resolution and renewal can be effectively anticipated and realized.

The influence and interplay of television on the American Sports Calendar also merit consideration. The particular timing and length of certain sports events and seasons are adapted to, or determine the broadcast schedules of, America's television networks. In order to expand the number of crucial games that can be telecast, the NBA has extended its playoff format to include more games, and Major League Baseball created the League Championship Series two decades ago before adding the "extra" preliminary play-off series in 1994. The number of college football bowl games has now swelled from fewer than ten that were telecast in the pre-cable era to more than twenty-five at century's end.

To accommodate a large television audience, the World Series now starts on a weekend (so that a seven-game series might consume prime-time slots on two weekends), and its former weekday games have been transferred to nighttime offerings to fit the prime time format and the Nielsen polling periods. Symbolically perhaps the most important accommodation of sports and their seasons to American television schedules was the intrusion of lights into Wrigley Field. The change was finally accomplished not to enable the Cubs to avoid the deadly slump of August in the midst of a typical, late-summer Chicago heat wave, but to facilitate the possibility of nighttime World Series telecasts and to increase the prime time television audience for WGN. Similarly, the starting times of some collegiate basketball games have been shifted to late night so that double- or triple-header telecasts can be presented, thus increasing the likelihood of a larger televiewing audience. The days and times of professional football games—now including not only Monday night, whose ABC telecast has now passed its twenty-fifth anniversary, but also expanding to Sunday nights, occasional Thursday nights, and Saturdays following the completion of the collegiate regular football season—have been diversified to accommodate national telecast. The emergence of the ESPN and FOX sports networks, as well as regional and local cable sports enterprises, has focused more attention on the span of sports seasons. Finally, in order to appeal to larger live audiences and the prospects of national telecasts, major sports rivalries have begun to coordinate their games with national holidays. In this way, certain sports events and spectacles are becoming identified with established civic holidays: the Indy 500 on Memorial Day weekend, the plethora of collegiate football bowl games on New Year's eve and New Year's day, the NBA on CBS on Christmas Day, and the football games at Dallas and Detroit on Thanksgiving afternoon.

The integration of the American Sports Calendar with television schedules is essential for the survival and profitability of television networks and professional sports enterprises. For the primary reason given for the purchase of new televisions is that of wanting to see sports,[11] and the pace setting multi-million dollar contract awarded to Cubs' second baseman Ryne Sandberg was directly related to WGN's superstation status and its number of prime time telecasts of the Chicago Cubs. In fact, the pervasive public support of professional sports has coincided directly with their increased exposure initially on radio, then on television, and most recently on dedicated sports cable networks.

Although we have focused thus far on the separate seasons of American sports and how they conform to a regular cycle that we can call a sports calendar, we must ask about its meaning in its entirety: What does the calendar of the sports seasons and holidays mean? In general, unlike a number of natural and religious seasons, the sports seasons do not get associated with celestial or agricultural phenomena, although elements of the these cosmic orientations remain. Baseball's season indeed begins in the time of spring, the time for celebrating fertility, and football's tearing up of turf occurs after the time of harvest. But their rude reflections of natural rhythms hardly signify the overall importance of the sequence of sports seasons and the development of a sports calendar.

Basically, the sequence of the sports seasons provides a kind of "symbolic syntax" of the year, a kind of "running commentary" on the progress and importance of time.[12] The establishment of a calendar manifests a cosmological orientation that strives to explain space and time—not necessarily in the natural recurrence of seasons, but to explore the mystical and metaphysical order of reality: Why and how does the world mean something rather than nothing? Why do events and festivals take on a special sense of significance?

Although the American sports seasons do not completely correspond to traditional periods of planting and harvesting, of cultivating and laying fallow, there are ways in which the shape of the sports calendar itself corresponds to religious or liturgical calendars, which often have developed in response to a perception of cosmic significance of natural cycles.

One of the significant dimensions of the Christian liturgical calendar is that it celebrates sacramental time, a time when mystery is manifest, a time when the hope and promise of the season are present. In a similar manner sports seasons cultivate the growth of hope (as with the eternal, recurrent optimism of Cubs' fans) and the ability to deal with thwarted possibilities and frustrated expectations by recognizing the prospect for a new season in a new year. Through its cyclical regularity, the American sports calendar ever celebrates the possible newness of life, of teams, of players, and of fans. Because the primary purpose of the sports seasons is to frame the possibility for realizing expectations and dealing with frustrations, to make it possible for another team to come out ahead next year after having suffered humiliation this season, the seasons begin and end with variant dates each year. This variation, however, merely indicates that the seasons conform to cosmic time rather than historical time, wherein the celebration of specific dates might be more significant. For time itself, as one liturgical guide has put it, "is not an abstraction, but a dimension of that which is born, lives, and dies. We can perceive it if, abandoning the realm of abstraction, we come to reflect upon ourselves."[13]

Even as the Christian liturgical year is not a neutral framework but an ordered celebration of seasons that address the variety of religious needs and concerns in a culture's life, so too the American sports calendar differentiates and repeats separate seasons that appeal to different sensibilities. It provides a series of patterns and festivals that differently appeal to sports fans and reflect their variant preferences: from the icy chill and violence of hockey to the open spaces and freedoms of baseball; and from the turf-bound conflicts of football to the transcendent gliding of players above hardwood courts in basketball. Each of the major seasonal sports manifests myths and rituals that distinguish them from the others, as essays throughout this volume attest.

The ephemeral, temporal, and cyclical character of seasons measures out the myths by which people order their lives.[14] Like most religious calendars, the primary function of the American sports calendar is to provide some kind of ritual transition from the chaos of secularity to the cosmos of sports, from cultural malaise to corporate hope. In other words, the sports calendar orients followers to the mythic origin and destiny of the sport and, by extension, themselves. The sports calendar thus reflects identity and wholeness of the American sporting enterprise and of the American competitive character itself.

Finally, the American sports calendar presents one series of festivals and seasons that occurs in overlapping and sometimes conflicting ways with other calendars—such as the Christian liturgical year or the Muslim series of religious holidays, cycles of ethnic festivals and occupational events, and the sequence of civic holidays that mark out the character of American mythic history. The convergence or competition of calendars does not reflect incoherence in American culture but its complexity. For it is possible for one person to be an Irish Catholic who celebrates St. Patrick's day in March, who attends to the significance of Lent and Easter, who awaits the first pitch in Cincinnati to signal the start of the baseball season, and who sheds tears while attending Memorial Day commemorations at a military cemetery.[15] Each person participates in a number of competing symbol systems, each of which commands certain forms of religious allegiance and affection, seeking to render some order to the world, to make sense out of one's experience, and to find hope or direction in the challenges and ambiguities that one encounters.

For American sports fans, then, it is often *through* the series of sports seasons that they find or establish order, that they experience wonder, that they calculate possibilities, and that they invest in opportunities. For them, the rhythm of the seasons is the measure by which they order their lives, consecrating and celebrating memories of the great plays and near-misses (like the '64 Phillies and the '69 Cubs, or the Tennessee Titans in Super Bowl XXXIV) and forecasting and forging hopes about the season yet to come, as certainly the die-hard Cubs and Red Sox fans do year after year, season after season, ever hopeful that the start of a new year will bring new life and its promise of fulfillment.

---

[1] Cf. Tom Boswell, *Why Time Begins on Opening Day* (New York: Doubleday, 1984).

[2] See my brief essay "The Super Bowl as Religious Festival" that follows in this volume.

[3] *Days of the Lord: The Liturgical Year, I,* written by Benedictines under the supervision of Robert Gantoy and Romain Swaeles, trans. Gregory LaNave and Donald Molloy (Collegeville MN: Liturgical Press, 1991) 11.

[4] Cf. Mircea Eliade, *The Sacred and the Profane: The Nature of Religion*, trans. Willard R. Trask (New York: Harcourt, Brace, and Co, 1959), especially chap. 2.

[5] Catherine L. Albanese, *America: Religion and Religions* (Belmont CA: Wasdsworth, 1981) 465.

[6] James A. Mathisen, "From Civil Religion to Folk Religion: The Case of American Sport," in *Sport and Religion*, ed. Shirl J. Hoffman (Champaign IL: Human Kinetics, 1992) 17-33.

[7] Eliade, *Sacred and the Profane*, esp. 29-36, 104-113.

[8] Mircea Eliade, *Cosmos and History: The Myth of the Eternal Return*, trans. Willard R. Trask (New York: Harper and Row, 1959) 51.

[9] Boswell, *Why Time Begins on Opening Day*, 300.

[10] James Mote, *Everything Baseball* (New York: Prentice Hall Press, 1989) ix.

[11] Cf. Gregor Goethals, *The TV Ritual: Worship at the Video Altar* (Boston: Beacon Press, 1981), especially chap. 1, "Ritual: Ceremony and Super Sunday."

[12] Cf. Jack Santino, *All Around the Year: Holidays and Celebrations in American Life* (Urbana: University of Illinois Press, 1994) 17.

[13] *Days of the Lord*, 1.

[14] See Theodore Gaster, "Seasonal Ceremonies," in Mircea Eliade, ed., *The Encyclopedia of Religion*, 16 vols. (New York: Macmillan, 1987) 16:148-51.

[15] Cf. Santino, *All Around the Year*, 1.

BASEBALL

THE PITCHER'S MOUND AS COSMIC MOUNTAIN
RELIGIOUS REFLECTIONS ON BASEBALL

Joseph L. Price

Introduction

During a Wrigley Field rain delay in the summer of 1986, several theologians and historians of religion overheard a conversation between two teenage boys in the bleachers. One asked the other: "Why is the pitcher's mound higher than home plate? Why is it the only part of the field that is raised?" His friend responded with technical data about the exact height of the mound and the historical observation that the height of the mound was reduced two decades earlier in an effort to give the batters a better chance to hit against such overpowering pitchers as Bob Gibson. Despite the correct and seemingly sufficient information reported by his friend, the first boy then mused, "No, that's not it. There must be some *real* reason why the pitcher's mound is higher."[1]

This story advocates my turn to religious studies in an effort to understand the lure and sufficiency of baseball for millions of Americans. It should not be surprising that some philosophical, or academic framework is applied to the game in order to understand its compelling attraction. Attempts have been made to interpret the game of baseball by looking at the physics of the phenomena, such as the difficulty of hitting a 90 mph fastball released only sixty feet away. With the ball traveling at a speed of 132 feet per second, it is easy to calculate that the batter has less than half of a second to judge the angle of approach, speed, and altering rotation on the ball in order to swing a bat of a little more than two pounds quickly enough to make solid contact with the pitch.

Other academic interpretations of the game have been summarized and offered by Roland Garrett, who finally opts for the sufficiency of a metaphysical approach. He has noted, for instance, that both mathematical and psychological models have been proposed for analyzing the appeal of the game. In terms of mathematical options, Garrett notes that implicit, incarnate trigonometric calculations enable an outfielder to time the speed of his approach to the point of a fly ball's descent. He notes the psychological—in this case certainly Freudian—attempt to explain the fascination with the game: "In baseball, it might be said, the competition of pitcher and batter represents the age-old conflict between father and son. The pitcher-father attempts to reach home with a thrown ball, representing semen, while the batter -son uses his bat, a phallus, to deflect and scatter the semen-ball. The pitcher-father gains success when a pitched ball either enters the strike zone or (after being hit) enters a glove of his teammates. The batter may be put out either way. But if, by getting a hit, the batter-son can prevent the pitcher-father from attaining sexual union at home, he can himself attain it by rounding the bases and reaching home again."[2]

Another set of reasons that provoke a religious interpretation of the game comes from the extensive attention and allegiance given to the game. Because this latter set of reasons can be dealt with more quickly, I will turn attention to it first. In this regard an appeal to statistical computations (which are one of the fascinations with baseball fanaticism) identifies the inordinate attention commanded by the game. After examining the extensive appeal of baseball, I will explore then the mysterious if not mystical dimensions of the teenage fan's query about the height of the pitcher's mound.

Fascination and Fanaticism

During the 1998 baseball season—which featured the home run chases and races of Mark McGwire and Sammy Sosa—more than 50 million fans walked through the turnstiles at Major League baseball games. According to attendance statistics released by Major League Baseball, the most popular team drew more than 3 million fans to its home stadium.

Yet most fans who watch the game do so via television by receiving local telecast signals, cable connections, or satellite dish reception. Each Major League team telecasts its games in addition to the NBC and FOX featured games, ESPN's offering of weeknight double-headers, and various regional telecasts on the affiliate networks of ESPN and FOX Sports. In fact, during the spectacular 1998 season, FOX and ESPN captured record television audiences, especially for the Labor Day game when McGwire hit his record tying homer. Add to these network telecasts the vast viewership of baseball favorites—the Cubs and Braves—on TV "superstations" from Chicago and Atlanta, and you can calculate the annual viewership of Major League Baseball in excess of 4 billion viewers—within the United States alone.

This seemingly astronomical figure of those who, in one way or another, attended the games by viewing them does not take into account the hundreds of millions of others who daily "attended" the games via radio broadcasts. These figures can be extended even further when one considers that the minor league teams—about 150 of which are somehow affiliated with the Major League teams—command local radio audiences for the faithful following of their games.

In addition to the kind of religious devotion to Major League Baseball that is evinced through attendance statistics, the trappings of Major League Baseball also bear remarkable similarities to the styles of reverence and rituals associated with established religious traditions. Like many religions, baseball has a binding creed, as Jim Murray, sports columnist for the *Los Angeles Times* has described its nearly inexorable set of traditional rules. "Baseball is a game that revels in its predictability.... It's not a sport, it's a religion. It takes on new beliefs with the greatest of reluctance." By contrast, he continues, "Football changes its rules, its concepts, as nonchalantly as a debutante changes her wardrobe."[3]

Along somewhat the same line of comparison, Murray Ross compares the attraction that fans have to sports like baseball and football. Classifying sport as some sort of popular theater (since it has a sort of rudimentary drama, type characters, and heroic or comic action action amidst story and character variations), he goes on to muse about the activity of sports spectating, which, he says, "involves something more than the vicarious pleasures of identifying with athletic prowess." In fact, he proposes "that each sport contains a fundamental myth which it elaborates for its fans, and that our pleasure in watching such games derives in part from belonging briefly to the mythical world which the game and players bring to life."[4]

In addition to its religious affections for rules, baseball has its temples—its stadiums—where the rites are performed—and its shrines—like the Hall of Fame. It also features various memorials to bygone heroes, like the busts in the Hall of Fame, the commemorative plaques beyond the centerfield fence in Yankee Stadium, and the retired numbers hanging from the upper deck at Fenway Park. Baseball has its cult of saints, its superheroes of bygone years now "enshrined" (as avid enthusiasts put it) in the Hall of Fame. Baseball, like religions, also has its relics, its tangible artifacts that help to call to mind the journeys to the games and the contact with the heroes. For the fan, the relics are called game balls, players' autographs, and the plethora of memorabilia—officially licensed souvenirs—that can be purchased at stadium souvenir stands. Like many religions, baseball has its sacred texts—the official tables of statistics and the official publications from yearbooks to the fans' weekly tract, the *Sporting News*, which for years bore the subtitle, "The Baseball Bible." Baseball also has its high priests, like All-Star pitchers and Cy Young Award winners, and its true believers, like the most faithful fans who, typified by Cubs' devotees, never give up even when hope has become unreasonable. Like some religions, baseball identifies its sins by calculating and tabulating errors for fielders, strike outs for batters, and walks, balks, and hit batters for pitchers. Finally, baseball has its own liturgical calendar—its own list of holy days or holidays that begins with the festive "new year" celebrations of Opening Day, includes national holidays like Memorial Day, July 4th, and Labor Day, features the All-Star Game, and concludes with the high holidays of the divisional playoffs and World Series.

The ability of baseball to establish a cohesive identity as a community—like that of an avid fan immediately and fully establishing communion with other fans who otherwise are strangers—and to evoke a sense of personal wholeness is neither fully derived from the public veneration of the game and its heroes nor from the personal thrill generated by great plays. By way of comparison, the fundamental character of religion is not fully located in its appeal (expressed in popular devotion and apotheosis) or in its power to evoke a peak experience. Including these appealing and powerful elements, a religion establishes its essential character with its ability to generate, orient, and sustain an identity in community; and a religion accomplishes this process by means of its narrative structure of symbols—its mythology—both in explicit and implicit ways.

Although a functional approach to an analysis of baseball as religious provides a useful index of the prominence of baseball in the life of Americans, I suggest that baseball, as America's national pastime, commands religious respect because its rituals and symbols manifest an underlying mythology that should be called religious. The mythology of baseball is displayed most clearly in its cosmology, its ritual action, and its dramatization of a kind of cosmic dualism.

The Cosmos of Baseball

The most significant, inherent reason that baseball can provide religious coherence for many Americans is that the game has a cosmology of its own. It has its own sense of order. As the philosopher Alfred North Whitehead once noted, "whatever suggests a cosmology, suggests a religion."[5] Historian of religion Peter Gardella specifically extends this cosmological connection to baseball. He proposes that a kind of cosmic reason determines the orientation of the field and the play of the game:

> Baseball diamonds organize space in the same way as the basilica of St. Peter at Rome, the altar of heaven at Peking and the great mosque in Mecca. What happens on baseball diamonds may seem to be only a sport, but the pattern of the field and the rules of the game also form a ritual. Understanding baseball requires the analytic tools of psychology and comparative religion.[6]

Although I differ with Gardella in determining the kind of mythic or ritual structures that underlie the game, I do agree that the lure and love of baseball can be explained most adequately (but certainly not exclusively) by appeal to the methods and insights of religious studies. For baseball claims the devotion, allegiance, indeed fanaticism of millions of persons and it serves as a center of meaning and hope for many players and fans who look to its order to provide a semblance of significance and order in their perhaps otherwise mundane, unfocused, or disorganized lives.

In baseball, the cosmos is structured in terms of the myth of the center, for the game itself—the field and the rituals of its play—has a sacred center and a highly developed cosmology that is connected to the pitcher's mound, the mythical center of the field. In mythological terms, it does not matter that the pitcher's mound is not the geographic center of the field, for the sacred center does not connote geographic or geometric centrality—a unique, exclusive kind of centrality—but mythological and metaphysical centrality—one of meaning and being.[7]

Baseball is structured by such a mythical and metaphysical center, one that signifies the cosmology of the game. This is not, however, to say that Abner Doubleday[8] or Casey Stengel comprehended the significance or even consciously apprehended the presence of the myth of the center in the structure of the game. For a myth does not have to be articulated, understood, or even recognized in order to manifest power and exert dominance in the shaping of an identity. There are some claims by Buddhist enthusiasts, however, that Doubleday, who was a member of the Theosophical Society, intentionally infused the game, as Helen Tworkov notes, "with mystical Buddhist numbers—nine (innings, players, yanas), three (strikes, jewels, vehicles), and four (balls, bases, noble truths)."[9] Although modern baseball historians have questioned the historicity of Doubleday's influence on the game, some of the enthusiasts have considered the shape of the baseball field as an oblique reference to the *Diamond Sutra*. One further coincidence, which Buddhologists often disregard since the mysteries of the universe underlie and eventually explain all such unusual convergencies, merits mention: "the 108 stitches (as in suture of 'sutra') on the hardball. This is the total of 9 x 3 x 4: the same number of Buddhist prayer beads on a sacred mala as well as the number used ritually and repeatedly throughout Buddhist cultures."[10]

The dominant myth in the game of baseball, however, is one that transcends the particularities of Buddhism and bears remarkable similarity to the myth of the center, or as it was first known at Delphi, the omphalos myth.[11] For ancient Greeks, the idea that the omphalos, or navel, was the center of the earth indicated not only that the sacred rock or cosmic mountain was the mythical center of the earth but also that the omphalos manifested a biological connection with the rest of the world, that is, that it was the point from which creation began. In the ancient world, the summit of the cosmic mountain often was identified with the navel of the earth, for at the highest point in the world (not necessarily the highest geographic point on the planet Earth but the highest mythical point for a people, their place of peak experiences) the gods first touched the Earth and began the process of creation.

Because of its relative height, it nearness to the heavenly arena of the gods, the cosmic mountain was thought to be the place of divine activity, the place of the world's beginning and the place for efficacious sacrifice to the gods. The myth of the center, as expressed in the designation of cosmic mountains, was not restricted to the Greeks or to cultures that embraced multiple deities. For native Americans in the San Francisco Bay region regarded Mt. Diablo as the dwelling place of the gods; and in the history of Israel's religions, for example, mounts Tabor, Hebron, Zion, and Sinai were thought at one time or another to be the center of the world, the place whether God both began the creation of the world and the nation of Israel.[12]

As the place of the origin of creation, the omphalos represents the point of intersection and interaction of the cosmic spheres: At the rock of the center, heaven, hell, and earth come together. As this point of cosmic intersection, the omphalos is the place where the axis from the center of heaven to the center of hell penetrates the earth. The omphalos thus provides the point of entry into earth from both the heavenly and chthonic realms. As such, the omphalos becomes the ideal location for duels between cosmic forces, between the creative powers associated with the heavenly gods and the destructive forces connected to chthonic forces. In addition to its concentration on creation mythology, the omphalos myth has several other motifs that are often found in conjunction with the sacred stone and the cosmic mountain. Some of these are snake worship, sun worship, chthonic rituals, and bisexual rituals.[13] Although all of these motifs are not found in baseball (except perhaps at Phoenix where the Arizona Diamondbacks utilize snake iconography), elements of some of them appear in the structure of the game, and their presence confirms the similarity of the implicit mythology of baseball with that of the omphalos myth.

For the omphalos myth and its exemplification in the game of baseball, the most important point of correspondence is the identification of the omphalos—the central, sacred stone—with the cosmic mountain. In the world of baseball, the cosmic center is the sacred "stone" that is atop the sacred mountain: The pitcher's rubber is located at the top of the pitcher's mound, a twelve-inch high rise that provides the only topographical elevation in the field.[14] Rising above the level contour of the field, the pitcher's mound corresponds to the cosmic mountains of old, and its stature as such is reinforced by the presence of the rubber at its crest.

As the mythical center of the field, the pitcher's mound is the point at which creation of the game begins. The pitcher, who starts play by throwing the ball to the batter, must stand on top of the pitcher's mound and must keep his foot on the rubber until he has released the ball. There is, then, an umbilical connection between the creative activity of the pitcher (as a high priest) and the omphalos itself.

The cosmic structure of the game is not limited to the centrality of the pitcher's mound and the creativity that begins there. Among the few essays that have been written on baseball as one form of American folk religion,[15] there has been little mention of the significance of the four bases, each of which lies at one of the cardinal direction points, thus forming the four corners of the world.[16] It is also interesting to note that the base-runners can find safety and security only at the four corners of the world, and that, in line with the omphalo-mythic practice of sun worship, the base-runners must follow the apparent course of the sun in its relation to the world. Like the apparent direction of the sun, base-runners move in a counterclockwise fashion, from home to first to second to third and back to home. Correspondingly, when a batter stands at home plate, the perspective of the sun's movement from right to left is determined by standing at the southern point, with east lying to the right and west to the left.

The cosmological correspondence between the omphalos myth and the structure of baseball extends beyond the points in the infield to the outfield reaches at the foul poles, which are misnamed since they stand in fair territory. Lying in a direct line from home plate (the southernmost corner of baseball's world) to first and third bases (the eastern and western corners of the world), the foul poles correspond to the sun and moon. Like the two astral bodies that in ancient times were thought to lie at the edge of the sky, the foul poles are found at the farthest reaches of the outfield, baseball's expansive northern territory. According to the mythic astral cosmologies, the sun and moon were thought to determine the course of events on earth; and similarly in baseball, the play of balls as fair or foul is determined by their relation to these two stellar poles.

Ritual Activity

Although the baseball diamond can be understood in omphalo-mythic terms, it also achieves its status as sacred space by the particular ritual of consecration that occurs at the beginning of each season and before each contest. The consecration ritual is not conducted by the players but by the grounds crew who are, so to speak, "the custodians of the temple." Their responsibilities include the care of the field between games, the immediate pregame preparation of the field, and the restoration of the field during the middle innings or after rain delays.

Baseball is the only team sport that, at the professional level of play, requires that the infield be covered with a tarpaulin between games in order to protect the field from the possibility of saturation with rain. In addition, baseball is the only team sport that can be postponed or halted during play because of rain. What this suggests is that the world of the baseball game can be threatened by the destructive waters of the mythic flood or the primeval waters of chaos, both of which are intimated or potentially conjured up by the waters of rain. The grounds crew bears the responsibility for protecting the game from such threat of destruction or from such chaos.

Before the players begin their pre-game practice, the grounds crew removes the protective covering; and the foretaste of order is brought to the field as the players throw and hit the ball. After the players on the opposing teams have taken batting and fielding practice, the grounds crew continues the ritual of preparing the field for play. Failure to adhere to the details of the ritual provides either team with "grounds" for protesting the validity of the contest. The grounds crew chalks the batter's box and the foul lines between home plate and first and third bases. The crew rakes the pitcher's mound, smoothing it off and filling in indentations. Members of the crew then drag the dirt portion of the infield, using screens to smooth the dirt, after which they finally sprinkle water on the dirt to settle the dust.[17]

At this point the correspondence or the waters with cosmic forces switches from the destructive threat of rain and chaos to the fructifying force of water as the bearer of life. The use of water in the final purification rites at the pitcher's mound signals the dual orientation of water rituals with baseball and connects the creative forces—those associated with birth and growth—with the center itself. Perhaps coincidentally, at Dodger Stadium the spigot that supplies water for the settling of dust is located on the back side of the pitcher's mound.

The final portion of the consecration ritual by the grounds crew is the placing of freshly whitened bases at the corners of the infield. Yet with the full preparation of the field, there is one final act that remains necessary to complete the consecration process—the fusing of the mythical with the political. With the performance of the national anthem, public sanction and political approval of the game are secured. The chaos that existed prior to batting and fielding practice is transformed into a cosmos ready for contest between two forces, the home team and the visiting team.

Just as the baseball diamond undergoes ritual consecration before it is made ready for play, so too does the ball require proper ritual preparation for admission into the game. Before a ball can be used in play, it must be introduced into the game by the home plate umpire. Not just any ball, however, is acceptable. Before every game the home plate umpire rubs each ball with a substance of Delaware River mud, taking the sheen off the ball by physically introducing it to the earth. When the pitcher receives the ball, he rubs it down, adding the particularity of his "priesthood" to the sacred object itself. If for some reason, such as intentionally scuffing or wetting the ball (as Joe Niekro and Gaylord Perry were accused of doing) or inadvertently getting marred after being hit, the ball becomes contaminated and gets thrown out of play by the umpire. Although the home plate umpire is the only one who can introduce a ball into play, the ceremonial "first ball" of the game will be introduced by a local or political celebrity who performs the ritual of "tossing out the first pitch." Such an action signifies the popular devotion to the game and the political appeal of the event.

As in the ball games and religious rituals of the Oglala Sioux, so too in baseball is the field itself identified with the world. Yet the *ball* also represents the world. There is no contradiction or duplication here, however, between the world represented by the ball and the world constituted by the diamond. They are mythical worlds, not exclusive or contradictory worlds but merely multiple worlds, each with its own realm of significance.[18] In baseball the ball itself is covered with horsehide, and it has a single row of 108 stitches, duplicating the number of beads in a rosary, that always appear as if it were two rows of stitches. The single row of stitches ties together two symmetrical, identical, reversed pieces, somewhat like the yin and the yang, whereby dualistic forces are bound together in a unified whole. In baseball, the ball is white, signifying the undefiled purity of creation,[19] and the stitching is red, the color of blood, suggesting the possibilities of both birth and death. The ball itself manifests the clear dualism of the game, consummately expressed in the conflict between the forces of creation (the pitcher delivering the pitch) and the forces of destruction (the batter swatting the ball).

Even as there are rituals of consecration for the field in order to distinguish it from ordinary space and even as there are rituals that govern the introduction of a ball into play, so too are there rituals that a pitcher must follow for a pitch to be valid. On one hand, a pitcher must take the sign from his catcher while his foot is in contact with the rubber. On the other hand, the pitcher cannot touch his mouth while he is on the pitcher's mound for fear that his own sputum will pollute the ball. The pitcher as high priest cannot allow that which is earthly to defile the purity of a new world in the process of creation unless, of course, the pitcher himself is perverse.

These two rituals of prohibition prevent contamination of the ball while within the area of the cosmic mountain. And other rules, as I have suggested, govern the delivery of a pitch. When runners are on base, most pitchers use a motion called "the stretch" rather than the full wind-up. In this way they hope to prevent base-runners from taking a large lead and stealing a base. But rules govern also the ritual of the stretch: The pitcher must bring his hands to a complete stop at or above his belt before resuming his motion to deliver the pitch. The pitcher must stride toward home plate when pitching to the batter. Failure to adhere to any of these strictures results in the umpire calling a "balk," thus awarding an extra base to the base-runners at that time.

Cosmic Dualism

One of the probable reasons that the game of baseball appeals to so may fans is that its cosmology, its mythical structure, is also connected to a drama of cosmic dualism that is constantly played out in both personal and social terms. A sense of dualism pervades the game: the confrontation of the pitcher with the batter; the opposition of two distinct teams; the structure of innings during which teams alternate turns at bat and turns in the field; the clear distinction between the play of balls as fair or foul; the position of pitches as either balls or strikes; the status of the batter or baserunners as either safe or out; the division of the Major Leagues into to two leagues whose champions vie for the World Series title; and the covering of the ball itself.

Classically, the dualistic, cosmic conflict pits the forces of good against the forces of evil, light against darkness, creation against chaos, or it presents the Gnostic tension between flesh and spirit. In baseball, although there may be occasions when the nature of the conflict appears to be that of good versus evil, the basic confrontation is between the forces of creation and those of destruction, the classic battle between life and death—safe or out, winner or loser. The dramatic action in baseball's version of the cosmic conflict occurs in the battle between the pitcher and the batter. As suggested earlier, the pitcher is the agent of creation, the one who, keeping his foot in contact with the rubber (the omphalos), hurls the white ball (the undefiled world) toward home plate (the southernmost point in the cosmos, the place of warmth and rest) in an effort to prevent the batter (the destructive force) from knocking the ball over the fence (beyond the reaches of the universe), circling the bases (circumnavigating the globe), and scoring a run. The battle between pitcher and batter, in fact, also reenacts the most ancient armed conflict, the wielding of sticks and the hurling of stones. It is appropriate that the battle between the cosmic forces begins at the cosmic mountain (the pitcher's mound), which is the point of intersection of the three cosmic spheres, and climaxes at *home* plate, the territory over which control is sought.

The alignment of the pitcher with the forces of creation is reinforced by the metaphorical designation of the warm-up area for pitchers as the bullpen, for the bull has long been associated with fertility and creation. The association of the pitcher with a bull, however, does not mean that the pitcher is singularly masculine. Indeed, the act of throwing the ball connotes the masculine act of ejaculation. But the pitcher also wears a glove, which is reminiscent of the womb and with which he hopes to catch or retrieve the ball in an effort to prevent the batter from getting on base and scoring a run. This bisexuality of the pitcher corresponds to some priestly rites often connected with the rituals and myths at omphaloi.

In contrast to the pitcher, who stands in touch with transcendent forces, the batter digs in at *home* plate, wielding the refined limb of a tree (usually either ash or hickory) that is the fruit of the earth. The batter is concerned about his present world, not creating a new world. He is earthy. He represents an earthly chaos that challenges the creative powers of the pitcher. The batter's charge is to knock the ball out of this world—to prevent the new world (the ball hurled as a potential out) from affecting this world—so that he can run around the bases safely and score a run. The pitcher attempts to create a perfect game, allowing no batter to reach base, while the batter attempts to destroy this quest for perfection and establish in its place a sense of completion, a full circling of the bases. In this way, Gardella notes, "Baseball demonstrates the difference between perfection and completion more clearly than any phenomenon of everyday life."[20]

On a larger, more social scale, the dualism of baseball pits the home team, always dressed in a predominantly white uniform (or as in the case of the Houston Astros' colorful splash, a uniform whose background is white), against the visiting team, always wearing road gray. The contrast in colors of the uniforms indicates the fans' estimation of the alignment of the two teams as representatives of the forces of good and evil, light and darkness, purity and contamination, in the cosmic conflict. The fans normally consider the home team as "good" and the visiting team, "bad." Yet there is no inherent reason why either team should be thought of as being "good" or "bad," as being representatives of cosmos of chaos, life or death, creation or destruction, since each team alternates in the roles of pitching/fielding and batting, of attempting to establish order and to disrupt it. The dual roles of teams as offensive and defensive forces is a social extension of the mythical bisexuality of the pitcher himself, who (until the advent of the designated hitter in the American League) also gets to take a turn at bat—to become one of the destructive forces of play while identifying with the hitting activity of his team. The fact that each team assumes both creative and destructive roles further supports the idea that baseball's structuring myth corresponds to the dualities of the omphalos myth.

At the end of the game, however, one team must prevail. Unlike football and hockey in which tie games are possible, baseball requires a winner and a loser. The winning team is the one that exercises greater control over baseball's cosmos by exerting power over the ball and its pure vision of perfection by pitching effectively, hitting authoritatively, and circling the bases often.

Conclusion

There is a story about Reinhold Niebuhr, the American-born theologian, taking fellow theologian Paul Tillich, who was a recent immigrant from Germany, to a baseball game. After several innings Tillich was still having trouble getting the knack of the game. As play progressed, an impressive "twin killing" or double play was started by the shortstop on the home team. Fans throughout the stands roared with approval and applause. Puzzled by such an overwhelming response to a play that had not seen the ball hit over the fence nor even far enough to score a base-runner, Tillich sought an explanation from Niebuhr. Failing to communicate the significance of the event in understandable baseball terms, Niebuhr finally said, "It's a *kairos*, Paulus, it's a *kairos*." With that explanation, Tillich understood. (For Tillich, *kairos* was the category of time and history that marks turning points, occasions of depth rather than events continuing the normal chronometric measure of time.) Although the story in its present form might be embellished or even apocryphal (in which case it would be emblematic of baseball's lore), it adequately encapsulates the way in which a heroic event in baseball is sometimes seen as an event wherein a force larger than life is present, an event wherein the course of events is transformed by the nature of the event itself.

In American culture, baseball has exhibited such power to compel allegiance, to generate meaning, to elicit and foster hope. Baseball has certainly manifest a number of characteristics of religion. Yet it is the mythos of baseball—its order through design, ritual, and conflict, the complex combination of which resemble the ancient omphalos myth—that underlies its compelling power, that undergirds its creation of meaning, and that nourishes its arousal of hope. For the fans and players, as Donald Hall has so eloquently and aptly put it, "the diamonds and rituals of baseball create an elegant, trivial, enchanted grid on which our suffering, shapeless, sinful day leans for the momentary grace of order."[21]

So we return to the rain delay conversation between two teenage boys in the bleachers at Wrigley Field. "Why," one asked, "is the pitcher's mound higher than any other part of the field?" The historian of religion wanted to turn and say, "Because it's a cosmic mountain. It adds order to the game by providing its center." But respecting the youthful love of baseball and its mysterious lure, the religious scholars remembered the remark without imposing academic analysis at a time when they shared some sort of liturgical experience of communion with the other faithful Cub fans enduring yet one more delay before defeat.

Writing about Americans' fascination with sports, Catherine Albanese, a historian of American religion, has noted that, "by setting up boundaries and defining the space of the game, sports have helped Americans fit a grid to their own experience in order to define it and give it structure."[22] In baseball, the myth of the center provides the structure around which the game is oriented, and its utilization of creation mythology links it to the dualism that pervades the game. The implied and exemplified myth of the center generates and sustains the religious import—"the momentary grace of order"—of baseball for millions of Americans who have often not analyzed their attraction and devotion to the game.

---

[1] Knowing of my previous work on baseball and religious myth, Professor Frank Reynolds of the University of Chicago Divinity School noted this conversation and reported it to me.

[2] Roland Garrett, "The Metaphysics of Baseball," *Sport Inside Out: Readings in Literature and Philosophy*, ed. David L. Vanderwerken and Spencer K. Wertz (Fort Worth: Texas Christian University Press, 1985) 645.

[3] Jim Murray, "Wanted: Playoff Memories," *Los Angeles Times*, October 9, 1983, III:1.

[4] Murray Ross, "Football Red and Baseball Green," *Sport Inside Out*, 716.

[5] Alfred North Whitehead, *Religion in the Making* (New York: The Macmillan Company, 1926) 141.

[6] Peter Gardella, "Baseball Samadhi: A Yankee Way of Knowledge," *Books and Religion* (September 1986): 15.

[7] Cf. Mircea Eliade, *Patterns in Comparative Religion*, trans. Rosemary Sheed (New York: Sheed and Ward, 1961) 231.

[8] The established tradition (yea we say oral tradition) of baseball has long recognized Abner Doubleday as the creator of the game of baseball. But in recent years, the process of demythologization has been applied to this *textus receptus*. See, for instance, Victor Salvatore, "The Man Who Didn't Invent Baseball," *American Heritage* 34 (June-July 1983): 65-67.

[9] Helen Tworkov, "The Baseball Diamond Sutra," *Tricycle: The Buddhist Review* (Summer 1993): 4.

[10] Ibid.

[11] For an alternate application of the omphalos myth to baseball, see A. Bartlett Giamatti, *Take Time for Paradise: Americans and Their Games* (New York: Summit Books, 1989) 86 ff. The former commissioner of Major League Baseball, Giamatti identifies home plate as the center, which distorts a number of the mythical directions that prove to be significant for a cosmogony of the game. Giamatti's work, which appeared posthumously, does not make reference to my earliest published account connecting baseball and the omphalos myth. See my, "'The Momentary Grace of Order': Religious Aspects of a Sport," *Journal and Times of the California Association of Health, Physical Education, Recreation and Dance* (March 1987): 16-19ff.

[12] Cf. Samuel Terrien, "The Omphalos Myth and Hebrew Religion," *Vetus Testamentum*, 20:319. For further comment on the general identification of the cosmic mountain with the omphalos, see Mircea Eliade, *Images and Symbols: Studies in Religious Symbolism*, trans. Philip Mairet (New York: Sheed and Ward, 1961) 43.

[13] Terrien, "The Omphalos Myth and Hebrew Religion," 320.

[14] At this point I recognize the intentional aberration that occurred at the old Crosley Field in Cincinnati, where the warning track (normally a band of bare dirt or cinders that provides a liminal area between the outfield grass and the homerun fence) was replaced by an upward sloping area of grass. In addition, at each field, the bases, which represent the geographic extremes of the cardinal directions, are artificially elevated, although only slightly. It is not insignificant that the slightly elevated portions of the base-paths are the only points of safety for a runner.

[15] James Mathisen, "From Civil Religion to Folk Religion: The Case of American Sport," in Shirl J. Hoffman, ed., *Sport and Religion* (Champaign IL: Human Kinetics, 1992) 17-33.

[16] The notable exception is Michael Novak's metaphysically oriented essays in his book, *The Joy of Sports: End Zones, Bases, Baskets, Balls and the Consecration of the American Spirit* (New York: Basic Books, Inc., 1976), especially chapters 2-4 and 7.

[17] In some of the "cookie cutter" ballparks that were erected in the early 1970s, such as Cincinnati's Riverfront Stadium and Pittsburgh's Three Rivers Stadium, there is an artificial playing surface that covers most of the area normally known as the dirt portion of the infield. At stadiums such as these, there are dirt portions around the bases that receive comparable ritual care by the grounds crew before, during, and after each game.

[18] Cf. Eliade, *Images and Symbols*, 39.

[19] Several years ago, Charles Finley, the former maverick owner of the Oakland Athletics, experimented with orange colored baseballs during spring training. Although he claimed that the fans enjoyed the color and that the hitters benefited by seeing the ball better, no serious thought was given by the commissioner or by the rules committee of the owners to making a change from the traditional white baseball.

[20] Gardella, "Baseball Samadhi," 15.

[21] Donald Hall, *Fathers Playing Catch with Sons: Essays on Sport (Mostly Baseball)* (New York: Dell Publishing Company, 1986) 51.

[22] Catherine Albanese, *America: Religion and Religions* (Belmont CA: Wadsworth Publishing Company, 1981) 322. In the context of her imaginative and illuminative chapter on cultural religion, Albanese also suggests that the contestative character of baseball establishes the sport as a model for promoting a cultural code of "loyalty, fair play, and being a good sport in losing" (322).

THE FETISH AND MCGWIRE'S BALLS

Paul Christopher Johnson

Longing on a large scale is what makes history.
Don Delillo, *Underworld*

As I write this introduction it is just a few days since Joe DiMaggio died. For the season of 1941 his hitting streak of fifty-six games provided a radio narrative that united the country. Joe, the immigrants' son made good, hero even to the Cuban fisherman of *The Old Man and the Sea*. In the 1950s there was Joe and Marilyn, perfect iconographic (con)fusion. By the 1960s, though, Paul Simon penned the lyrics, "Where have you gone Joe DiMaggio?/...Joltin' Joe has left and gone away." Joe the center-fielder now Joe the relic and, like the bones of saints, signalling both presence and absence, the last shred of a lost golden age. No wonder DiMaggio didn't understand the lyrics in Simon's song.

The next time a baseball story would hold the national gaze as hypnotically was the 1998 season as Mark McGwire and Sammy Sosa chased and surpassed Roger Maris's home-run record. Once again, fans half a continent away or on a Caribbean island asked each other by the newsstand or by their fishing nets, "Did he get one today?" In this essay I want to redirect the question, from "Did he get one?" to the sign-value of the Ball itself; in other words, to the query, "What did he (and we) get?"

As we begin, consider for a moment an image from Woody Allen's recent (1997) film, "Deconstructing Harry." Harry Block is a writer who experiences his own life only as it is mapped out in and over against his creative world of fiction. Family members and ex-lovers are mere signs, props for his fictions. One woman, trying to move Block from his voyeurism, proffers an astute gift, a sign from the "real world" he can unequivocally love. She gives him a ball autographed by the 1951 New York Giants, including Bobby Thomson who hit the pennant-winning home run, the "shot heard 'round the world." Harry is thrilled. He squeezes and tosses the Ball at the close of the film, as he is cured of his writer's block (denoted by his name) and again has an idea for a story.

In "Deconstructing Harry," the Ball makes but a brief appearance, but in Don Delillo's 1997 novel *Underworld* the Ball supplies the entire subtext of the overt narrative. The Ball hit by Bobby Thomson in 1951 is the object marker against which multiple lives are mapped through time. Its trajectory, arcing into section 35 in the left-field stands and then passed from collector's hand to collector's hand, is the tangible anchor in an ever-increasing garbage bin of chaotic human lives of the nuclear age, and the waste those lives and weapons emit.

Delillo has not conjured the only reappearance of the Ball, however. The final months of the 1998 professional baseball season were dominated by the scrambles for Mark McGwire's and Sammy Sosa's record-setters. The stories, equally mythic in proportion, were remarkably similar to Delillo's fictional version: of bitten hands and broken legs in the Ball's retrieval, disputes of monetary value, IRS statements on potential tax consequences, congressional rebuttals, and heroic acts of generosity to "fix" the Ball(s) finally in museum shrines for all to pilgrimage towards in Cooperstown at the Baseball Hall of Fame. As observers and analysts of the signs and structures of contemporary American culture, we cannot but be quickened by the stadium and media mêlée. After considering both Delillo's account and the "real world" narratives from the 1998 baseball season, I offer here an analysis of the power of objects by comparing them under the rubric of the oft-maligned term of the "fetish." By comparing objects that sixteenth-century Portuguese traders called *feitiço* to McGwire's record-setting balls, I will explore the use of set-apart-objects, objects heavy with significance, as they become anchors of memory and history-making.

Embodied Competencies and "History-Making"

By now it is surely passé to claim that history is constructed, interpreted, and narrated instead of simply observed and documented. Equally familiar is that such narratives are politically loaded and interested; they are not objective but rather a "memory that flashes up in a moment of danger," to recall Walter Benjamin's memorable phrase.[1] Already in the early 1970s, Hayden White wrote that "just as there can be no explanation in history without a story, so too there can be no story without a plot by which to make it a story of a particular kind."[2] In a similar vein, in the mid-1980s Marshall Sahlins theorized that history is a litany of "events" set apart and marked as culturally significant. "Events," in turn, are happenings attributed with significance according to structures of interpretation.[3] These approaches viewed history-making primarily as a literary, or in White's terms, "tropic," enterprise. What has been less discussed, however, are the non- or extra-textual processes by which we narrate ourselves into temporal and spatial orders.

Among such novel conceptualizations of history-making, Paul Connerton declared "history" a shared social memory, differentiated into three types: personal, cognitive and habit. It is the third, "habit memory," he argued, which most informs ritual performance.[4] It is memory coded in the bodily repertoire, that which is entailed in the ability to reproduce a certain performance even when that memory cannot be discursively refracted into words. It is the knowledge in the fingers to play a tune on the piano, the sureness in the dancing feet of a possession priest, or the legs of Michael Jordan driving the lane.

Paul Stoller[5] expanded from Connerton to argue that such bodily codes articulate not only ritual knowledge in the sense of an Eliadean model of the return to non-historical, "original" time, but also ritual knowledge which is emphatically historical and politically conscious. In studies of the Songhay of Niger, he demonstrated how possession performances present to consciousness a distinctly historical memory: colonial forces like the ferocious hauka spirit possessions recorded by Jean Rouch in his film first screened in 1954, "Les maîtres fous."

In a different context, that of North American popular culture, George Lipsitz wrote of "counter-memories" that are voiced in storytelling, popular novels, and other common acts of everyday life; and they run across the grain of historical master-narratives. To my reading, Lipsitz is describing the resistance, not necessarily conscious, to ruling ideas rationalized in academic texts and other authorizing venues: "Counter-memory is a way of remembering and forgetting what starts with the local, the immediate, and the personal. Unlike historical narratives that begin with the totality of human existence and then locate specific actions and events within that totality, counter-memory starts with the particular and the specific and then builds outward toward a total story. Counter-memory looks to the past for the hidden histories excluded from dominant narratives. …[It] forces revision of existing histories. [It] embodies aspects of myth and aspects of history…."[6]

Similar in seeking popular sources of "history," Luce Giard built on Lévi-Strauss's structural treatments of culinary habits to analyze eating as memory: "Eating, in fact, serves not only to maintain the biological machinery of the body, but to make concrete one of the specific modes of relation between a person and the world, thus forming one of the fundamental landmarks in space-time."[7] Giard cites Bachelard on this score: "This glass of pale, cool, dry wine marshals my entire life in the Champagne. People may think I am drinking: I am remembering…."[8] These recall Emmanuel Ladurie's description of "the special time of the farmer, the shepherd and the craftsman," where temporal orientation was not abstracted but rather measured in the walking distance between intervals, or the body's periodic ingestion of a meal.[9]

Viewed as a set, these studies attempt to describe how memory and "history-making" occur in bodily practice and popular culture through what Pierre Bourdieu referred to as "embodied competencies."[10] They suggest that rituals, songs, foods, popular legend, and objects may preserve distinct histories, counter-memories, to those recorded in textual master-narratives linked to hegemonic paradigms of doxa, "natural" or "commonsense" knowledge. The set of approaches also hints at the role of objects in history-making. History-making relies not only on literary strategies of interpretation and "spin," on constructed sequences of "events"[11] given a narrative style,[12] but also on objects and their sensual perception. Think, for example, of what Sir James Frazer called "sympathetic magic" evoked by contact with objects, a more direct path, though less "true," to working on the world than religion with its intermediarary powers.[13] Whatever Frazer's faults—viewing the manipulation of objects as failed science rather than as a semiotic system or as performative expression—he had a keen sense of the importance of objects in locating and "working" sacred power.

Frazer was not alone in this. Many scholars of religion, especially after the appearance of Durkheim's *Elementary Forms*,[14] became attuned to the mnemonics of the sacred—the totems and icons through which power is condensed, "worked," and redistributed. We have been less attentive, though, to the workings of objects in our own societies. Perhaps the cosmogonic task of temporal orientation, history-making, can be usefully interpreted in relation to the symbolic loading and periodic sensual contact with objects-set-apart.

Such objects I will call "fetishes." I will not, however, locate "fetish" primarily in the twentieth-century Freudian and Marxian vernaculars, but rather in the Portuguese colonialist use of *feitiço* as a description of West African sacred objects.

The Fetish and Narrative Fixation

The fetish, like other terms in the history of the study of "primitive" religions—totem (from the Ojibwa *ototemi*), shaman (from the Tungus *saman*), taboo (from the Polynesian *tapu*)—was extracted from a particular historical context and applied to general theories of cultural evolution and "primitive thought." The fetish is unusual among such terms in that it does not derive from any indigenous term—nowhere is there a fetish as such—but rather from the colonialist "encounter" between cultures, from the attempt to locate and describe the Other. It is in its very roots comparative, in this rather like the term of *Kultur* itself—popularized by Herder only in response and opposition to *civilization*[15]—in the sense that it instantiates difference as much as it does similarity. The fetish as classifying label denotes less of a specific definition or location than it does an itinerary or, as better befits a discussion of baseballs, an arc or trajectory. Following the fetish from 1) religion and the problem of objects (its original invocation as *feitiço* by Portuguese traders) to 2) the issue of primitive thought in social evolution (de Brosses, Comte) to 3) the commodity in capitalism (Marx) to 4) sexual deviation and displacement (Binet, Freud), we learn more about the history of the West than about any of the problems the fetish is supposed to describe.

In spite of this opacity, or perhaps because of it, the fetish is still very much with us. Having virtually disappeared from anthropological writing after the turn of the century in favor of magic (Frazer), animism (Tylor), pre-animism (Marett) and the like, it never was eliminated from popular discourse. Rather, it was subsumed into Marx- and Freud-derived vernaculars of the commodity fetishism and sexual fetishism—social and individual neuroses, respectively, which though distinct retain the common attribute of falsely ascribed value. The fetish has remained with us in their sense but elsewhere as well, notably in labels for "primitive" art. It seems always ready to resurface when indigenous religions do, especially in

Africa. In the February 14, 1999 *New York Times*, for example, the rebel boys' army in Sierra Leone is described as adorned with "fetishes made of twine, shells and mirrors...."[16] The old term resurfaces with the "old" (albeit contemporary) religion. The fetish, the magic, the violence—all of it almost, dare we name it, erotic in semantic transgressions.

Of course there are counter-examples where the fetish is deconstructed by applying it to elements of our own culture, where the one-way glass allowing the view of the primitive Other is transformed into a mirror, such that now the fetishizers are us: David Chidester's fetish of Coca-Cola,[17] or Michael Taussig's "state fetishism."[18] Similarly, Homi K. Bhabha called attention to the racial stereotype of the Other as fetish, as a distorted "fixation." Here he relies, among others, on Edward Said's comments in *Orientalism*: "...anyone employing orientalism, which is the habit for dealing with questions, objects, qualities and regions deemed Oriental, will designate, name, point to, fix, what he is talking or thinking about with a word or phrase, which then is considered either to have acquired, or more simply to be, reality...."[19]

In Bhabha's account, such "signifiers of stability" are an exercise of imperialist power. Very well—this is also at the root of Derrida's push towards the "historicity of history" or "spectrality" versus a constraining ontology of presence.[20] What is elided in this view, though, is the earlier argument that consciousness of the self in time relies on, even demands such fixations, and that any critical historical consciousness at all depends on this. "Signifier of stability" is comparable to "event" in Sahlins's version of history-making; or to "self located in time-space" in Giard. The paradox is that such stabilizers reify and essentialize in potentially distorting ways; and yet we must classify the world into livable distortions. Fixation is not an option; it is the sine qua non of social memory and thus of history-making. Fetishes, then, are fixations, yes, but not necessarily in Freud's pejorative sense of developmental arrest, or Said's/Bhabha's/Derrida's sense of socio-political arrest. At the very least we must acknowledge that such points of fixation cannot be wholly superseded; and quite possibly a critical historical consciousness even depends on them.

Fortunately, since it is a comparative term, the fetish has no etymological anchor heavier than "that which is made," and can always be spun in the opposite direction. Hence James Clifford's revision:

> ...we can return to them...their lost status as fetishes—not specimens of a deviant or exotic 'fetishism' but *our own* fetishes. This tactic, necessarily personal, would accord to things in collections the

power to fixate rather than simply the capacity to edify or inform. African and Oceanian artifacts could once again be *objets sauvages*, sources of fascination with the power to disconcert. Seen in their resistance to classification they could remind us of our *lack* of self-posession, or the artifices we employ to gather a world around us....[21]

Clifford suggests that, despite its baggage, the term can be inverted to cast illumination on our own classifying systems and where they fall short. Using the inversion of the fetish to reveal the power of objects to elude classification and to examine the process of classifying fixation itself, there is no reason to assume that the fetish has outgrown its academic use- (or exchange-) value. Perhaps it merely requires a bit of dressing up to once again entice and seduce.

Towards this end, William Pietz has written a series of remarkable essays over the last fifteen years documenting the history of the idea of the fetish and has co-edited a volume on the fetish as cultural discourse.[22] In Pietz's history, the fetish is finally not an object but rather a cognitive and existential problem of location; it is about issues of relating the self to time and space. It is about territorialization, or Giard's *terroir* of cuisine that responds to the terror of dislocation or the "crisis of historical memory" that Lipsitz calls the constitutive problem of our time.[23] The fetish is "a singularly fixating encounter,... a crisis moment of infinite value."[24] The fetish as response to this crisis yields structure:

> each fetish as a singular articulated identification. . . . Unifying events, places, things, and people, and then returning them to their separate spheres.... Certain structured relationships—some conscious, others unconscious—are established, constituting the phenomenological fabric...of immediate prereflective experience.[25]

The fetish functions as an ordering, a location where the self is related to time, space, and power.

There is little to disagree with here, other than to note that the fetish is not unique in this sense of the fixation of memory. History is always constructed in part by mnemonic reference to places, objects, monuments, and texts that transfix the human gaze, where time and space are focussed into legible patterns: flags, statues, engagement rings, photo albums. These are also locators and fixers of memory and experience. But are these all usefully conceptualized as fetishes? The issue seems to depend on the ability to manipulate the object with the aim of altering one's own or another's experience of the order of things. In this sense, most of our everyday mnemonic objects only become fetishes in extraordinary circumstances: the flag when burned or trampled, or a wedding band when melted down or flushed in the commode.

Fetish may be best viewed as a mode of action rather than a kind of object itself. It is a condensation of social powers onto an object in order to reconfigure them. "To fetish" would therefore be more apt than "fetish." Viewed in this broad sense, it is a structuring technique of human consciousness in time, not an evolutionary stage of the false attribution of power to objects, a stage now surpassed. (Is it even worth mentioning the fetishization of the year 2000?) We will return to the fetish as verb, as history-making, shortly.

In sum, if one means of reclaiming the fetish is tracing its etymology and usage, the other is by changing its arrow of valuation from denoting that which is other to that which is right under our noses. That is to say, there may be social/cultural phenomena which are most usefully understood under the rubric of the fetish; phenomena whose primary criterion is their materiality and condensed signification. Obvious examples named above include a wedding ring or a photo of the beloved. Wittgenstein, in his notes on Frazer's *Golden Bough*, wondered about the example of Schubert's brother, who after the composer's death cut his scores into pieces and gave them to his pupils.[26] We need not detain ourselves with Schubert, however, since another opportunity has recently been lofted into our section of the bleachers.

McGwire's Balls

On September 8, 1998, all the major television networks interrupted normal broadcasting for a special news update, not of the latest missile strike against Iraq, but rather of Mark McGwire's smash of his sixty-second home run. The shot broke Roger Maris's revered record of 1961 which had knocked Babe Ruth from the home run throne. As Tom Verducci of *Sports Illustrated* narrated the event, it was "mythic" in mysterious correspondences. Prior to the game, McGwire sat in the very clubhouse where Maris had dressed during his last two seasons as a player. "Then Jeff Idleson, the Hall's director of communication, showed McGwire the 34.5 inch, 32-ounce bat Maris had used to club his 61st home run in 1961. McGwire clutched the bat, rubbed the barrel over his heart and said, 'Roger, you're with me.'"[27]

"McGwire's blow, a bases-empty shot off Steve Trachsel of the Chicago Cubs, occurred two days before what would have been Maris's sixty-fourth birthday. Earlier in the day the stock market soared 380.5 points, the first day of trading after a Labor Day weekend in which which McGwire hit number sixty—measured at 381 feet—and number sixty-one. Coincidence?"[28] The sixty-first, we should note, he hit on his father's sixty-first birthday, adding to the aura of mysterious inevitability and fate. "As I was driving to the ballpark I said, 'This is meant to be, to give him this birthday present,' Mark would later say."[29]

"'I got the ball! I got the ball!" groundskeeper Tim Forneris yelled to equipment manager Buddy Bates. Bates ran it into his office, closed the door behind him, put it into a wall safe and called baseball security officials. They quickly arrived with a black bag containing a black-light lamp. When they turned it on and placed the ball under it, it glowed with the invisible ink devised specifically for the occasion."[30] "Baseball security officials, working with the US Treasury Department, had marked the balls so that McGwire's sixtieth home run and those thereafter could later be authenticated. They covered them with an invisible ink that glows when placed under an infrared light...."[31]

Commented Verducci, "Sixty-two would belong to the rest of us, a welcome touchstone in a cynical age."[32]

Meanwhile, one million dollars was proposed as the monetary value of the Ball, a conveniently symmetrical sum quickly picked up as authoritative on media wires nation-wide. Interviewed fans awaiting other Balls, however, were not necessarily measuring value in dollars and cents. Many returned home-run balls from numbers sixty to sixty-nine for no monetary reward at all. The balls, in St. Louis at least, were regarded as communal objects, in this closer to religious icons than saleable commodities. Yet even if they elected not to cash in economically, they were pleased to line their pockets ideologically, as many echoed McGwire himself by crowing how great it felt to "take part in history," "witness history," and even "*make history.*"

The story of the seventieth ball begins at the same point as the sixty-second, as hide and string at Rawlings Sporting Goods in Turrialba, Costa Rica. On September 27, 1998, McGwire hit it over the fence at Busch Stadium for his last home run of the year. Philip Ozersky won the scramble for the Ball, took it home in his pocket, and kept in a drawer beside his bed. After showing it to friends at Washington University Medical School, where he works, he stored it in a safety deposit box at his local bank. After a few scattered appearances, the Ball's flight ended in January when Todd McFarlane, a thirty-seven year-old cartoonist, purchased the Ball at auction for $3,005,000.

McFarlane seemed at once pleased with the camera-attention and reticent to burden the Ball with too many words. Probably he sensed that its object-value (fetish-value) could not be linguistically formulated in any way that would not disfigure the Ball, or appear foolish. Nevertheless, he haltingly hazarded a brief explanation: "Sports make you forget death, taxes, and politics, and all the other garbage that goes on in life." McFarlane will, he claims, occasionally allow the Ball to be publically displayed; in return, he has requested twenty batting-practice swings in every Major League ballpark.

As critical observers of culture and society, how should we account for many Americans' fascination with the home-run race, and with the Ball itself? What are the processes that transformed its commodity-value from a few bucks to three million dollars? It will not be sufficient to shrug and say, "the market." If the Ball's only power is as commodity-fetish, why did so many claimants to balls 60 to 69 return them for nothing? It also begs the question of what undergirds its commodity status. That is, even if McFarlane purchased the Ball as an investment, what is the cultural logic that will sustain and augment its exchange-value? To argue only that the Ball's field shifted from one of use-value to one of exchange-value ignores the issue of why some memorabilia become commodities while others do not, and therefore explains nothing. Is the Ball perceived to contain McGwire's charisma? If so, what are the processes by which it has come to contain this power—again the idea of magical contagion and mimesis, perhaps, such that to touch the Ball will lead to a sensation of heroism, or perhaps even to heroic acts of one's own? To answer the question of the power of objects better than Frazer did, we will need to back up about five centuries to the birth of the fetish.

The Idea of the Fetish

Pietz's articles extrapolate four principles that inform even historically variant versions of fetish discourse: 1) the fetish is a material object in which power is localized; 2) the fetish is radically historical; it arises in a historical event and represents the "enduring capacity to repeat this singular process of fixation"; 3) the meaning and value of the fetish depend on a particular social order; and 4) the fetish works in relation to the human body, such that the idea of an autonomous human body is subverted.[33] Here I will highlight a few of the historical moments described by Pietz in which these principles were articulated.

The fetish began as the Portuguese *feitiço* (fetisso) sometime during the fifteenth-century trade along the West African coast, most probably in trade with the Fon of Dahomey in the Bay of Benin, and the BaKongo of present-day Zaire, Angola, and Congo. The term *feitiço* was derived from the Latin *facticium*, suggesting "that which is made" and, more specifically, that which is made by humans instead of by God. Pliny, in his *Natural History*, contrasted *facticium* to that which is made by nature. Tertullian's *De Spectaculis* denounced body-building and wrestling as idolatry since these try to reform the body beyond God's creation, creating an "artificial" body, *facticii corporis*. Augustine, in *Contra Faustum*, discriminated "natural" eunuchs (*nativum*) and man-made eunuchs (*facticium*) from voluntary eunuchs (*voluntarium*). The latter manifest authentic spirituality since the "castration" is an act of will, of the soul moving within unaltered nature. What is key here is that facticium relies on artifice and manufacture; it is value-less and even evil insofar as it alters creation. It was this cargo of comparison and relative valuation that the Portuguese *feitiço* carried: fetish as "made," material, arbitrary since not intended by nature or God, and ultimately fraudulent. True spirituality, unlike fetishism, at least in neo-Platonic influenced interpretations of Christianity, is non-material; bestowed by God through nature or revelation, it is intended and significant.

The first foreign religious objects noted by Portuguese sailors descending the West African coast were Muslim amulets of Qur'anic scripture in leather pouches worn around the neck, quite similar to the *nomina* containing biblical texts common in Europe.[34] Further down the coast, from the ports of Benin to the Congo, a new sort of object was observed, an object differentiated from idols based on its being worn in close proximity to the body, and on its immediacy of effect without apparent divine mediation. What were these objects?

From a contemporary perspective, the idea that these objects did not refer to anything beyond themselves, or that the fetish was pure material power without reference to gods, myths, or social values, was clearly false. The objects observed along the Bight of Benin may have been what the Yoruba call *awure*, charms that bring luck and may be worn close to the body, or enclosed in small houses. So Clapperton observed an Oyo Yoruba ceremony after which "the performers all retired to the fetish house."[35] These "fetish houses," though, likely referred to *ile orisa*, to small temples that protected icons mediating *ashe*, or transforming power ultimately derived from Olorun (Olodumare), or "God."[36]

In the Kongolese case, further down the West African coast, Wyatt MacGaffey demonstrated from texts recorded early in this century that statues or other objects called fetishes in fact condensed myth, gods, ancestors, and human needs in complex designs. Called *minkisi*, these were and are potentially powerful objects, but only after receiving appropriate ritual treatments, just as the Catholic Eucharist chalice is merely a cup until sacramentally blessed. *Minkisi* are also symbols that evoke and render present to consciousness entire cosmologies through the common ritual processes of metaphor, metonymy, and condensation.[37] Portuguese sailors' impressions of the *feitiço* as that which is in itself powerful were erroneous. Again, the fetish does not refer to any object or culture of West Africa in reality, but should rather be understood as "an idea and a problem…which originated in the cross-cultural spaces of the coast of West Africa…."[38] To this we should add that these spaces were not even-handed spaces of cultural exchange but rather discursive "spaces" designed to ideologically justify Portuguese slave trade and gold extraction.

Within this middle space, the fetish arose as a concept to "naturalize" the socioeconomics of mercantile exchange in the fifteenth and sixteenth centuries as a mediating term for securing trade and determining cross-cultural value. This cut in several ways: the fetish was a brokered item of trade since "fetishes" were one of the main sources of gold sought by Portuguese traders; but trade alliances were also sealed over the fetish as witnesses. Here the Portuguese relied on indigenous Kongolese views of the fetish as deadly if betrayed. So the fetish itself could hold value (in gold) and also acted as the mediator of value (as a seal of a contract).

Hints of Marx's and Freud's fetishes are present very early in this trade history. The fetish was a source of gold, but West African societies also mixed other metals with that gold, so it was impure. The fetish thus had value, as gold, but it was also mere "fetish gold," that is, tainted with falsehood.[39] Freudian interpretation is similarly present in the earliest uses of *feitiço*: African women were said to "fetish" themselves, that is, adorn themselves in sexually enticing ways in order to gain "false" sexual access to

Europeans.[40] African eroticism was thus "fetish" eroticism, and "to fetish" was a verb implying physically real, but socially counterfeit, sexuality.[41]

The Dutch trader Willem Bosman's account brought fetish into common northern European parlance in the early 1700s, and here, not surprisingly, "fetish" became a pejorative label grouping African religions with Catholicism. Wrote Bosman: "...the Roman-Catholics would succeed better than we should (at converting the Africans), because they already agree in several particulars, especially in their ridiculous ceremonies."[42]

The Protestant polemic against fetishism as "ridiculous ceremony" is indicative of an emerging scholarly discourse of the fetish. Charles de Brosses's 1760 use of *fetiche*, and for the first time, *fétishisme* as a stage of human development,[43] was elaborated by Auguste Comte as a sub-area of his tripartite schema; and the rest of the story is a familiar one in the history of the study of religion. De Brosses's and Comte's "*fétichisme*" was replaced by "animism" under the Tylorean evolutionist paradigm, and then by Marett's "pre-animism," before being dealt a final death blow, at least in its denotation of a particular religious mode, by Durkheim and Mauss.[44]

What has remained? Occasional descriptions of the object-as-fetish have persisted until today, as in the *New York Times* example proffered above—what Jean Pouillon[45] has called the "fetish without fetishism," the denotation of a specific kind of object or perception without invoking its location within an evolutionary stage of human rationality. Usually, though, when "fetish" is still printed in popular publications, it is in the Marxian/Freudian senses of misascribed value: hence (to Republicans) Bill Clinton's "fetishizing" of health care reform. To call something a fetish in our time still casts a shadow—it describes an obsession or attraction as false consciousness, as valuing what is counterfeit.

Baseball and Fetishes

Let's return now to baseball, keeping in mind the ordering principles of the fetish as documented by Pietz. Recall that these included 1) the fetish's untranscended materiality; the material object as locus of power; 2) the fetish as a historically singular point of origin that can be partially repeated through the fixation on the fetish; 3) the fetish's dependence on a particular set of social relations for its meaning and value; and 4) the active relation of the fetish to the human body. Condensing these, we can view the fetish as an expression of radical historicality, as fixed "event" which as object-set-apart marks the body and locates the self in time. It is a touchstone to which one may repeatedly return through contact or mimesis, or what I earlier referred to as a mnemonics of human temporality.

How are popular forms of memory, such as those involved in baseball, a form of "making history"? Such power does not reside, to be sure, in the sense in which fans uttered it, "witnessing history" as if it were outside of them, passively observed like a river flowing by into which one suddenly plunges, drowning now "in history." Rather, by constructing the Ball's value through their attention to it, and then seeing/touching it or otherwise experiencing its presence, they (we) frame and articulate a relation between the self and time. History becomes a "livable distortion," a "signifying stabilizer," a "fixation."

Alternatively evaluated, per Sahlins, the contact with the Ball becomes an "event." To reiterate, as Sahlins described the construction of historical "events" at the outset of *Islands of History*, history is made of significant "events." Such narrative-generating "events" involve an equation: a "happening" plus a structure of interpretation. To this equation we now add a third and fourth term, such that (historical) "event"= "happening" + structure of interpretation + modes of representation/reproduction (the object) + contact with the object. The Ball is just such a mode of representation/reproduction, a point of symbolic condensation over which many Americans construct communal memory, or "make history."

Delillo and "The Shot Heard Around The World"

The mythic role of select, "contagious" baseballs in the construction of American (and not only North) memory and identity are present in more than just the 1998 homerun race. It is a common literary and filmic trope as well.[46] Perhaps the most eloquent fictional depiction of the baseball-as-fetish comes to us in Don Delillo's recent novel, *Underworld*.[47]

Underworld opens with a scene from October 3, 1951. The New York Giants are facing the Brooklyn Dodgers in the pennant race that has divided the city. It is the bottom of the ninth and the Giants are losing 4-2, with runners on second and third, one out, and Bobby Thomson in the batter's box. On the second pitch, the count at a strike and no balls, Thomson smashes a line drive into the lower deck of section 35, and the Giants win the pennant, 5-4. The announcer Russ Hodges keeps screaming into his microphone, "The Giants win the pennant!," but already a new competition in section 35, invisible to the radio audience, has been launched. It is the quest for the Ball: "The game is way behind him now. The crowd can have the game. He's after the baseball now and there's no time to ask himself why.... It's the ball they play with, the thing they rub up and scuff and sweat on."[48]

But what, precisely, does he hold? Even the boy, Cotter, isn't yet sure. Walking home trying to elude his insistent rival and pursuer, "he sees the Power of Prayer sign and carries the ball in his right hand and rubs it up several times...."

Whatever it is, it is important that it is the thing the players "rub up and scuff and sweat on," and which he now can rub. To Manx, his father, the pennant-winning ball is not to rub or hold to feel its magic, but rather to sell, to exchange for more useful things like sweaters. That night while the boy sleeps, Manx strikes a deal with Charles, a man who buys the ball for his own son at the price of $32.45. Yet after the exchange, Charles is unsure of what, precisely, he holds: "'Now that the ball is mine, what do I do with it?' Manx retakes the flask. 'Show it around. Tell your friends and neighbors. Then put it in a glass case with the fancy dishes. You saw those crowds go crazy in the street. This is bigger than some wars I seen.'"[49]

Eventually it passes into Marvin Lundy's hands. Marvin is an obsessional collector of baseball memorabilia. "This is history, back-page. From back to front. Happy, tragic, desperate." And, "In this trunk right here I have the one thing that my whole life for the past twenty-two years I was trying to collect." He is not sure why. "I said to myself a thousand times. Why do I want this thing? What does it mean? Who has it?" He cannot answer these imponderables, except that it is a mystery, "all around him, every street deep in some radiant amaze.... It was work of Talmudic refinement, zooming in and fading out...."[50]

It is from Marvin Lundy that the main character of *Underworld*, Nick, finally acquires the Ball. Dining with friends, he is pressed by Sims for the reason why he bought it, for $34,500.

> "What do you do, take the ball out of the closet and look at it? Then what?"
>
> "He thinks about what it means," Glassic said. "It's an object with a history. He thinks about losing. He wonders what it is that brings bad luck to one person and the sweetest of good fortune to another. It's a lovely thing in itself besides. An old baseball? It's a lovely thing, Sims. And this one's got a pedigree like no other."

"He got taken big-time," Sims said. "He's holding a worthless object."[51]

These are good questions that Nick's friends raise. Where does the Ball's value lie? In what does its value reside? Nick does occasionally take it out and look at it. More importantly, he touches it:

> Usually I kept the baseball on the bookshelves, wedged in a corner between straight-up books…. But now I had it in my hand. You have to know the feel of a baseball in your hand, going back a while, connecting many things, before you can understand why a man would sit in a chair at four in the morning holding such an object, clutching it… You squeeze a baseball. You kind of juice it or milk it…. The ball was a deep sepia, veneered with dirt and turf and generational sweat.[52]

A short while later, Nick reflects on the Ball's power to grant him a sense of memory and location: "I felt calmer now. I felt all right. My arm hung over the side of the chair and I squeezed the baseball, listening to Marian sleep-breathe—squeezed it hard, the veins leveling on the back of my hand, going dead flat."[53]

In Delillo's *Underworld*, the Ball is a sub-text to the main story, an object that anchors and, through its passage, marks the passage of time. It is the object-pivot to a story that leaps, hurly-burly, between the decades of the 50s, 60s, and 70s. As a stabilizing signifier, the reader holds onto it as desperately as Nick does, clinging to it like a ring-buoy in the rushing waters of the multi-layered, multi-voiced narrative. It links macro-historical political events, such as the rise and proliferation of nuclear weaponry as the master-myth of the Cold War period,[54] to the life of a particular country, to the life of particular persons who squeeze memory out of the Ball. The reader, like Nick, is forced to fixate on it. The reliance of Delillo, Nick, and the reader on the Ball raises many questions. The text returns over and over to mystery and religion. "I don't know," or to Talmudic inquiry, or to the Power of Prayer Temple. We read, and feel, that the object is powerful, that it signifies, that it involves issues of memory and history and the emotions that accompany them. But how? The ritualization of touch is suggestive: Cotter's rubbing the ball previously rubbed; Nick's periodic retrieval of the Ball to squeeze it until the sweats cease and the panic recedes.

Interpretations

What will McGwire's seventieth mean to Todd MacFarlane, now that he has it? Perhaps he holds nothing more (but nothing less!) than a sense of the self "in history," "making history" through the periodic bodily link to what we have all taken part in constructing in our gaze on number 70. For Nick, the Ball returns him to 1951 and to a simpler, less cluttered time (Where have you gone, Joe DiMaggio?). Holding the Ball, he resurrects through the magic of contact a time prior to the culture of waste and the Cold-War master narrative that defined his generation. McFarlane, the buyer of McGwire's seventieth, reveals something akin to Nick in his statement, "Sports make you forget death, taxes, and politics, and all the other garbage that goes on in life." An alternative sort of power, a "return" to a time set apart, an Eden without death or garbage.[55] Baseball as innocent America, pre-Cold War, pre-Viet Nam America. Baseball and apple pie.

It is here that Lipsitz's notion of popular culture and "counter-memory" are intriguing. If we consider the importance of the Ball as a mnemonic object constructing a "counter-memory," we are obliged to consider the question of what it "counters." We can hardly help but note that the other narrative demanding the public eye during the same period, a narrative both "popular" and "national," was President Clinton's affair with the young White House intern, Monica Lewinsky. For all its celebrity sex appeal, this narrative also left a sense of distrust and jadedness; *pace* the leads of Georges Bataille, a combination of guilt before a clear taboo and a transgressive pleasure in being there. Baseball, with all its DiMaggio magic of a purer America, served as the structural opposition, perhaps even antidote, to this collective obsession. The home-run race with the Ball as its sign, its fetish, was the trope (in the sense of turning) for configuring a counter-memory.

It is not that the McGwire image was so utterly pure. McGwire presented his own form of sensuality during his tanktop press-conferences after the game, fresh from the kill and reeking of testosterone.[56] Any direct erotic allure, though, was abridged, sieved through the images of McGwire-as-single-father.[57] With his son the bat-boy ever on his shoulders after the game, McGwire presented the image of an eroticism appropriately submitted to the duties of family, team, and public. The Clinton narrative, meanwhile, proffered the structural opposite: a family and country compromised by an egregious lack of sexual control. The structural diagram is not difficult to draw:

> McGwire : Clinton ::
> erotic restraint : erotic excess ::
> civic and family duties : breach of civic and family duties

"Reading" America in relation to the home-run race narrative returned us to Ruth and DiMaggio—to innocent inter-war America and solid, suffering Joe carrying his flowers to Marilyn Monroe's grave year after year. "Reading" America in relation to the Clinton-Lewinsky narrative returned us other philandering presidents, JFK and LBJ, to the Viet Nam era and the crisis of identity, to the breakdown of trust in public institutions. The contrast between narratives, McGwire's and Clinton's, is reflected in Paul Simon's lyrics, which we could add to the bottom of our structural chart:

> McGwire : Clinton ::
> "Here's to you, Joe DiMaggio" : "Joltin' Joe has left and gone away"

Obviously this is only one such possibility for how we might read the baseball narrative as "counter-memory," and the fact that we can tease such structures to the surface does not mean there are not manifold other possibilities. Furthermore, an important risk here is that of misconstruing professional baseball as populist resistance (Lipsitz's counter-memory) when it in fact is also a dominant media production. In the final analysis, the Clinton narrative and the McGwire narrative present equivalence as much as opposition. They both *sold*; they both "moved product."

Fortunately, for the purposes of this essay we need not determine the precise narrative content conveyed in baseball mythology, since we are here concerned with baseballs as condensation points, as fetish; with the use of the Ball in generating historical narrative, not the content of the narrative itself. Even in this sense, the ritual elevation of a home-run Ball may appear a long stretch from what the Yoruba or the BaKongo did with their *awure* and *minkisi*, besieged by European traders with their strange notions of value. The *feitiço* brokered differences even as it highlighted them and threw them into relief. It presented a mediating vocabulary of value for West Africans and Portuguese sailors, even as this vocabulary instantiated hierarchies of economic and "rational" control. But it also reveals something about the importance of condensed materializations of social relations and memory, of tangible points that, when "worked," revivify that memory of the past for purposes in the present.

The text, the ring, Shubert's cut-up musical scores, regional cuisine: these present epistemological lenses through which we see ourselves in the present, backlit by the past. Through these lenses we adjust the view. McGwire's Ball is not the same as the *minkisi*, most obviously in the sense that it does not refer to gods or spirits, nor that it is a colonized symbol. In the case of the *minkisi*, present experience of the body in time-space was and is (re)constructed through the objects' ritualization. Americans' use of McGwire's Ball is less clearly defined; but like the ritualization of sacred objects, it depends on principles of condensation, contact, metaphor, metonymy, and mimesis. The Ball is approached, whether in Cooperstown or through the television, in order to approach a larger-than-life, super-human presence that transfixes the gaze, mediates between and structurally locates social groups by generating a shared symbolic grammar, and allows contemplation of the self-in-time. We touch the Ball to evoke memories of the past, to "return" and thereby recharge our sense of the real in the present.[58]

Remember that the fetish is a fluid, mediating term, an idea about objects, not an object itself; a mode of action, "to fetish." It is not important to determine whether a baseball is or is not a fetish. What is important is that by looking at baseball in terms of the concept of the fetish, we begin to see the fixation on contemporary memorabilia in a new light. In order to understand ourselves "in history," a spectral history without master narratives—Lipsitz's crisis of memory or Benjamin's flash in a moment of danger—along the latest and most virtual bend of the late-modern turn, it is possible that we require the fetish, the fixation on objects, more than we did a half-century ago. More likely is that we have always relied on objects to stabilize memory and to animate history, suggesting again that Tylor's "animism" and Frazer's "sympathetic magic" were not stages of religious evolution but rather stable, persistant modes of human consciousness.

Does the return of the idea of the fetish surprise? Were the decades of post-colonial rehabilitation enough? The rehabilitation is that the fetishizers are we, that the fetish never left, and that its return only surprises under the "common-sense" regime of Protestant and Enlightenment discourses against the animating power of objects, a six-inning slumber after which we now stand to stretch.

[1] Walter Benjamin, "Theses on the Philosophy of History," *Illumniations*, ed. Hannah Arendt (New York: Schocken Books, 1968) 255.

[2] Hayden White, *Tropics of Discourse* (Baltimore: Johns Hopkins University Press, 1978) 62.

[3] Marshall Sahlins, *Islands of History* (Chicago: University of Chicago Press, 1985) xiv. Cf. Andrew Abbot, "Conceptions of Time and Events in Social Science Methods," *Historical Method* 23 (1990):140-50; William H. Sewell, Jr., "Three Temporalities: Toward an Eventful Sociology," *The Historic Turn in the Social Sciences*, ed. Terrence J. McDonald (Ann Arbor: University of Michigan Press, 1996) 245-80; and William H. Sewell, Jr., "Historical Events as Transformations of Structures: Inventing Revolution at the Bastille," *Theory and Society* 25 (1996): 841-81.

[4] Paul Connerton, *How Societies Remember* (Cambridge: Cambridge University Press, 1989).

[5] Paul Stoller, "Embodying Cultural Memory in Sonhay Spirit Possession," *Archives de Sciences des Religions* 80 (1992): 53-68; Paul Stoller, *Embodying Colonial Memories: Spirit Possession, Power, and the Hauka in West Africa* (New York: Routledge, 1995); and Paul Stoller, *Sensuous Scholarship* (Philadelphia: University of Pennsylvania Press, 1997).

[6] George Lipsitz, *Time Passages: Collective Memory and American Popular Culture* (Minneapolis: University of Minnesota Press, 1990) 213.

[7] Luce Giard, "Plat du Jour," *Living and Cooking*, vol. 2 of *The Practice of Everyday Life*, ed. Michel de Certeau, Luce Giard, and Pierre Mayol, trans. Timothy J. Tomasik (Minneapolis: University of Minnesota Press, 1998) 183.

[8] Giard, "Plat du Jour," 188.

[9] Emmanuel Le Roy Ladurie, *Montaillou: The Promised Land of Error*, trans. Barbara Bray (New York: Vintage Books, 1979) 277.

[10] Pierre Bourdieu, *Outline of a Theory of Practice*, trans. Richard Nice (Cambridge: Cambridge University Press, 1977) 81.

[11] Cf. Sahlins, *Islands of History*, and Sewell, "Three Temporalities."

[12] Cf. White, *Tropics of Discourse*.

[13] Sir James Frazer, *The Golden Bough*, Imperial one-volume abridged edition (New York: Macmillan Company, 1958) 12.

[14] Emile Durkheim, *Elementary Forms of Religious Life*, trans. Joseph Ward Swain (New York: Free Press, 1915).

[15] Marshall Sahlins, *How Natives Think: About Captain Cook, for Example* (Chicago: University of Chicago Press, 1995) 9-13.

[16] Jan Goodwin, "Sierra Leone Is No Place to Be Young," *New York Times Magazine* (February 14, 1999).

[17] David Chidester, "The Church of Baseball, the Fetish of Coca-Cola, and the Potlatch of Rock 'n' Roll: Theoretical Models for the Study of Religion in American Popular Culture," *Journal of the American Academy of Religion* 59/4 (1996): 743-66.

[18] Michael Taussig, "Maleficium: State Fetishism," *Fetishism as Cultural Discourse*, ed. Emily Apter and William Pietz (Ithaca: Cornell University Press, 1993).

[19] Homi K. Bhabha, *The Location of Culture* (London and New York: Routledge, 1994) 71.

[20] Moishe Postone, "Deconstruction as Social Critique: Derrida on Marx and the New World," *History and Theory* 37 (1998): 370-87.

[21] James Clifford, *The Predicament of Culture: Twentieth Century Ethnography, Literature, and Art* (Cambridge: Harvard University Press, 1988) 229.

[22] William Pietz, "The Problem of the Fetish, I," *Res* 9 (1985): 5-17; William Pietz, "The Problem of the Fetish, II," *Res* 13 (1987): 23-45; William Pietz, "The Problem of the Fetish, IIIa," *Res* 16 (1988): 105-123; William Pietz, "The Spirit of Civilization: Blood Sacrifice and Monetary Debt," *Res* 28 (1995): 23-38.

[23] Lipsitz, *Time Passages*, viii.

[24] Pietz, "The Problem of the Fetish, I," 12.

[25] Pietz, "The Problem of the Fetish, I," 13.

[26] Stanley Jeyaraja Tambiah, *Magic, Science, Religion, and the Scope of Rationality* (Cambridge: Cambridge University Press, 1990) 60.

[27] Tom Verducci, "Making His Mark," *Sports Illustrated* 11 (1998): 32.

[28] Verducci, "Making His Mark," 30.

[29] Verducci, "Making His Mark," 34.

[30] Verducci, "Making His Mark," 31.

[31] Verducci, "Making His Mark," 33. Sosa's sixty-second homerun, meanwhile, would not be authenticated and validated as "real" with such rational and bureaucratic precision. While it is not the objective of the present essay, we could treat these select balls as "social texts," and wonder about the treatment of Sosa's sixty-second in comparison with McGwire's. Why no US Treasury ink for Sosa? Was the perfect rational specificity only necessary for the California native, and not for the Dominican? Was Sosa a potential usurper of the throne of "America's game"?

[32] Verducci, "Making His Mark," 34.

[33] Pietz, "Problem of the Fetish, II," 23.

[34] The key reference for this assertion is in a footnote from Andre Alvares d'Amada, *Tratado breve dos Rios des Guinâe do Cabo-Verde desdc o Rio do Sanagâaatâe aos baixos de Sant' Anna* (Porto: Commercial Portuense, 1841 [1594]) 100.

[35] H. Clapperton, *Journal of the Second Expedition into the Interior of Africa* (Philadelphia: Carey, Lea and Carey, 1829) 87.

[36] The translation of Olódùmaré as "God" is contested, but is articulated most forcefully by E. Bolanji Idowu, *Olodumare: God in Yoruba Belif* (New York: Original Publications, 1995).

[37] Wyatt MacGaffey, *Art and Healing of the BaKongo Commented by Themselves: Minkisi from the Laman Collection* (Bloomington: Indiana University Press, 1991); and Wyatt MacGaffey, "African Objects and the Idea of the Fetish," *Rsh* 25 (1994): 123-31.

[38] Pietz, "Problem of the Fetish, I," 5.

[39] Pietz, "Problem of the Fetish, IIIa," 110.

[40] Pietz, "Problem of the Fetish, IIIa," 111.

[41] Though Freud followed Alfred Binet in referring to sexual deviance as fetishism, he is certainly the most notorious. See Sigmund Freud, "Unsuitable Substitutes for the Sexual Object: Fetishism" (1905) and "Fetishism" (1927), *The Standard Edition of the Complete Psychological Works of Sigmund Freud*, trans. James Strachey, 7 (London: Hogarth Press, 1953).

[42] Pietz, "Problem of the Fetish, II," 39.

[43] Charles de Brosses, *Du culte des dieux fétiches, ou Parallèle de l'ancienne religion de l'Egypte avec la relation actuelle de Nigritie* (England: Westmead, Farnborough, Hants, 1970) 10.

[44] E.g., Durkeim, *Elementary Forms of Religious Life*, 203.

[45] Jean Pouillon, "Fetiches sans fetichisme," *Nouvelle revue de psychanalyse* 2 (1970): 135-47.

[46] Though here we may wonder about the range of a contagious object's power. Can an object anchor us in time as we witness its manipulation on film or page? This would conform to Frazer's second mechanism for passing power, magical imitation or homeopathy. Through imagined mimesis, we copy the actual contact with the object performed on screen or in fictional text. Watching contact and finding it meaningful, second-hand magic would therefore be a combination of the two mechanisms, contact and mimesis.

[47] Don Delillo, *Underworld* (New York: 1997).

[48] Delillo, *Underworld*, 45-48.

[49] Delillo, *Underworld*, 653.

[50] Delillo, *Underworld*, 174, 175, 176-77.

[51] Delillo, *Underworld*, 99.

[52] Delillo, *Underworld*, 131-32.

[53] Delillo, *Underworld*, 133.

[54] This is consistently the master-narrative against which Delillo's characters battle. In *End Zone* it is football that proffers an antidote through its structure and purity, though finally it is a failed solution. In *White Noise*, the protagonist seeks redemption from the fear of death by watching his child sleep; the remedy again only partial and temporary.

[55] Mircea Eliade, *The Myth of the Eternal Return*, trans. Willard R. Trask (New York: Harper Torchbooks, 1959).

[56] The said testosterone level was later found to be, along with his biceps, chemically enhanced.

[57] It would be remiss not to clarify here that we are only considering the mythic, constructed McGwire, not McGwire-as-such.

[58] Cf., Eliade, *Myth of the Eternal Return*.

EVERY RELIGION NEEDS A MARTYR
THE ROLE OF MATTY, GEHRIG, AND CLEMENTE IN THE NATIONAL FAITH

Peter Williams

Heroes and Martyrs

In the great old boxing movie *Body and Soul,* John Garfield takes gamblers' money to fix his fight. He gets into the ring planning to take a dive, but then he has a Hollywood change of heart: He can't go through with it, and he knocks the other fighter out. On the way back to the dressing room a battered Garfield is stopped by a gentleman in a gray fedora, who fixes him with what cliché experts would call a steely glare. Garfield glares right back. "What're ya gonna do, kill me?" he says. "Everybody dies."

Miguel de Unamuno could not have put matters more simply or bluntly: The fact that everybody dies is indeed the tragic sense of life,[1] the irreducible kernel and prime source of everybody's subliminal malaise, and you can go from Unamuno all the way back to the "J" creation story for corroboration. Adam is in pretty good shape at the outset of Genesis, since he stands to live forever. At the end of that story, though, evicted from the timeless world by a super power carrying a flaming sword, he knows he can count on physical extinction, and that any chance he might have must always be clouded by the doubt we call faith. In George Orwell's very scary phrasing, when a man dies, it's not just one mind less; it's one world less.[2]

There's more to the story and to death, of course, although as a lapsed Irish Catholic I tend to brood more over death than over sin, Adam's other curse; but orthodoxy, religious or mythic, does tend to treat the two equally. Milton, for example, posts Death and Sin on either side of the gate to Hell, and being told you're going to have to live a life of sin is an important part of the tragic package, even though it may not pack the emotional wallop of being told that your life will surely end both inexplicably and unpredictably. The bottom line is this: we don't want to die, ever; and we'd rather be good, not just sometimes, but always.

What then? Genesis and every good book since tell us to forget it: We are fallen, imperfect in body (we'll die) and in soul (we'll sin). Ironically, the only vestige of perfection left to us is our ability to conceive perfection. We can imagine perfect virtue, and yearn for both that and endless life. In brief, we can imagine Adam before the fall: This is how we make our heroes.

Our first impulse, of course, is to make morally and physically invincible heroes of ourselves. As kids, we put on paper hats, grabbed a plastic bow and arrow, and turned the back yard into Sherwood Forest and the unpleasant neighbor into the bad Sheriff. We have what the cartoonist Steig called "Dreams of Glory," and since the innocence of childhood lasts a lot longer at night, these dreams will sometimes persist well into adulthood. Let me confess a few of my own adult dreams of glory to you: the time I was president, sitting in the Oval Office and handling the affairs of the nation with perfect aplomb; the time I was one of the Beatles, although I couldn't tell you which one; the time I opened the Met season, singing the tenor lead in a weird amalgam of "Tosca" and "Boheme," and brother, they loved me; the time I sat patiently on the Seventh Avenue local during rush hour, going to work at Cape Canaveral in my astronaut suit; the time, in a sparring match, when I kept knocking Ali down, while he got more and more frustrated and more and more irritable. I was just a little faster, just a little stronger, and every time he got up, that amazed look on his face, I'd pop him again, always with a left jab, and down he'd go again. In the dream, I felt bad. I saw no reason for hard feelings, since I myself felt none, and I tried to explain to Ali that there was nothing personal in it.

You laugh? Hypocrites, *lecteurs—mes semblables, mes frères!* The only thing that's keeping many from this year's fantasy baseball camps is the requisite thousands of dollars. Still, when we try to make ourselves into perfect heroes, we have to laugh, since our real, non-heroic world is always too much with us. Therefore, if it's going to succeed, the impulse to create Adam-like heroes has to go further afield. We can only make heroes out of persons we have never met, individuals whose real selves have been replaced by the two-dimensional, artificially tinted photos on antique baseball cards. We delude ourselves into believing in these cardboard images, first, because we have absolutely no direct contact with the humans from whom they were shaped, and, second, because our desire to believe is nothing short of desperate.

Thus far I have suggested that there are two stages to the hero-making phenomenon. First, we imagine or dream the unfallen Adam, a cluster of flawless principles in an eternally healthy body; then we find a public figure, sufficiently distant from our real world, whom we can transfigure. Nietzsche, in suggesting that Apollo presides over our capacity to imagine perfection a priori, is talking about the first stage;[3] Jessie Weston, in maintaining that Adonis began his mystic career as a real individual, is talking about the second.[4] The resultant hero is a man whom we know to exist in the real world, but who also has reached the idealized and Edenic state that is our own fondest wish. The hero thus conceived is our perfect surrogate; in believing in him, we can live the flawless life vicariously.

Can such a hero die, especially when he is still young enough to be contemporary with his own achievements? Not in the world we imagine, of course, and it must be remembered that, for us, this is his only world. But the imagined and imaginary world of idealized heroism is supported by the real world—we couldn't believe in the idol were it not for our knowledge of the existence of the man—and the real world is always at liberty to withdraw its support. When a hero returns to the real world and dies young, you might expect a shocked and disillusioned awakening on the part of the idolaters, a realization that this clay-shod person was fallible, after all; but that's not what happens. Martyrdom is the mode of death that creates a more permanent life; something new is born, an unchanging stone to forever trouble the living stream. If the hero's myth is strong enough, his death in the real world will only fix and enhance his image in the ideal one. Repeatedly, popular rumors arise that JFK has been found some place, still alive, if somewhat the worse for wear, and that Elvis is still hanging out in or around Grand Rapids. As far back as Elia Kazan's "Viva Zapata!," the peons refuse to believe their hero has been killed despite the contrary evidence of several hundred very large bullet holes and a peculiar lack of activity on the part of Emiliano himself. At the end of the movie, a couple of them look up at the mountains, where they see Zapata's horse. They decide that Zapata, still very much alive, has found some way to get inside the horse. Personally, I think that sounds a bit kinky, even for Marlon Brando, but suffice it to say that martyrdom does not take stature away from the hero; if anything, martyrdom increases that stature and preserves it more efficiently.[5]

Clemente as Hero

Let's turn at last to baseball. The heroes we create in baseball are no different from our heroes in any other area: they, too, represent our effort to reverse the effects of Adam's curse. Look at the distinction between "prowess" and "ethical" heroes, for example.[6] The former is physically heroic, the latter spiritually; taken to logical extremes, they represent immortality of flesh and perfection of soul. The perfected prowess hero knows not death; the perfected ethical hero cannot sin: These are the qualities of Adam before the fall.

While it could certainly be argued that anyone good enough to play big-league ball would have to be a prowess hero, it's also true that here, as elsewhere, image is more powerful than truth. Thus Christy Mathewson, Lou Gehrig, and Roberto Clemente are all ethical heroes, notwithstanding their respective 373 wins, 2130 successive games, and 3000 hits. Their ethical heroism becomes important when each of their lives takes its tragic turn. The fact is that we feel the ethical hero's martyrdom more deeply than that of the prowess hero. It's particularly obvious in the case of Gehrig. Following the diagnosis of his fatal disease, he lingered for a couple of years and finally died, exactly prefiguring what would happen to Ruth later in the same decade. But, although Ruth was just as much the martyr in the real world, he was a prowess hero, not an ethical one; although his illness and death were nationally mourned, they were less of an emotional catastrophe than the passing of Gehrig.

To be a proper baseball martyr, then, one must be an ethical hero, like the three players under consideration. Of these three, the most distinctive may be Clemente, for two reasons: he is the only one of the three to die without warning, and he is the only one whose ethical heroism was primarily active; in other words, he died, as he had lived, doing charitable work for the disadvantaged. In this, he was very much a hero in tune with the social activism of his time; and the response to his death, showing an awareness of this, ended by strengthening a heroic image that was already well established.

Clemente's plane went down in the sea off San Juan as he was trying to fly supplies to the survivors of the great earthquake in Nicaragua. He had no need to make the trip; this time he had decided to ride shotgun, because profiteers at the other end had been ripping him off, and he wanted to make sure this load of relief supplies got through. His plane went down on New Year's Eve, 1972; appropriately, on the most self-indulgent holiday of the year, Clemente was using his time to help others.

Reaction to his death was severe, especially in Puerto Rico, where three days of official mourning were declared and Governor-elect Colon canceled his inaugural ball. Back in the continental United States, Tom Seaver said the word for Clemente was "compassion," and Willie Stargell cried in public. Both Leonard Koppett and Danny Murtaugh noted that the manner of Clemente's death was consistent with the generous nature of his life. Bowie Kuhn, unsurprisingly, dipped into his executive cliché bin, saying, "words seem futile." The only person to use the word "hero" was Nicaraguan dictator Somoza, who may have been one of those responsible for diverting Clemente's aid. If Somoza was one of the profiteers, of course, he was also partly responsible for Clemente's having taken that plane.[7]

On January 2, at Colon's inauguration, the language of the eulogists indicated that the conversion of simple hero into transfigured martyr had begun. Colon lamented the man, saying "our youth have lost an idol," but his secretary of state welcomed the immortal martyr: "We have with us today the spirit of a man…who helped teach [us] how to…become better citizens," he said.[8]

For the rest of that first week, the public reaction remained largely one of sincere shock, with President Nixon calling Clemente "a generous and kind human being."[9] In Pittsburgh, the mayor proclaimed Roberto Clemente Week, two fans began circulating a petition to re-name Three Rivers "Roberto Clemente Stadium," and the ALCON electric message board on Mt. Washington flashed, "ADIOS AMIGO ROBERTO" in enormous letters over the city. The Mellon Fund donated $100,000 in Clemente's name to help the quake victims, and the Pirates quickly matched that sum.[10] The Baseball Writers Association of America and the Hall of Fame cleared the way for Clemente's immediate installation at Cooperstown, using Gehrig's similar case as precedent. Back in San Juan, efforts were begun to rename both the coliseum and the airport after Clemente while, in a brief and grisly return to the real world, a navy salvage expert said they'd better find the body soon if they wanted to find it at all. "They [bodies] tend to disintegrate in salt water," he said.[11]

Two weeks after the crash, the memory of the event was still fresh enough for a class of nine-year-old children in the Bronx to write down their reactions in their study of Puerto Rican history. The language the kids used, with its innocent emphasis on permanence, further demonstrates the paradoxical power of martyrdom to revivify. Darria Tucker called him a generous man, whom "everybody should remember," and she concluded that "he will always be a hero." Robert Zabala, saying that Clemente "died because he really cared," suggested that death had really made little difference, since Roberto was "a great hero in life and death."[12]

By February, however, it became difficult to separate sincere tribute from exploitation. In New York City, at a salsa concert at the Garden, Symphony Sid asked everyone in the crowd to light a match to observe a moment of silence, after which, of course, they all got up and danced, jubilant and carefree.[13] The CYO, at their annual sports dinner, added a special posthumous award for Clemente; the other two honorees were promoter Bill Fugazy, the Don King of that era, and Bowie Kuhn.[14]

Clemente was a hero for his time, and his name kept stubbornly cropping up all year long. Who knows how genuine the ceremony was in Pittsburgh on opening day in the spring of 1973? No doubt the fans loved him, and the Galbreaths, the owners of the Pirates who planned the show, are gracious people; still, the anthem was sung by one Paul New, whose only qualification seems to have been that he wrote "The Ballad of Roberto Clemente," a song that had become, according to the paper, a "best-seller."[15] Later, in May, Vera Clemente, Roberto's wife, was given the Presidential Citizens Medal by President Nixon. The Watergate investigation was just about to begin, and the commander-in-chief, having sensed a great photo opportunity, was shown with the widow, grinning from ear to ear.[16] But there were undeniably real tributes, too: Clemente's name was used for a new PAL center in a Hispanic ghetto,[17] for a major intersection in a Hispanic business area,[18] and for a new low-income housing project. He was being fixed in American myth as an archetype for a certain kind of hero, the kind who actively helps the poor.[19]

Gehrig as Hero

Gehrig was just a nice guy. It's nearly impossible to find a picture of him lacking that famous smile, which always invites observers to shuffle up next to him. He never got out there in the trenches like Clemente; he didn't have to. The low-keyed manner and the smile were all he ever needed, and he probably even skipped beatification on his quick trip to the saintly calendar. It's terrific what image can do; even Eleanor Gehrig seems to have been unscarred by Lou's marital lapses. Beyond the familiar distinction between real person and image, however, there is something that makes Gehrig's case unique: everybody knew he was sick, maybe terminal, for two years before he actually died.

The story begins in the fall of 1938. He had a terrible spring camp and a worse April. The writers wondered in print, the fans wrote to the writers asking them to leave the poor guy alone, and the writers told the fans they'd be happier than anyone if they could find positive things to say. On May 2 Gehrig asked to be benched, and McCarthy, benched him.

There are three distinct periods in Gehrig's martyrdom: first, the month and a half following the end of his career; second, the two years of his illness; finally, the period after his death.

The first of these begins with eulogies for his career. His biggest advocate was always Joe McCarthy, who was so blinded by affection for the man that he thought him the greatest player in history. After Gehrig stepped down, McCarthy said he had done "the proper thing," adding that Gehrig was "a perfect gentleman, a credit to baseball" and "too grand a fellow" to have waited for the fans to boo him.[20]

It's unlikely the fans ever would have. A sad silence maybe, but no boos. Ordinary fans like Lester H. Goodking wrote to the papers in the same spirit. "He will take out of baseball the highest regard of all the fans," Lester said, of fans "who respect him as an outstanding player and a clean one, too." Then, exactly one month after he benched himself, Gehrig revealed that he was going up to the Mayo Clinic for tests. He said not to worry, that he was all right, but Yankee Coach John Schulte was more up front: "Lou is a sick man," he gravely told reporters. Gehrig agreed that "a thorough examination will be a good idea," but he said again that he was "feeling all right," attributing overreaction to everybody: to the press, to his teammates, to the fans, or, as he said, "the boys in general." Something certainly seemed wrong.[21]

Gehrig got to Rochester on June 13, and the physicians worked over him for the next four days. On June 17, a Saturday, he got a weekend pass, and sailed up the Mississippi at the request of one of his doctors. He was back in the clinic on Monday, when he received an envelope containing the diagnosis. He read it, but he declined to reveal the contents to the press; it was a Yankee matter, he said, and McCarthy would have to handle it. His refusal to talk was affable, of course; he was just observing the chain of command. Then he packed his stuff and got ready to fly back home. It was his thirty-sixth birthday.

What Arthur Daley called "the shocking news" broke three days later, on June 22. Ed Barrow, not McCarthy, made the announcement. "Gentlemen, we have bad news," he said. "Gehrig has Infantile Paralysis."

The writers were astonished, but Gehrig, saying he'd have to "accept the bitter with the sweet," only grinned. The *New York Times* ran a four-column picture showing Lou in uniform in the dugout, telling his story to Joe Gordon, Lefty Gomez, Bill Dickey, and Coach Schulte. In that picture, Gehrig, of course, is smiling. Only Dickey, Lou's best friend and roommate, looks cheerless. Daley, who was there when the picture was snapped, reported that Dickey "sat there morosely" the whole time, saying nothing at all.

The second period of mourning began then. First there was a retrospective look at how Gehrig had received the news. In Rochester, he had simply said, "I suspected something was wrong." Then he'd attended a small birthday party, never revealing what he had just been told. Later, at the airport, he "autographed a ten-cent baseball for a small boy."[22]

There were eulogies again. In an editorial, the *Times* said Gehrig had left "a record of good sportsmanship and clean living that has been a shining example for every boy who ever stepped on a playing field," and it looked as if every fan in the country wanted personally to solace him. By June 23, he had taken home "four huge boxes of mail and telegrams." Gehrig himself, who must have been feeling a good deal more mortal than mythic, was genuinely "stunned" by all this.[23] The culmination, of course, was Lou Gehrig Appreciation Day, on, to complete the mythic elevating, July 4. It should be remembered that this was less than two weeks after everybody had been told that, fairly soon, Gehrig would be either crippled or dead.

The emotional catharsis of Lou Gehrig Day is too well known to need any summary here, although it may be noted that Mayor LaGuardia got into the act for the fist time. LaGuardia always seemed to be motivated more by charity than by a need for headlines in his efforts to help Gehrig. At the stadium that day, he called Lou "the greatest prototype of good sportsmanship and citizenship," clearly indicating how the man was becoming the archetypal figure of myth.[24] In the months to come, LaGuardia was just as sympathetic to the stricken man, making sure that he always had a dignified job in city government. In August, Gehrig was made honorary youth director of the New York World's Fair, and Grover Whelan, with a sidelong glance at Lou's building immortality, told Lou that the "virtues" he "displayed in the world of today will live because of you in the world of tomorrow."[25] In October, Gehrig was appointed to the Municipal Parole Board. In a compassionate gesture, LaGuardia made sure he was given a ten-year term. A photographer for the *Times* posed Lou reading a book called *Crime and the Community*, and he was, as ever, dimpled and smiling; but in the picture, he looked uncharacteristically thin.[26]

The public continued to praise him. The warden of Alcatraz said the kids of the country wanted "more models like Lou Gehrig and Joe DiMaggio to emulate,"[27] and the Massachusetts branch of the Women's Christian Temperance Union gave Gehrig its commendation for his "contribution to good living."[28] In mid-November, at a benefit gala involving Jascha Heifetz, Tallulah Bankhead, Jimmy Walker, George Jessel, and Barbara Stanwyck, Gehrig got the most applause.[29] By the first week of January he was still getting regular coverage in the press. It was announced that his number would be retired, this being the first time this honor was ever accorded to any baseball player (George Selkirk, in fact, wore #3 for the Yanks that year).[30] He was shown being sworn in for his job at the Municipal Parole Board, and when he was asked to pose for photographers, he put away the pipe he'd been smoking. Why? "Well, I don't want to be shown smoking in pictures because of the possible effect on young boys," he said. "I can't encourage kids to smoke."[31]

On January 7, he "laughed at reports that his weight had dropped to 130."[32] On January 9, he went back to the Mayo Clinic, thus ending the second period of public mourning.[33] Astonishingly, nothing at all about Gehrig appeared in the *New York Times* for well over a year. Possibly his story had become too heartbreaking to deal with, and everybody was in a state of denial. For whatever reason, we are told nothing more about Gehrig until June 3, 1941, and then we are told that he is dead.

Once again, public reaction indicated how the man was becoming the archetype. Here are a few comments. Colonel Ruppert: "one of the finest characters who ever participated in the game." Joe McCarthy: "the world loses a great man." Joe DiMaggio: "a great individual; he was a good influence on us young ball players, to whom he was an inspiration." Will Harridge: "his conduct and sportsmanship on and off the playing field will remain an everlasting monument to his memory." Eddie Brannick: "a great example to the youth of America." Warren Giles: "a great, great guy." Joe Cronin: "one of the greatest gentlemen." Frankie Frisch: "a credit to the game and a grand fellow." Walter O. Briggs: "he was the ideal for American youth—a great player, a great sportsman and a fine gentleman." Governor Lehman: "he...always stood for fair play and clean sport; he was a fine type of American whose example may well be followed by the youth of our state." Judge Landis: "a real gentleman whose conduct on and off the field set a standard to which all players may well aspire." Bill Terry: "we had the highest respect for the way he lived." Bill ("Bojangles") Robinson: "it seems impossible that such a good fellow has gone." Ruth: "Lou was a clean ball player." Frankie Crosetti: "everybody loved Lou; you couldn't help it."[34]

Indeed you couldn't. Nor could you deny that, in death, he had become something greater and more permanent than simply a talented individual with a pleasant demeanor. He had become an "inspiration," a "monument," and an "example," an "ideal" and a "type" who "set a standard." Gehrig was, all of a sudden, "everlasting." He had become, not so much a real man, but a mythic figure who "stood for" abstract qualities, like one of the gods of Greece, Rome, or his own Germany.

Gehrig was now an undecaying idol, ethically perfect and immune to change, like one of Yeats's figures stuck in the gold mosaic of a wall. When his monument was dedicated a month later in Yankee Stadium, Mayor LaGuardia, "visibly affected," said "Lou typifies all that is good in American manhood," and, no, that's not a mistake—LaGuardia used the present tense.[35] The last coverage of Gehrig's death appears in the *Times* on September 16, 1941, when his grave site is finished and his ashes are taken to the cemetery in, believe it or not, Valhalla, New York.[36]

Mathewson as Hero

Gehrig's martyrdom would seem tough to top, but in fact there is another saintly figure who probably would rate a higher position in Dante's great rose of Paradise. Certainly this has nothing to do with Christy Mathewson, the real individual, being a better person than Gehrig; if anything, he was probably worse. He seems to have been a shrewd gambler, his behavior after the Merkle incident was certainly suspect, there is even doubt about his war record—and, worst of all, it's known that he started out as a football player. What Matty had going for him was that he was, like Clemente, the right hero for the time. Just as Ted Williams's tough-minded independence was wrong for the forties and fifties, Gehrig's Eagle Scout was inappropriate in the era of Ruth, Dizzy Dean, and Hack Wilson: Matty, though, was just what the fans had ordered. The best illustration of their adulation is probably the fictional portrait in Greenberg's

The Celebrant, in which Matty sometimes appears as Christ, sometimes as the unfallen Adam, a "perfectly formed" man who stands "at the center" of his teammates and looks "young as an April morning."[37]

Since Matty was, like Gehrig, afflicted with a potentially lethal disease, the fans were also warned of his possible martyrdom. However, probably because his tuberculosis had been cured once before, less notice was taken of his final illness in 1925. On April 30, it was reported that he had a cold, but also that "his condition cannot be considered serious or in any way alarming."[38] On July 9, his wife said reports that he had had a tubercular relapse were "absolutely untrue."[39] On August 6, Matty himself said he was "feeling fine," but it was disclosed that he would remain in the clean air of Saranac Lake for "several months,"[40] and on August 12, claiming he felt still better, he celebrated his forty-fifth birthday there.[41] On September 9, his TB specialist, Dr. Edward Packard, downplayed Matty's condition, saying he "is all right.... His condition is nothing to cause alarm." The following day, Dr. Packard emphatically denied that Matty was "battling for his life," insisting that all he had was a slight fever.[42] When Matty died on October 7, Packard made no comment as to his condition, although he did sign the death certificate.[43]

I should pause here to point out that there is another aspect of martyrdom, one suggested by the foregoing discussion of Gehrig, one that is made even more obvious in Matty's case. It is an alternative way of denying the hero's death. In addition to making the player immortal in his mythical persona, we can gain further consolation from the notion that he has a spiritual heir. The king is dead; long live the king. In Gehrig's case, the heir was DiMaggio; in Matty's, it was Walter Johnson. By a marvelous and reassuring coincidence, Matty died on the day Johnson, that era's other preeminent nice guy, was winning the first game of the World Series. The report of Johnson's win and Matty's obituary were printed side-by-side in single-column stories on page 1 of the *Times*; a baton has seldom been so melodramatically passed.[44] Mythically, it seems, if Johnson could win a World Series game, then Matty, or the spirit of Matty, was not dead after all.

For a few days after his death, Matty was eulogized, as Gehrig would later be, as the All-American ethical hero. It turned out that he loved three things: baseball, motor cars, and checkers. In fact, "he loved checkers almost as dearly as he loved baseball." He had been "the idol of the nation's fandom over a span of more than two decades," and he was " a symbol of the highest type of American sportsmanship."

Individuals paid tribute. John McGraw said Matty "stood out as a man, …one of the most admirable figures baseball has ever known." Emil Fuchs, not a man known for his sentiment, was "grief stricken," calling Matty "an example of all that is good in baseball." Hughey Jennings said baseball had lost "its greatest idol"; "Matty was the idol of the kids, many of whom patterned their lives after him," he said. Even Mayor Curley of Boston understood that Matty was now more than an individual, calling him the "exemplar of the national game."[45]

Matty had requested burial in Lewisburg, Pennsylvania, where he had attended Bucknell and where he had met his wife; when the train arrived at Grand Central in New York, nobody was there to greet it. Word passed quickly among the trainmen, though, and a bunch of them went to the baggage car to stand around the coffin. When the undertaker arrived, they helped him load the coffin into the hearse, and it was driven across town to Penn Station, where Francis X. McQuade of the Giants, heading the mourning party, took over. McQuade and a number of others, including McGraw and Harry M. Stevens, rode the train to Lewisburg, where they were met by a delegation of Bucknell students and Mrs. Mathewson's parents, who still lived in town. The ceremony was brief and simple. McQuade and McGraw were both pallbearers. The official eulogy, delivered by the Reverend Frank B. Everitt, emphasized Matty's "standards." "Christy Mathewson lived on the athletic field to establish those standards," Everitt said. "He did more than any one man to stabilize the moral standards of modern sports. He has left behind him more than memory."[46] Again, this language clearly indicates that Matty had now progressed beyond being just "any one man" to a mythic condition in which he was inseparable from the abstract standards for which he stood. He had become, in the bargain, a good deal "more than memory."

Conclusion

It may be difficult to determine objectively which of these three real men has become the greatest martyr, the most powerful archetype of virtue brought low by fate. Despite the fact that in life he was clearly the best man, it seems to me that Clemente was just as clearly the weakest martyr, notwithstanding Gehrig's great dimples. This is partly because Matty was the sort of hero his time demanded. It may also be because the lack of radio or TV allowed a greater distance between individual and image, thus making it easier for the fans to ignore their man's blemishes. In any case, there is no way I can see Matty as a man of forty-five, a little jowly, in jacket and tie and wearing a businessman's hat. That picture exists, of course; the *Times* printed it when Matty died. But it's not Matty. Matty is a big kid wearing a small baseball cap, with a frank expression on his face and a clear, blue-eyed gaze. His hair has been artificially tinted a light brown. You can only see the top part of him, but out of sight, below the frame, he's got a very small leather glove on his left hand. He's as young as an April morning, and that's the way he'll stay, through time and beyond it, world without end. Amen.

[1] Miguel de Unamuno, *Tragic Sense of Life*, trans. J. E. Crawford Flitch (1921; New York: Dover Publications, 1954).

[2] George Orwell, "A Hanging," *Shooting an Elephant and Other Essays* (1950; New York: Harcourt Brace Jovanovich, 1978).

[3] Friedrich Nietzsche, *The Birth of Tragedy and the Geneaology of Morals*, trans. Francis Golfing (Garden City NY: Doubleday and Company, Inc., 1956).

[4] Jessie L. Weston, *From Ritual to Romance* (Garden City NY: Doubleday Anchor Books, 1957).

[5] I use "martyr" to mean not just a fallen champion or defender of a group, but also the most typical and admired *representative* of that group, a figure who, once fallen, becomes "a sacred symbol of an authority [or spirit] around which the society [or group] rallies." (Samuel Z. Klausner, "Martyrdom," in Mircea Eliade, ed., *The Encyclopedia of Religion*, 16 vols. [New York: Macmillan Publishing Company, 1987] 9:231.) For a more extensive discussion of my use of the term, see my *Sports Immortals* (Bowling Green OH: Bowling Green State University Popular Press, 1994) 95-99.

[6] These are distinctions made by Tristram Coffin, *The Old Ball Game* (New York: Herder & Herder, 1971).

[7] Leonard Koppet, "Clemente a Player On and Off the Diamond," *New York Times*, January 2, 1973, 48; Sam Goldaper, "Puerto Rico Goes into Mourning," *New York Times*, January 2, 1973, 48; Joseph Durso, "A Man of Two Worlds," *New York Times*, January 2, 1973, 48; and (unsigned) "Clemente, Pirates' Star, Dies in Crash of Plane Sending Aid to Nicaragua," *New York Times*, January 2, 1973, 1.

[8] *New York Times*, January 3, 1973, 17.

[9] *New York Times*, January 3, 1973, 32.

[10] *New York Times*, January 5, 1973.

[11] *New York Times*, January 7, 1973, L16.

[12] *New York Times*, January 14, 1973, L5.

[13] *New York Times*, February 4, 1973, 53.

[14] *New York Times*, February 15, 1973, 56.

[15] *New York Times*, April 1, 1973, L2.

[16] *New York Times*, May 15, 1973, 35.

[17] *New York Times*, February 3, 1973, 24.

[18] *New York Times*, July 18, 1973, 41.

[19] *New York Times*, December 6, 1973, 51.

[20] *New York Times*, May 3, 1939, 28.

[21] *New York Times*, June 2, 1939, 30, *New York Times*, June 4, 1939, L6; and *New York Times*, June 14, 1939, 31.

[22] *New York Times*, June 22, 1939, 22.

[23] *New York Times*, June 22, 1939, 22.

[24] *New York Times*, July 5, 1939, 1.

[25] *New York Times*, August 6, 1939, L1.

[26] *New York Times*, October 12, 1939, 27; October 17, 1939, 14.

[27] *New York Times*, October 20, 1939, 15.

[28] *New York Times*, October 18, 1939, 23.

[29] *New York Times*, November 16, 1939, 28.

[30] *New York Times*, January 7, 1940, L1.

[31] *New York Times*, January 3, 1940, 23.

[32] *New York Times*, January 7, 1940, L1.

[33] *New York Times*, January 9, 1940, 25.

[34] *New York Times*, June 3, 1941, 1, 25.

[35] James P. Dawson, *New York Times*, July 7, 1941, 19.

[36] *New York Times*, September 16, 1941. Gehrig's ashes had been kept in Ed Barrow's mausoleum until Lou's own "modest monument" could be completed.

[37] Eric Rolfe Greenberg, *The Celebrant* (New York: Penguin, 1986) 29, 20.

[38] *New York Times*, April 30, 1925.

[39] *New York Times*, July 9, 1925, 15.

[40] *New York Times*, August 6, 1925, 15.

[41] The Associated Press said that he was "fighting and apparently winning another battle for his health," *New York Times*, August 12, 1925, 17.

[42] *New York Times*, September 9, 1925, 29; and October 25, 1925.

[43] In fairness to the doctor, the headline *did* say that Mathewson had died "unexpectedly." *New York Times*, October 8, 1925.

[44] *New York Times*, October 8, 1925.

[45] *New York Times*, October 8, 1925.

[46] *New York Times*, October 8, 1925.

FOOTBALL

THROUGH THE EYES OF MIRCEA ELIADE
UNITES STATES FOOTBALL
AS A RELIGIOUS "RITE DE PASSAGE"

Bonnie J. Miller-McLemore

In the last several years we have witnessed the publication of a wealth of material on sports from research on game and play to studies of the psychology and sociology of sport. The latter reveal that ancient, non-literate societies regarded games as dramatic reenactments of cosmic struggles. Spectators and players adopted important religious roles. From the Timbira Indians of Brazil to the Mayans and Aztecs of South America to the Athenians in the early Olympian Games, persons have envisioned sports as played ceremoniously for the gods to secure favors, prolong life, expel evil, and so forth.[1]

These instances suggest that religious aspects could reemerge in modern sports. While some critics lament an absence in contemporary secular culture of religious belief and practice, I suggest that we take a closer look at American culture and its sports fascination.[2] If mainline institutional religion no longer holds sway among the dominant culture as it once did, what has replaced it? What does draw attention, fascination, and in the long run, pious devotion? Without doubt, sports has become a twentieth-century American obsession.

In the three decades coinciding with Pete Rozelle's tenure as commissioner of the National Football League, the merger of the American Football League and the National Football League, and the big money involved in contracts and television rights, football has blossomed into a cultural phenomenon of national proportion. Statistics confirm football's rising curve of popularity. The Super Bowl, for instance, has become the most lucrative and most widely viewed annual spectacle in American mass-mediated culture. More than 170 million viewers or around 40 percent of all households watched the game in 1996.[3] It does not seem completely far-fetched, then, to say that football exhibits a proclivity towards becoming a new kind of secular faith, even more so than other forms of popular culture.

But this speculation needs better theoretical exploration than it has received thus far in more theoretically ungrounded works that name sports without any qualification *the* religion of modern-day America. It is easy to declare that we act fanatically about football or any other enthusiasm for that matter. But are there really religious or quasi-religious dimensions to this fascination? If so, what are they and how do they work? Certainly football serves other significant functions in American society. I do not mean to exaggerate its religious role. Nor do I want to deride football in order to prove the merits of traditional religious practice or of other forms of so-called "high culture." But I do think that we should take seriously its possible religious dimensions.

Convinced that the sacred is often camouflaged in the commonplace, historian of religion Mircea Eliade[4] provides ready entrance into the hidden religious mysteries of modern sports. An observer of myth and ritual, Eliade always maintained keen interest in the connections between the religious world of "archaic man" and the popular expressions of faith in modern life. Convinced that the human has a deep need for and sense of the sacred, he finds manifestations of the religious in the most ordinary. His appreciation of the significance of piety for human life suggests that football might function as a powerful religious manifestation that speaks directly to what he names the "fragmented existence" of contemporary secular culture. Modern persons tend to believe that they live in a completely profane world. Yet we remain unconsciously enmeshed in and nourished by glimpses of the sacred that reappear in certain camouflaged myths and degenerated rituals. Modern veneration of the winter sport of football from preseason contests to Monday night games to Super Bowl festivities provides one fascinating illustration.[5] Eliade's concepts of myth, ritual, and the sacred can help us unmask the gods within the pastime.

Secularization and the Rise of Popular Culture

Distinct among formative scholars in the methods of history of religion, Eliade possesses an uncanny ability to bring together a phenomenological and ontological analysis of the religious. He differs from the usual practice of those in his field in so far as he does not limit himself to any one aspect of the history of religions. Nowhere in his writings does one come across attempts to outline historical stages of religious development or to classify religions into neat categories. Rather, he orders manifestations of religious phenomena and then seeks to penetrate their essential theological or spiritual significance. He studies early religions in order to discover what aspects of life are religious in and of themselves. To find his way into the mental universe of "archaic man" as a representation of the religious person *par excellence*, he explores myths, symbols, and customs rather than explicit beliefs or doctrines. In this way, he gains access to a plethora of "religious" material from that of prehistoric Australians to ancient Egyptians to Europeans in the Middle Ages to the modern Picasso and Beckett. While an expert in phenomenological analysis of premodern beliefs, he remains driven by the desire to discover universal characteristics of religious behavior and experience.

Eliade does not give a precise definition of religion. Nor does he see this as a genuine problem. We can best discern his view of religion by looking at the first word in a series of terms that he places in opposition: the sacred and the profane; "archaic man" and "modern man"; sacred time and myth and historical time and history.

Sacred and Profane. Distinct from Rudolph Otto's classic study of the nature of religious encounters as irrational, Eliade holds immense respect for the human experience of the "sacred in its entirety." By the sacred he means that mode of existence oriented toward a revelation of that which is "preeminently the real, at once power, efficacity, the source of life and fecundity."[6] This ultimate reality reveals itself as a quality transcending ordinary experience and as a powerful, efficacious force and source of all life. The revelation is paradoxical: the sacred makes itself known in and through ordinary forms of nature. Not belonging to this world, it is manifest in and through it. The "wholly other," transcendent reality sanctifies and makes this world real.[7] In *The Sacred and Profane*, Eliade avers that "the sacred tree, the sacred stone…are worshipped precisely because they are hierophanies, because they show that it is no longer stone or tree but the sacred…. In other words, for those who have a religious experience, all nature is capable of revealing itself as a cosmic sacrality."[8] Paradox is woven into the very structure of religion. As cause of both life and death, useful and dangerous, accessible and inaccessible, the sacred remains essentially ambivalent.

Archaic and Modern. Behind the idea of the sacred lies the notion of "archaic" or "primitive man" as opposed to and distinct from "modern man." By archaic, Eliade does not mean mental inferiority or primordial stupidity. He refers, rather, to the premodern, ahistorical, non-literate cultures or, more importantly, to those that orient their cultural life around concrete manifestations of the sacred. He views the premodern person then as *the* religious person *par excellence.*[9] The premodern lives "in a universe steeped in sacredness."[10] She or he thinks about and responds to the world as an organic whole or cosmos and participates in being itself by living as close as possible to consecrated objects. Remaining always and naturally in a sacred place by repeating ceremonial archetypal actions, the primitive person experiences eternity and shares in the drama of creation in even the homeliest acts.

Myth and History. These dualisms of sacred and profane and primitive and modern correspond to a final pair of terms: myth and history. The world becomes a cosmos, says Eliade, when persons continue to re-experience its creation in *illo tempore.* The religious person actualizes this by remembering and modeling the deeds of gods and heroes at the moment of creation in the beginning of time through particular myths and rituals. The myth recreates original events. Every true ritual redeems the eternal in time. In this way, myth and ritual tap a source of renewal that lies beyond the immediate wastage of time and death. When the religious person successfully unites with this spiritual non-material power, mythical time and divine ecstasy replace the meaningless, isolating character of historical, profane time. In Eliade's view, religion awakens and sustains consciousness of another world through a "corpus of historical techniques and rituals" that reveal and manifest the sacred.[11]

The Rise of Popular Culture. One can define the sacred, Eliade remarks, as simply the opposite of the profane. To recognize the profane we need only to look at "the broken and alienated existence lived by civilized man today."[12] This existence contrasts sharply with the organic, imaginative life and the rich unity and diversity of "primitive man."

Eliade does not see secularization as an evolution from lower to higher forms of religion. "Such an evolutionary hypothesis might have been possible a few generations ago," he notes, "but is now completely impossible."[13] The major religious attitudes came into existence "once and for all" when persons first saw themselves in relation to the universe.

However, we can organize the history of religion in terms of the drama of the losing and re-finding of certain religious values, a loss and rediscovery that goes on for all time. Technological society bears a close resemblance to what Eliade describes as the case of the "otiose god" in which the "Supreme Being" is "forgotten." God withdraws from humankind and loses "*religious actuality*." In the modern scientific world, we observe a "progressive descent of the sacred into the concrete."[14] Modernity entails an eclipse of the sacred in which people endeavor to pass from the profane to the sacred less frequently than primitive peoples did. For example, while the premodern person saw the sky as a supreme hierophany, revealing the transcendence and changelessness of the infinite both in itself and through the earliest sky gods who abided in it, today many people see the sky simply as the area of space explored by astronauts and satellites and remaining to be fully conquered by science. It no longer functions primarily as a source of power or meaning. When children express awe before the moon, stars, space, or thunder, many people feel somewhat surprised by the phenomena that they have long ceased to notice. The triumph of the experimental sciences, an intellectualized rationality and technology, and the artificial environment these foster, create a chasm between the sacred and the profane. Modernity generates a remarkable detachment from the wider cosmos, its rhythms, and mythical history.[15] The distinctiveness of the modern person "lies precisely in his determination to regard himself as a purely historical being, in his wish to live in a basically desacralized cosmos."[16] The profane of modern society does not even constitute a "world" according to Eliade. It possesses an "unreal" quality of the "uncreated," of "nonexistence."

Instead of possessing a sacred mythology, modern persons have a secular and political one. Modern symbols and rituals suffer a similar degenerative fate. Symbols have only social or artistic value; ritual has fallen into a state of "superstition and economic-cum-aesthetic value."[17] In short, "the life of modern man is swarming with half-forgotten myths, decaying hierophanies and secularized symbols."[18] As a result, people achieve the transition from temporal, profane time to sacred timelessness with greater difficulty than in other historical periods.

Yet Eliade believed in the "myth of the eternal return," as he subtitled one of his books. The United States has not yet become a society completely void of myths and symbols. Although demythologization and desacralization have reached alarming proportions, the modern still has significant vestiges of religiosity.[19] Certain forms of mythical behavior and thought survive today because they comprise basic constituents of human nature. The nostalgia for the regeneration of time remains a universal: "we find in man at every level, the same longing to destroy profane time and live in sacred time."[20] People remain in need of myths. Hence residues of religiosity continue to reappear despite all efforts otherwise.

In *Birth and Rebirth*, for instance, Eliade demonstrates that many so-called non-religious festivals reproduce forms of archaic ritual. Various symbols of initiation survive, not necessarily as rites properly speaking, but in the form of folk customs, games, and literary motifs.[21] In *Myth and Ritual* he traces the process of demythologization and then discusses the camouflaged survival of myths with reference to Christianity, art, and modern ideologies. He notes reappearances of myth throughout history: the eschatological myths in the Middle Ages; the "philosophies of history" during the Enlightenment; and the revolutionary stories and movements of the Reformation, the French Revolution, and Marxist Communism.[22] Each instance reflects a deeply rooted hope in a cosmic myth of a universal renewal by an exemplary hero in some form, whether martyr, reformer, revolutionary, or party leader. Even the process of secularization cannot extinguish this hope: "Mythical thought transcends and discards some of its earlier expressions outmoded by History, and adapts itself to the new sociological conditions and new cultural fashions—*but it resists extirpation.*"[23]

Eliade applies these hypotheses to certain aspects of popular culture. Specifically, we find residues of myth in certain forms of mass media, especially in the United States, and in literature. Certain books, though "apparently 'secular,' in fact contain mythological figures camouflaged as contemporary characters and offer initiatory scenarios in the guise of everyday happenings."[24] The modern passion for the novel expresses the continuing need to find one's way into "foreign" universes and "to hear the greatest number of 'mythical stories'…camouflaged under 'profane' forms."[25] Today Eliade might have expanded these comments to include cinematic dramas such as *Rambo, Star Wars, Rocky, E.T.,* and the Indiana Jones trilogy. The compulsive desire to follow the complexities of the "twofold reality" of literary characters reflects an undeniable revolt against historical time and a desire to "escape from Time" into the imaginary worlds of novels and films:

> It is hard to conceive of a human being who is not fascinated by "narrative," that is, by a recounting of significant events, by what has happened to men endowed with the "twofold reality" that…on

the one hand…reflect the historical and psychological reality of members of a modern society and, on the other,…possess all the magical power of an imaginary creation.[26]

These new myths perform the same basic functions of myths in earlier societies even though they may have different overt meanings.[27] Comic strips, Superman, the detective novel, and even the glorification of public figures through the mass media represent modern variations of folkloric heroes caught in exemplary struggles between Good and Evil, with the Demon, with Wealth. Eliade believed that modern phenomena such as the drive for corporate success, the mass exodus to suburbia, and the frenzy surrounding annual sales of new cars, reflect a primordial "nostalgia" for perfection and salvation through transcendence of the limits of the human condition.[28] Again he might have expanded his analysis today to include the current craze about physical fitness, the appeal of therapy and self-help literature, the voyeuristic viewing of television court dramas and talk shows, and perhaps, the mania about football.

Homo Religiosus: A View from the Sidelines

It is precisely in this context that we might situate the fascination with football. Insights into the religious character of traditional societies allow us to penetrate our own spiritual heritage and the mental universe of modern religious consciousness. Religious experience occurs in the midst of daily life without our notice. We overlook the significance of many of our obsessions and routines precisely because they seem so ordinary. Their meanings seem obvious and common. But the sacred makes itself known through the ordinary and through the temporary suspension of the ordinary. Such is the case with modern football. Noticed or not, football expresses a complex system of coherent affirmations about ultimate reality through its myths and rituals—through its creation of sacred time and sacred space.[29]

Recreation of a Mythic Cosmos. The structure of almost all play and sport possesses a certain mythic quality. Play and sport by their very nature alter reality. In his classic work on play, Johan Huizinga writes, "In the form and function of play, man's consciousness that he is embedded in a sacred order of things finds its first, highest, and holiest expressions."[30] Pierre

Coubertin, the renovator of the Olympian Games, sees modern athletics as "an impassioned soaring": The "deep play" of the games, the ultimate sporting event, resolves paradoxes and occasions the "revelation of higher order, non-contradictory truths."[31] Theologian David Tracy, following philosopher Hans-Georg Gadamer, likens the experience of disclosure in religious revelation to the act of playing a game. When we truly enter into this act, we lose our-usual self-consciousness and find ourselves gripped by "a happening, a disclosure" that has the power to transform and renew.[32]

We can find more than a few mythic characteristics in the spectacle of football. According to Eliade, myth is the narration of a sacred history. It relates "an event that took place in primordial time." Myth depicts the creation of reality through the deeds of supernatural beings, whether "the whole of reality, the Cosmos, or only a fragment of reality."[33] "Living" a myth, either by ceremonially telling the myth or by performing the ritual that the myth explains or justifies, implies a genuinely "religious" experience insofar as it differs from the ordinary experience of everyday life. "One ceases to exist in the everyday world and enters a transfigured auroral world" impregnated with the presence of the creative acts of powerful figures—"the Supernaturals."[34] Myth is the most effective means of awakening consciousness of another world beyond.

Football's mythic quality has less to do with the hype, excitement, and cheering, as some might suppose on first impression, than it does with some of the forms and structures of the game itself. Particular rules, regulations, limits, and goals create a sense of cosmos within a cosmos, a world unto itself, and carefully prescribe the clean lines of an ultimate "cosmic struggle." The arena of the stadium centers around a contest between two opposing teams. The field becomes the "staging area" for micro-level demonstrations of life. For the game to work, people must accept these cosmic boundaries as "true" and "sacred" and as definitive of "reality." The boundaries restrict the player's actions to a certain highly defined form.

At the same time, distinct from other forms of popular culture, immense freedom and potentialities exist within the limits. A dynamic of possibility thrives within the bounded universe. In the typical Saturday, Sunday, or Monday night game, almost anything can happen. Each play has an expansive variety of outcomes. The actual events of the game remain forever unrehearsed. They involve unexpected and exceptional performances in a situation always characterized by a sense of uncertainty and lack of control. A sequential drama develops before our eyes. It issues forth in heroes and happiness or losers and tragedy. Watching a series of plays entertains and intrigues fans precisely because it moves them outside all routines of ordinary life to an imaginary world and at the same time creates a world that feels more real than all other ordinary moments. As one editorialist put it, where once the game may have been a "harmless diversion," now it has become "our major *raison d'être*"; sports substitutes for life and we accept the field of play as "a more meaningful reality than our own."[35] Thus the play-by-play announcer gravely calls a football game "war," a player's grit "courage," and injuries "tragic."

When we reduce the game by calling it mere entertainment, we overlook the extent to which the viewer as well as the participant becomes involved. As Eliade states, one "lives" a myth "in the sense that one is seized by the sacred exalting power of the events recollected or re-enacted."[36] We deceive ourselves when we assume that the players do the work and the fans only look on and watch. To a greater depth and seriousness than most forms of popular entertainment, the outcome of the battle has affective repercussions for the viewer. Where else do "observers" jump to their feet at one with a sympathetic crowd and shout, "Go," "Fight," "Kill 'em"? The exploits and failures of the team have power to exult or depress. The greater the degree of participation, the more the onlooker takes on the characteristics of a member of a family or tribe: the person shares the elation of victory or the despair of defeat, learns the secrets and the lore (e.g., the season's schedule, the players' names, the statistics), wears its symbols (e.g., colors, hats, mascots, flags), complains about the decisions of its chiefs, and fundamentally, hates the opposition.

A deep sense of communal participation arises. A televised game permits simultaneous viewing by a mass audience of a significant event in their corporate lives. Television cameras use large amounts of non-playing time to scan the crowd and to build this syndicated sense of unity of all believers. In an odd sort of camaraderie among strangers, viewers and participants care about each other in joy at a play well-executed; they grieve with each other over the one point loss during the final few seconds. The outcome of each game would have little meaning or existence beyond that shared by this wide collective of observer-participants and the meanings that they construct and believe in together.

Not only does football create a mythic cosmos for communal participation but, it also occasions a particular cosmos for a particular group. Eliade states, "Myths cannot be related without regard to circumstances.... They are not recited before women or children, that is before the uninitiated."[37] Regardless of the progress of women's sports in the past several years, football belongs to the world of men. It creates a "brotherhood" for which "sisterhood" has no equivalent, although the rise of popularity of women's sports has increased markedly since the establishment of Title IX regulations. Nonetheless, broadly speaking, men still express greater interest in football than women. Certainly in terms of conversation, men talk about football more frequently than women, and men often use their "Monday morning quarterback" discussions as a way of establishing a group's unity.

This is not to accuse football of male chauvinism or to exclude women from participating and enjoying the sport. Now, perhaps more than a decade ago, more fans are women. But the very nature of football itself dictates that it remain male-dominated. Football is a contact sport. It requires physical prowess and strength. In current practice, there is no doubt about sexual differences. Even the name, "tackle" football, reminds women that this world involves injury and threatening contact, especially for persons with smaller physiques. Women can cheer men on from the sidelines but a quick review of the record books comparing achievements of men and women confirms football as uniquely a man's world. Even the presence of a woman announcer strikes the viewer as somewhat discontinuous. The football uniform and the outfits donned by the cheerleaders further pronounce sexual distinctiveness. Tight pants, exaggerated shoulder breadth, tapered waist, and straight hips heighten and even caricature the male's physique as do the necklines, tight sweaters, short skirts, and boots of the female cheerleaders. Male and female are placed in their historical roles in patriarchal society of heroic achiever and sexual sustainer.

Among the viewers, the game unites an otherwise distant and uncommunicative group of initiates—men—in universal dialogue of a unique sort. Football speaks to men nationwide through a *world of action*. It promotes a sense of public achievement through competition in much the same way, though to a lesser extent, that the *world of words* of soap operas has served to answer the private needs of women at home. Frequently, women find religious proclamation through the world of words of the soaps, and men find manifestation of the sacred through the world of action of sports. Football announcers, journalists, coaches, players, and fans use a common vernacular that is mysterious to the uninitiated, largely women. The latter are hardly welcome participants; when they make comments about the outcome of a particular play or game, their words often seem to possess less credibility or potency. As Eliade notes, "The 'story' narrated by the myth constitutes a 'knowledge' which is esoteric, not only because it is secret and is handed on during the course of an initiation but also because the 'knowledge' is accompanied by magico-religious power."[38] Many women simply do not learn the language and hence cannot possess the power.

Like specific myths, each game transports historical figures into the plane of mythology and creates an "exemplary model for all significant human action."[39] Myths teach "how to repeat the creative acts" of the Supernaturals or of our heroes. The mythic lore of football recalls and venerates the mighty feats of figures like "Mean Joe" Greene, Bronco Nagurski, Dick Butkus, Red Grange, Johnny Unitas, and Walter Payton. These select few are enshrined in halls of fame, trophy cases, or more mundanely nowadays, through stardom doing television commercials. These heroes, tempered and steeled in the great white heat of competition, possess a certain influence and charisma over masses of fans. They model wholeness, bodily control, self-sacrifice, and joy. Most of all, they have attained the goal—a moment of perfection. This moment comes with sustained effort, discipline, and alas, chance. When it's fourth down and two to go, a minute remaining with the score six to zero, and the game's most valued player completes a pass, throws an effective block, or dances over the goal line, the perfect form has been attained. The miraculous has happened, as with the Tennessee Titans' final trick play against the Buffalo Bills in the 1999 playoffs. All attentive fans somehow subconsciously recognize this as a moment of beauty and striving toward excellence. They bask in the sense of satisfaction it carries.

A final critical ingredient in the myth of the football, however, lies somewhere else—in the isolated presentation of a cosmic struggle between two sides, good and bad, life and death, amidst a controlling power beyond our power, fate. Each game is a game of chance; its outcome depends in part upon the grace of unexpected luck or upon the injustice of getting a "bad break." A good game will only heighten and accentuate this element of risk. It matches the antagonists as closely as possible and makes stakes as final as possible. Specific rules determine the exact amount gained or lost in the standings by winning or losing. The computed point differential and the number of games won and lost determine a team's place in the playoffs. Often a team's chances for success rest upon the calculation of a long string of wins or losses of other teams. Even the team unbeaten and statistically proven the better may be "defeated" in such calculations.

So "death" remains an ever-present "reality." Announcers remark poignantly, "So, the Dallas Cowboys struggle to stay alive" or "The Bears hang in there." Victory heralds abundant life and vivacity. The team has tested fortune and fate and come out ahead. The victors have survived the battle by a grace of power not quite all their own. They have the opportunity to live on to the immortal status of the Super Bowl. On the other hand, defeat brings silence, anguish, withdrawal, and bleakness. The loss comes like the dying of a small, unglorified death. Fate has judged and proven the players less worthy.

Similar to the reenactment of the *agon*, the struggle of the Sun God, in the Olympic Games, the match reenacts the struggle to persist in the face of hardship, suffering, injustice, physical strain, unequal odds, and the uncertain probabilities dealt by fate. The opponent is not merely the other team but the unseen antagonist, death, ready to wield its mortal blow. The cosmic myth of football does not hide or diminish the tragic, the irrational, or the unjust cruelty of fate. Rather it harnesses, orders, and even nourishes these elements and specifically shapes them into an enemy to conquer. At some point, no matter what, each team is placed in a situation doomed to fail. Each new success in the string of wins only heightens the suspense, the anticipation, and ultimately, the tragedy of the defeat that some day must come. In the end, all must lose. No team goes undefeated. As in life, all must die. The game then becomes an exercise in coming to terms with this harsh reality. It is a lesson in learning to live within the rules and conditions while striving to transcend the limits of finitude.

And with the turn of season, when the Super Bowl and various college bowl games roll around, select teams triumph over death. Their victories assure us that ultimately life is stronger than death and that winter will again turn to spring. As Eliade observes, "The world must be annually renewed" through myth and ritual; "the end of one cycle and the beginning of the next are marked by a series of rituals whose purpose is the renewal of the world...."[40] With the conclusive "super" event, each team receives the promise of resurrection and the permission to start over. Talk about life's possibilities in the season ahead begins anew.

The timing of the Super Bowl and college bowl games is more than coincidental: "The greatest of renewals," remarks Eliade, "takes place at the New Year."[41] The most privileged college bowl games are played on January 1. Our Christianized American culture may lack formal religious new year rites of repentance and renewal, but the Rose Bowl, Orange Bowl, Sugar Bowl, and Fiesta Bowl games aptly serve the same purpose. They bring resolution to the past year's struggles and herald new beginnings in the year to come. Amidst life's trials, the final victors emerge and their brilliant performances live on in the memories of the participants and fans. Through fall, winter, and spring—colloquially known as football, basketball, and baseball seasons respectively rather than as changes in weather and foliage—fans participate in the tides of nature through the structure of sports. As one reporter commented in his tongue in cheek portrayal of football, "Obviously football is a syndrome of religious rites symbolizing the struggle to preserve the egg of life through the rigors of the impending winter."[42]

Creation of Sacred Time and Sacred Place. Living the myth "also implies that one is no longer living in chronological time but in the primordial Time."[43] In Eliade's view, by narrating and acting out the myth, "archaic man" abolishes profane time. That is, the religious person forgets his or her entrapment in time by "transforming successive time into a single eternal moment."[44] By "sacred time," Eliade means intense, momentary, eternal presence. "Profane time" has duration, a past as well as a future, and is characterized by practical mediocrity. Though more apparent in primitive experience, the modern person also dislikes the deceptive, boring, frustrating, inescapable, irreversible qualities of time—what Eliade calls the "terror of history."[45] We too fear the human predicament of being caught in time, and we try to escape it in various ways.

In the play of football, major alterations in the sense of time occur, similar to the primitive's periodic attempts to stop profane time. The so-called sixty minutes of official play take more than two hours of normal time. Yet the total time of live play action and contact in a typical telecast may turn out to be much less than thirty minutes.[46] We bask in the power of controlling time. Time halts and the gods rest during half-time. Time-outs may be called and the clock stops under certain conditions. The most exciting moments occur when one team tries to "slow the clock" or "stop the time with six seconds left and nine yards to go."

Almost all participants and many observers have at some point experienced the suspension of ordinary time. An hour elapses unnoticed in what seems an instant. Persons become completely immersed in the present due to the high intensity and the extreme concentration and mental attention necessary for perfect execution The return to ordinary time feels like moving from one reality to another. Player John Brodie's testimony provides an excellent example of this phenomenon:

At times, and with increasing frequency now, I experience a kind of clarity that I've never seen adequately described in a football story. Sometimes, for example, time seems to slow way down, in an uncanny way, as if everything were moving in slow motion. It seems as if I have all the time in the world to watch the receivers run their patterns.... I know perfectly well how hard and fast those guys are coming and yet the whole thing seems like a movie or a dance in slow motion.... Here-and-now awareness, clarity.... Life can feel like a box after a game. You can get into another order of reality when you're playing, a reality that does not fit into grids and coordinates that most people lay across life....[47]

The fixed roles and codified rules help the game become "as large as life" and break the bounds of historical and chronological time. Cultural theorist John MacAloon and social psychologist Mihaly Csikszentmihalyi have talked about "sacred time" in terms of "deep play" and the "flow experience."[48] In a series of interviews with rock climbers, they found sufficient evidence to hypothesize the presence of an "eternal moment" or flow experience under certain conditions. A degree of uncertainty is necessary; stimuli of ordinary life are screened out; danger is accepted and even utilized; the terror of death is managed. Some climbers talk figuratively about the "away-from-it-all qualities," a "sufficiency of the present," and a "sense of participation and immediacy."[49]

The rock climber as well as the football player reaches or discovers a state rare in normal life—a "flow experience." This experience lifts persons out of time and disengages them from internal and external clocks. The timing of the "flow" is not quite within even the best athlete's control. Football requires long periods of cognitive planning and physical recuperation as well as bursts of intensity. A truly dramatic play that has the power to transform time comes only in its own good time. Years of practice and preparation can increase but never entirely determine either their advent or their frequency. Even the people in Eliade's study of premodern societies only acquire the escape from time for a relatively brief period and never completely.

Space also acquires sacred importance in the life of *Homo religiosus* according to Eliade. The center of the world, represented by shrines, temples, and cathedrals and conceived of as an organized cosmos unto itself, becomes preeminently the zone of the sacred.[50] The construction of the football stadium itself resembles an organized self-sustaining cosmos. At the farthest concentric circle arise walkways for spectators. Next, beside each entrance ramp to the center arena, are the necessities of life: food stands, restrooms, first aid, police, and ushers. Moving inside, the space becomes increasingly narrowed and focused until all eyes move to the nave, the middle of the playing field, where the referees and the two opposing team captains stand for the coin toss at the beginning of the game—the first symbolic act of fate. The intricate patterns of five- and one- yard line markings, the rectangular plots at both ends, and above all, the sacred space in the air marked by the two goal posts give the central space further meaning and "reality." Within the infinite reaches of the universe, the competition is carefully measured out and centered around a small segment of reality. When the ball leaves these boundaries, the sacred time of the game stops. Fans who have rushed into this special territory in the excitement of the crowd in the last seconds of a victory know the awesome quality of the space which only minutes earlier excluded them from its playing surface.

Certain stadiums acquire special status as unique Meccas for authentic football fans. They become consecrated places where important events occur or where heroic deeds have happened. Pontiac Michigan's Silverdome or Chicago's Soldier Field, for instance, probably surpass, or at least rival, the importance of structures built under the aegis of religion. As Michael Novak points out facetiously, "Suppose you were an anthropologist from Mars.… Flying over the land in a rocket, you notice great ovals near every city."[51]

The structure of football works to make the forces of nature and creation integral aspects of the sacred space of the playing field. Owners expend immense amounts of money maintaining the beauty of turf, whether artificial or real. The contest occurs regardless of rain, snow, or shine (or even fog off the lake in Chicago). If the person is not there to experience the weather, the announcer always paints a vivid picture of it. The heartier fan or player is the one who seemingly unaffected can withstand temperature extremes. The game brings the urbanite, oblivious of nature's changes of season and weather, back into contact with its capricious character. Like the "archaic man" oriented to the recurrent fundamentals of life and nature within the wider universe, the fans and players situate themselves in a certain niche within the larger cosmos beyond them.

Transformation through Ritualized Mass Activity. The conversional affect of sacred time and space comes not only through the retelling of the myth but also through the repetition of sacred actions as outlined in the myth, that is, through ritual. As Eliade demonstrates, "archaic man" comes to know and assume the sacred through the initiation rite. The ritual process endows the novice or initiate with a sacred sense of existence totally different from the profane sense of "historical man." Ritual recreates in dramatic form the passage from death to life and the passage from the human condition to eternal bliss.[52]

Anthropologist Victor Turner has developed this idea of initiatory rituals further. His study of the middle phase of "liminality" in particular illuminates the ritual processes of football. Liminality,[53] or the marginal phase of mid-transition, Turner says, exists not only in tribal rites but also in "the prolixity of genres found in modern industrial leisure."[54]

In many ways the event of football resembles a ritual organized around the classic scheme of *rites de passage* and their three movements of separation, liminality, and re-aggregation. The football event is a "liminal institution" in the sense that it exists outside the boundaries of the normal social order while remaining sustained as an important adjunct to that order. The actors and audiences of the game pass through non-ordinary states of being and temporarily adopt liminal status and roles. This allows them to experience novel meanings of reality and then return to ordinary life renewed and changed.

As with any true ceremonial cycle, football includes a beginning phase of separation from normal structures of daily life, a middle period when one sits "betwixt and between," neither here nor there, and a final movement of reentry, rejuvenated and altered, into the originating structures.[55] Each game requires pregame activities that stress asceticism, dedication, preparation for the impending battle, seclusion, and indoctrination. Players must control and restrict their diet, social habits, sleep patterns, and physical exertion. The opening ceremonies bring a colorful procession of musical bands and mascots, the entrance of the opposing teams with accompanying shouting and singing of symbolic songs, sometimes a pre-game moment of silence to honor heroes who have died in the line of duty, and finally, the playing of the national anthem. All these various factors represent "quasi-liturgical properties" of the first phase of *rites de passage*, rites of separation from "ordinary life."[56] They set up and initiate a period of public liminality. As Joseph Price notes, even the pause of memorial silence is "reminiscent of an act of prayer."[57] While opposing teams and fans are juxtaposed at opposite extremes of the stadium, the national anthem relays a solemn, respectful sense of their ultimate unity before a common fate. The anthem closes with a cheering outburst of the crowd in their heightened excitement for the battle's determinative outcome. And the game begins.

The contest itself, marked off clearly in time and space, reflects the middle state of liminality and its *rites of initiation and selection* for the athletes and then, vicariously, a *rite of intensification* for the spectators. As in religious *rites de passage*, some of the goals of this phase include the abolition of profane time, the return to the mythical sacred time of the past, and a decisive alteration in the status of the initiates. Conceivably, the game may transport the entire community, including those viewing through live telecast, beyond the ordinary boundaries of space and time. Life's normal rules and regulations shift: male players hug each other and dance; they jeer, swear, and occasionally aggressively attack an opponent who has angered them; fans shout, drink, talk to complete strangers, take off their shirts, decorate their faces, wear silly hats and clothes. Those in the liminal state experience the "emergence of communitas,"[58] a strong feeling of camaraderie and community across boundaries that normally separate and segregate. Most characteristic of the mid-liminal phase, a sense of paradox arises:[59] success amidst failure, life amidst death, good breaks and bad breaks, altruism and violence, cooperation and competition, risk and security, chance and skill.[60] A "grounding down" process occurs: ordeals of physical exercise and endurance, struggles with bad luck, threats of severe injury, adverse weather conditions, and so forth. And a rebuilding process occurs: instruction, new plays, "tribal esoterica" of signals, strategies, momentary glories, and so on. Football preserves the tradition of a half-time when each team retreats to seclusion for the express purpose of "reciting sacred myths," showing sacred objects, sharing pedagogical advice, and rekindling the spirit. Will pitted against will under the selection of fate, by the final quarter one team emerges as victor and the ritual drama is resolved.

The closing ceremonies reflect the *rites of closure* and *"re-aggregation"* within the normative order—the third and final phase of *rites de passage*. Norms of daily life return. Players have their status clearly established. They are either heroes or losers. Civilly they exchange handshakes and disappear beneath the stadium. Fans may continue some of what now becomes more abnormal behavior, shouting, joking, jumping, hugging, but eventually they will once more don their everyday appearances. The formal opposition of the fans fades away into a "spontaneous communitas" as the assembled thousands, having weathered a common ordeal together, vacate the space they once occupied and file out side by side. As they move back into the mundane world, some feel the sharp contrast between the order of the game and that of "ordinary life." However, the "truth" revealed in play is preserved, though transformed now from the indicative to the subjunctive; the "is" becomes another great "could" or "ought" in the retelling. The reality becomes part of the lore of retrospective possibility as fans and players rethink the game.

MacAloon proposes an intriguing theory. He contends that in modern culture "spectacle" has triumphed over three other genres of sport—festival, ritual, and game—as the dominant genre in the Olympian Games and in general. However, the decline of ritual, festival, and game does not mean their demise. In fact, the spectacle may "serve as a recruiting device, dissembling suspicion toward 'mere ritual' and luring the proudly uncommitted."[61] So those who believe that they come simply to watch a secular spectacle are drawn unwittingly into an experience of ritual renewal and reformulation. Football may embody what MacAloon predicted: A "ramified performance type" would emerge as a "sort of servo-mechanism" or "meta-genre" that would re-integrate festival, ritual, and play. Beneath the guise of spectacle, football continues to foster ritual, festival, and play. Sacred forces are evoked, and social and spiritual transformations effected.

Eliade believes that understanding the structure and function of myths in traditional societies "not only serves to clarify a stage in the history of human thought but also helps us to understand a category of our contemporaries."[62] This is certainly the case with the sport of football. Viewed in this light the game of football has assumed significant religious roles and dimensions. Carefully camouflaged beneath the more obvious aspects of spectacle and sport, it embodies the ongoing power and survival of myth and ritual in popular culture. The game initiates a passage into a re-created state that reverses the oppressions of profane existence and brings about a moment in the presence of the sacred. Winning does not simply mean crushing the opponent. It signifies conquering fate and quieting adversities stronger than opposing teams. Losing tests and trains the spiritual capacity to adjust to the limits of life, while still retaining hope in the face of finitude. Brief encounters with the sacred during the game itself give us a glimpse of the possibility that ultimately we might transcend these limits.

[1] Allen Guttmann, *From Ritual to Record: The Nature of Modern Sports* (New York: Oxford University Press, 1978) chap. 1.

[2] Others have made similar contentions in other arenas. See, for example, Paul Tillich, *Theology of Culture*, ed. Robert C. Kimball (London: Oxford University Press, 1959), especially chapter 4, or Langdon Gilkey, *Naming the Whirlwind* (Indianapolis: Bobbs-Merrill Co., 1969). This essay represents a variation of what Tillich described as a critical "theology of culture," "the attempt to analyze the theology behind all cultural expressions, to discover the ultimate concern...." (*Systematic Theology*, 3 vols. [Chicago: University of Chicago Press, 1951-1963] 1:39).

[3] Cf. Michael R. Real, "The Super Bowl: Mythic Spectacle," *Television: The Critical View*, ed. Horace Newcomb (New York: Oxford University Press, 1979) 170.

[4] In the years since first conceiving this essay, I have become aware that the work of Mircea Eliade has come under sustained criticism from various sources focusing on his methodological sophistication, the accuracy and adequacy of some of his "field notes," and some of his personal relationships that might have unduly influenced some of his perceptions and productions. Despite these criticisms, which have been effectively dealt with by Bryan S. Rennie, *Reconstructing Eliade: Making Sense of Religion* (Albany: State University of New York Press, 1996), I continue to think that Eliade's perspective provides an illuminating lens through which we can understand professional football and our fascination with it.

[5] See Joseph L. Price, "The Super Bowl as Religious Festival," *The Christian Century* (22 February 1984): 190-91, for a brief look at how the 1984 Super Bowl specifically functioned "as a major religious festival for American culture," signaling "a convergence of sports, politics and myth." [This essay is reprinted as the following essay in this volume.].

[6] Mircea Eliade, *The Sacred and the Profane*, trans. Willard R. Trask (New York: Harcourt, Brace and World, 1961) 28.

[7] Eliade, *Sacred and the Profane*, 11.

[8] Eliade, *Sacred and the Profane*, 12.

[9] Eliade, *Sacred and the Profane*, 165-66, 187.

[10] Mircea Eliade, *Patterns in Comparative Religion*, trans. Rosemary Sheed (New York: Sheed and Ward, 1958) 445.

[11] Eliade, *Patterns in Comparative Religion*, 95.

[12] Eliade, *Patterns in Comparative Religion*, 447.

[13] Eliade, *Patterns in Comparative Religion*, 97.

[14] Mircea Eliade, *Myth and Reality*, trans. Willard R. Trask (New York: Harper and Row, 1963) 93-99.

[15] Mircea Eliade, *The Myth of the Eternal Return or Cosmos and History*, trans. Willard R. Trask (Princeton: Princeton University Press, 1965) xiii.

[16] Eliade, *Sacred and Profane*, 13.

[17] Eliade, *Patterns in Comparative Religion*, 446.

[18] Eliade, *Sacred and Profane*, 93.

[19] Eliade, *Myth and Reality*, 97, 111-13.

[20] Mircea Eliade, *Rites and Symbols of Initiation*, trans. Willard R. Trask (New York: Harper Torchbooks, 1965) xv.

[21] Eliade, *Rites and Symbols of Initiation*, 122-36.

[22] Eliade, *Myth and Reality*, 162-84.

[23] Eliade, *Myth and Reality*, 176 (emphasis added).

[24] Eliade, *Rites and Symbols of Initiation*, 135.

[25] Eliade, *Myth and Reality*, 191.

[26] Eliade, *Myth and Reality*, 191-92.

[27] Eliade, *Myth and Reality*, 190-91.

[28] Eliade, *Myth and Reality*, 184-86.

[29] A cautionary note should be added. As cultural theorist John J. MacAloon points out in his analysis of the Olympian Games, a sports event should not be lumped under any single rubric, whether ritual, game, festival, or spectacle. All four genres appear in every event and are intimately interconnected to one another on all levels ("Olympic Games and the Theory of Spectacle in Modern Societies" [Paper prepared for participants in Burg Wartenstein Symposium No. 76, 1977]). It remains beyond the scope of this article to unpack the presence of the other genres of game, festival, and spectacle within the performance system of football. I will look primarily at myth and ritual and only allude to the complex relation between these and game, festival, and spectacle.

[30] Johan Huizinga, *Homo Ludens: The Play-Element in Culture* (Boston: Beacon, 1955).

[31] Pierre de Coubertin, *The Olympic Idea: Discourses and Essays*, ed. The Carl Diem Institute (Stuttgart: Verlag Hoffmann, 1967) 99, quoted by MacAloon, "Olympic Games and the Theory of Spectacle," 23.

[32] David Tracy, *The Analogical Imagination: Christian Theology and the Culture of Pluralism* (New York: Crossroad, 1981) 113-14; see also Hans-Georg Gadamer, *Truth and Method* (New York: Seabury, 1975) 91-119.

[33] Eliade, *Myth and Reality*, 5.

[34] Eliade, *Myth and Reality*, 19.

[35] Joseph Bauers, "Sports, Our Drug of Choice," *Chicago Tribune*, March 16, 1989, 25.

[36] Eliade, *Myth and Reality*, 19.

[37] Eliade, *Myth and Reality*, 9.

[38] Eliade, *Myth and Reality*, 15.

[39] Eliade, *Myth and Reality*, 6.

[40] Eliade, *Myth and Reality*, 42.

[41] Eliade, *Myth and Reality*, 41.

[42] Real, "Super Bowl," 175.

[43] Eliade, *Myth and Reality*, 19.

[44] Eliade, *Patterns in Comparative Religion*, 407.

[45] Eliade, *Myth and Reality*, 137, 192.

[46] Real, "Super Bowl," 175.

[47] Quoted in Michael Novak, *The Joy of Sports* (New York: Basic Books, 1976) 178.

[48] John J. MacAloon and Mihaly Csikszentmihalyi, "Deep Play and the Flow Experience in Rock Climbing" in *Beyond Boredom and Anxiety* (full citation unknown); Mihaly Csikszentmihalyi, "Flowing: A General Model of Intrinsically Rewarding Experiences," *Journal of Humanistic Psychology*, cited by Victor Turner, "Variations on a Theme of Liminality," in *Secular Ritual*, ed. Sally F. Moore and Barbara G. Myerhoff (Assen: Van Gorcum, 1977) 48-52. Csikszentmihalyi defines flow as the "'holistic sensation present when we act with total involvement,' and is 'a state in which action follows action according to an internal logic which seems to need no conscious

intervention on our part.'" See also the more extensive analysis of "flow" in Mihaly Csikszentmihalyi, *Flow: The Psychology of Optimal Experience* (New York: Harper and Row, 1990).

[49] Cf. Joseph L. Price, "Naturalistic Recreations," *Spirituality and the Secular Quest*, ed. Peter H. Van Ness (New York: Crossroad, 1996) 423-27.

[50] Eliade, *Cosmos and History*, 12-17; for more detailed attention to sacred space, see Eliade, *Sacred and the Profane*, chap. 1.

[51] Novak, *Joy of Sports,* 155.

[52] Eliade, *Rites and Symbols of Initiation*, x.

[53] For a succinct discussion of the concept of liminality, see Mark Kline Taylor, "Liminality," *A New Handbook of Christian Theology*, ed. Donald W. Musser and Joseph L. Price (Nashville: Abingdon Press, 1992) 293-96.

[54] Turner, "Variations on a Theme of Liminality," 43. Turner based his work on the formula of Arnold Van Gennep, *The Rites of Passage*, trans. Monika B. Vizedom and Gabrielle L. Caffee (London: Routledge & Kegan, l909) for what Gennep called rites of passage. Gennep's formula has become "an anthropological commonplace, perhaps even a cliché" according to Terence S. Turner ("Transformation, Hierarchy and Transcendence: A Reformulation of Van Gennep's Model of the Structure of Rites De Passage," in *Secular Ritual*, 53). For a more detailed description of Turner's development of this formula, see Victor Turner, *The Forest of Symbols: Aspects of Ndembu Ritual* (Ithaca and London: Cornell University Press, 1967) chap. 4; and *The Ritual Process: Structure and Anti-Structure* (Ithaca: Cornell University Press, l969) chaps. 3 and 4. Like Eliade, Turner also draws our attention to the "similarities between the leisure genres...in complex industrial societies and the rituals and myths of archaic, tribal, and early agrarian cultures," including the leisure activity of football ("Variations on a Theme of Liminality," 42-43). For an engaging historical analysis of leisure in American society, see Witold Rybczynski, *Waiting for the Weekend* (New York: Viking, 1991).

[55] Turner, "Variations on a Theme of Liminality," 36-38.

[56] Turner, "Variations on a Theme of Liminality," 44.

[57] Price, "Super Bowl as Religious Festival," 191.

[58] Turner, "Variations on a Theme of Liminality," 46-47. Turner defines communitas as "social antistructure, meaning by it a relation quality of full, unmediated communication, even communion, between definite and determinate identities, which arises spontaneously in all kinds of groups, situations, and circumstances."

[59] Turner, "Variations on a Theme of Liminality," 37.

[60] Turner, "Variations on a Theme of Liminality," 36.

[61] MacAloon, "Olympic Games and the Theory of Spectacle," 36.

[62] Eliade, *Myth and Reality*, 2.

THE SUPER BOWL AS
RELIGIOUS FESTIVAL

Joseph L. Price

When the Dallas Cowboys are at the top of their game, winning routinely and decisively, one of the favorite quips that circulates in north Texas concerns Texas Stadium, where the Cowboys play their home games. The stadium has a partial roof that covers much of the stands but none of the playing field. Cowboy fans say that God wants to be able to see his favorite football team more clearly.

This is the attitude that ancient societies brought to their games. In ancient Greece, for example, the Olympics were only one set of athletic contests which were performed in honor of the gods. Among the Mayans in Central America, the stadium was attached to an important temple, and the stands were adorned with images of the gods and reliefs of sacred animals. The ball game started when the high priest threw the ball onto a circular stone in the center of the field: the sacred rock, the omphalos, considered the sacred center and associated with creation mythology. Thus the game was connected to the Mayan story of the world's origins.[1]

Professional football games are not quite so obviously religious in character. Yet there is a remarkable sense in which the Super Bowl functions as a major religious festival for American culture, for the event signals a convergence of sports, politics, and myth. Like festivals in ancient societies, which made no distinctions regarding the religious, political, and sporting character of certain events, the Super Bowl succeeds in reuniting these now disparate dimensions of social life.

The pageantry of the Super Bowl is not confined to the game itself, nor to the culture heroes who attend it—e.g., Bob Hope, John Denver, Dan Rather and other celebrities—for the largest audience watches the game via television. Likewise, the political appeal of the festival is not restricted to its endorsement by political figures such as President Reagan, who pronounced the 1984 Super Bowl's benediction. The invocation is a series of political rituals: the singing of the national anthem and the unfurling of a fifty-yard-long American flag, followed by an Air Force flight tactics squadron air show.

The innate religious orientation of the Super Bowl was indicated first by the ritual of remembrance of "heroes of the faith who have gone before." In the pre-game show, personalities from each team were portrayed as superiors, as demigods who possess not only the talent necessary for perfecting the game as an art but also the skills for succeeding in business ventures and family life.

For instance, one of the most effective segments was about Joe Delaney, the former running back for the Kansas City Chiefs who died while trying to save two children from drowning. In a functional sense, Delaney was being honored as a saint. The pre-game moment of silence in honor of the life and contributions of George Halas, the late owner of the Chicago Bears and one of the creators of the National Football League, was even more significant: I am not sure whether the fans were silent in memory *of* "Papa Bear" or whether they were offering a moment of silence to him. Nevertheless, the pause was reminiscent of an act of prayer.

Bronco Nagurski, a hall of famer (which stands for official canonization), had the honor of tossing the coin at the center of the playing field to signify the start of the game. The naming of a Most Valuable Player at the end of the game was a sign of the continuing possibility for canonization.

But the Super Bowl and its hype could not dominate the consciousness of many Americans without the existence of a mythos to support the game. Myths, we know, are stories that establish and recall a group's identity: its origin, its values, its world view, its *raison d'être*.

Two dominant myths support the festivity and are perpetuated by it. One recalls the founding of the nation and the other projects the fantasies or hopes of the nation. Both myths indicate the American identity.

The first concerns the ritual action of the game itself. The object of the game is the conquest of territory. The football team invades foreign land, traverses it completely, and completes the conquest by settling in the end zone. The goal is to carry the ritual object, the football, into the most hallowed area belonging to the opponent, his inmost sanctuary. There, and only there, can the ritual object touch the earth without incurring some sort of penalty, such as the stoppage of play or the loss of yardage.

This act of possession is itself reflective of cosmogonic myths, for, as Mircea Eliade has noted, "to organize a space is to repeat the paradigmatic work of the gods."[2] Conquering a territory and bringing order to it is an act equivalent to consecration, making the space itself sacred by means of recalling and rehearsing the primordial act of creation.

The specifically American character of the mythology has to do with the violent nature of the game. Not only does it dramatize the myth of creation, it also plays out the myth of American origins with its violent invasion of regions and their settlement. To a certain extent, football is a contemporary enactment of the American frontier spirit.[3]

Amidst the ritual of the forceful quest, there is the extended "time out" of half time, a time of turning from the aggressions of the game to the fantasies of the spirit. During the half-time show, the second dominant American cultural myth is manifest. It revolves around the theme of innocence. The peculiarly American quality about this myth is that even in our nation's history of subjugation, a sense of manifest destiny was often associated with extending the nation's boundaries. Indeed, the idea that a divine mandate had authorized the people to move into a place to which they had no claim, other than getting there and staying there, indicates that the people did not think they bore final responsibility for the displacement of natives or infringement on their hunting space. In other words, the assignment to God of the responsibility for territorial expansion was an attempt to maintain the illusion of blamelessness among those who forcibly took alien lands.[4]

In the 1984 Super Bowl, the theme of righteousness was acted out in a three-ring circus that featured 2,100 performers from Walt Disney Productions. Although acts took place in the outer rings, which were colored blue, attention was focused on the largest center ring, which was white. In this area, most of the performers wore white or pastel shades of yellow. The visual effect was an overlearning sensation of cleanliness and purity. And the extravaganza's music reinforced the impressions of the "whiteness" of it all; the harmonies sung by the Disney troupe were simple and syrupy, a kind of white sound with less harmonic complexity than that of most Muzak renditions.

The overall effect was one of feigned innocence and the nice hope often exemplified for Americans by Walt Disney's vision. Finally, the transition from this scenario was accomplished by the explosion of fireworks along the perimeter of the field. The fantasy and violence of exploding Roman candles shifted the scene back to the play of the American frontier, simultaneously reviving intimations of the festival's patriotic character. Fireworks are the hallmark of the Fourth of July, and evoke the national anthem lyrics' imagery—"the rockets' red glare, the bombs bursting in air."

As a sporting event, the Super Bowl represents the season's culmination of a major American game. As a popular spectacle, it encourages endorsement by politicians and incorporates elements of nationalism. And as a cultural festival, it commands vast allegiance while dramatizing and reinforcing the religious myths of national innocence and apotheosis.

[1] See the essays in Vernon L. Scarborough and David R. Wilcox, eds., *The Mesoamerican Ballgame* (Tucson: University of Arizona Press, 1991), especially chapter 12, John W. Fox, "The Lords of Light Versus the Lords of the Dark: The Postclassic Highland Maya Ballgame."

[2] Mircea Eliade, *The Sacred and the Profane: The Nature of Religion*, trans. Willard R. Trask (Harcourt, Brace, and World, 1959) 32.

[3] Richard Slotkin, *Regeneration through Violence: The Mythology of the American Frontier, 1600-1860* (Middletown CT: Wesleyan University Press, 1973).

[4] The religious concept of Manifest Destiny, which had been implicit throughout much of the colonial experience in America, became articulated during the period of frontier expansion.

AMERICAN SPORT AS FOLK RELIGION
EXAMINING A TEST OF ITS STRENGTH

James A. Mathisen

That a relationship exists between sport and religion in America has become nearly axiomatic. Stadia are temples; by-gone heroes are saints; fans are faithful worshipers; the litany goes on. Various commentators on American life, including James Michener[1] and Christopher Lasch,[2] have sought to describe the apparently religious character of sport.

Meanwhile among academics, the interpretations of the relationship between sport and religion have been more conceptual and ethereal, but also more diverse. Religionists, philosophers, historians, communications theorists, and especially sociologists have joined the discussion. Is sport a religion,[3] a quasi religion,[4] a civil religion,[5] a surrogate religion,[6] or a secular religion?[7]

If those were the only five alternatives, perhaps the best option would be that sport can be a civil religion. Philip E. Hammond, for example, has explained that competitive sports may be "crucial social structures for the transmission and maintenance of America's civil religion."[8] While admitting that sport, especially at national and international levels, may look like a civil religion, elsewhere I have argued that really it is not.[9] Martin Marty,[10] Donald Jones and Russell Richey,[11] and Gail Gehrig[12] have distinguished varieties of civil religion, the most viable being Robert Bellah's transcendent, universal model.[13] But such a civil religion is elitist, the "product of the scholar's world."[14] By contrast, sport, as Americans know and practice it, is a common, everyday phenomenon with little sense of a civilly religious transcendence or elitism.

Others have been more suspicious of attempts to depict American sport in religious terms. Robert J. Higgs has cautioned that "sports are like religion in many ways just as they are like war in some ways, but they are not equatable with either."[15] Edwin L. Cady has been more emphatic in rejecting sport as religion. In his description of American university sport, the "Big Game" may function as a "ritual expressing and communicating a secular religion of the American Dream…. As religion it is altogether a metaphor, …at best, sort of sacred."[16]

The problem then is partly definitional, partly conceptual, partly functional. Sport looks like a religion, but it is not one. It is sort of like civil religion, but not quite. The best conceptual response amid this uncertainty is to interpret American sport as a contemporary folk religion. In making that case, I will take two lines of argument: 1) definitionally, sport satisfies the requisite characteristics of a folk religion; and 2) demonstrably, sport operated as a folk religion when tested from within in the form of a professional football players' strike in the late 1980s.

The Character of American Sport as Folk Religion

In approaching sport as a folk religion, one must ask two prior questions: What is folk religion in general? And what have been the peculiar features of American folk religion? Answering the first question is easier. Folk religion is a combination of shared moral principles and behavioral customs. For Robert Linder, it is folk religion that "emphasizes the common religion of a people as it emerged out of the life of 'the folk.'"[17] Robin Williams previously declared that "every functioning society has to an important degree a common religion. The possession of a common set of ideas, rituals, and symbols can supply an overarching sense of unity in a society riddled with conflicts."[18]

More important for our purposes than merely a working definition are the peculiar features of American folk religion. Anthropologist Anthony Wallace noted that in America

> religious belief is inextricably interwoven with secular aspects of the world view and cosmology…. While for analytical purposes they [religion and the secular] can be distinguished, …in daily life the individual is apt to employ sacred beliefs and values to rationalize all aspects of his behavior.[19]

In an earlier day A. Roy Eckardt,[20] W. Lloyd Warner,[21] and Franklin H. Littell[22] described varieties of folk religion, and Will Herberg put his finger on Williams's "common religion"[23] and on Marty's "religion-in-general"[24] and labeled it the folk religion of the "American way of life."[25] "[It] is, at bottom, a spiritual structure, a structure of ideas and ideals, of aspirations and values, of beliefs and standards.... The very expression 'way of life' points to its religious essence, for one's ultimate, over-all way of life is one's religion."[26] Later, he affirmed that

> spiritually it is best expressed...in that special kind of idealism which has come to be recognized as characteristically American. But it is in its vision of America, in its symbols and rituals, in its holidays and its liturgy, that it shows itself to be so truly and thoroughly a religion.[27]

A final aspect of folk religion is its provision of "salvation," which "consists in the condition of positive relationships of the folk community" as "a mystic 'life' which binds all together."[28]

The key issue for this discussion is the manifestation of American sport as a folk religion, if one assumes that a common religion emerging from the life of the folk can take various forms and that sport is one example. Religious historian John F. Wilson has pointed out that

> the world of sports has become central to American popular culture.... The emphasis upon success, closely identified with money, derived from brute power melded with technical expertise, is perhaps the most direct and telling dramatization of the content of the American culture.... This culture created and sustained through the modern means is linked to public religion in America.[29]

Similarly, while Novak's argument that sports are natural religions tended toward excess, he accurately suggested how sport may "provide an experience of at least a pagan sense of godliness. Among the godward signs in contemporary life, sports may be the single most powerful manifestation.... Sports constitute the primary lived world of the vast majority of Americans."[30] Sport, then, by its emphases within, and its experiencing of, our culture fits the descriptions of a folk religion suggested above by Wallace, Herberg, and others.

Another issue, however, in establishing sport as a folk religion has been a semantic one. For example, one of the earlier and more perceptive analyses of American sport as a folk religion comes from journalist Robert Lipsyte, who identified a "SportsWorld" as a dangerous and grotesque web of ethics and attitudes, an amorphous infrastructure that acts to contain our energies, divert our passions, and socialize us for work or war or depression.... The melting pot may be a myth, but we will all come together in the ballpark.... A man must prove his faith in sports and the American way by whipping himself into shape, playing by the rules, being part of the team, and putting out all the way. If his faith is strong enough, he will triumph.... [SportsWorld] extolled the game as that William Jamesian absurdity, a moral equivalent of war, and the hero of the game as that Henry Jamesian absurdity, a "muscular Christian." It has surpassed patriotism and piety as a currency of communication, while exploiting them both. By the end of the 1960s, SportsWorld wisdom had it that religion was a spectator sport while professional and college athletic contests were the only events Americans held sacred.[31]

To extend these notions of anthropologists, sociologists, historians, religionists, and journalists, let me suggest three specific ways in which sport manifests itself as a folk religion. First, American sport as folk religion consists of a distinctive set of myths, values, and beliefs. Howard Slusher emphasized how sport "evolves into a symbolically developed *ideology*. Sport becomes both what it is and a declaration of the culture.... [One] need look no further than the Americanization of sport in keeping with the technological and materialistic values of our society."[32]

At this level of values and ideology, on the one hand, sport encapsulates, magnifies, and reflects key beliefs and norms of the surrounding culture. Sports' beliefs are "accepted on faith by great masses of people...from the president of the United States down to the most humble bootblack. These beliefs are stated primarily in the form of perceived attributes of sports and are widely disseminated."[33] On the other hand, sport raises up particular values and myths of its own and projects them onto the culture with a normative certitude. It is this second half of the relationship that more closely characterizes a folk religion.

At an interpersonal level, for example, if I believe the myth that "sport builds character," then I will guide my children toward youthful athletic participation with a virtually untestable certainty that, without experiences as a shortstop or as a left wing, their lives will be morally deficient. Furthermore, I will infer that the "character" of successful Americans who happen to have participated in sport at some point in their lives is what it is because of comparable participation in sport. Selective perception guarantees that I will interpret biographies in terms of the ideology and mythology of sport. Not to do so would be a demonstration of lack of faith and of irreligion.

Surely, a similar belief works on a larger scale in the drive of relatively small colleges to play an NCAA Division I intercollegiate basketball schedule. For many, for example, Oral Roberts University became a real school on the day it made such a commitment, regardless of any other criteria by which academic institutions are evaluated.[34]

At a community-wide level, when I have bought into the ideology of the folk religion of sport, I will be convinced of its value and efficacy as a symbol of social legitimacy and achievement. If I am a community leader of Chicago, for example, and the Chicago Bears are muttering about leaving town because of having to play in an outdated stadium (as they often have been in recent years), then one way to guarantee Chicago's continuing status in the eyes of fellow Americans who believe in the sport ideology will be to muster every available resource to retain a National Football League franchise in Chicago. Similarly, Green Bay, Wisconsin is clearly different from all other cities of comparable size and resources. Public policy and budgetary decisions will be based in part on what the presence of institutional sport, in this case professional football, says about Chicago, Green Bay, and countless other American communities.

Second, sport is an American folk religion in its collective cultic observances. Sport is a "magic elixir" that "nourishes the bonds of communal solidarity."[35] Conceivably, "the arenas and coliseums are little more than shrines for spiritual activity."[36] For Novak, "going to a stadium is half like going to a political rally, half like going to a church."[37]

Folk religion is myth and belief as cited above, plus practice; ritual, cultic practices reinforce the values shared by a community of believers. The small town in Indiana or Kentucky hardly will think twice about building a high school gymnasium with a capacity as large as, or larger than, the town's population for those Friday and Saturday night gatherings of the clan during the winter and early spring. Woe be anyone in town foolish or presumptuous enough to schedule another event at the same time as the game. In introducing her study of soccer, Janet Lever noted that

> By accepting that a particular team represents them symbolically, people enjoy ritual kinship based on that common bond.... Sport spectacles belong to the world of the sacred

rather than the profane: fans who say sport provides an escape from "real life" in effect sustain this religious distinction.... Like the effect of a religious celebration, sport fosters a sense of identification with the others who share the experience.[38]

In one sense, a particular sport such as basketball may be a sect-like version of the common, folk religion. On the one hand, being a sport fan is comparable to being religious—it's a taken-for-granted, American thing to do. But on the other hand, we may also have a further allegiance to one sport not unlike a denominational, religious affiliation. Here, additional sociological variables including social class, ethnicity, and level of education intervene. Personally, I am a sport fan first, a basketball fan next, and a college basketball fan next, but I also clearly feel little affinity for the professional basketball denomination of American folk religion.

Thus being identified with sport through its collective cult "creat[es] a dramatic, autonomous, and real 'world' of its own. Sports symbolism creates a 'bracketed world' emotionally segregated from the everyday worlds that people inhabit; this is a powerful source of its appeal."[39]

Third, besides sport's ideological and cultic manifestations, it has an historical character as a common religion. In traditional religion, charismatic founders pass from the scene, and the early converts soon give way to second and third generation adherents. Not only must the beliefs *per se* be transmitted, largely through the shared, cultic observances, but the developing history and tradition of the group take on their own added religious significance. Weber's classical analysis of the traditional means of legitimizing authority bears witness to the power of "that's the way we've always done things here."

Sport thus operates as a folk religion in its evoking senses of history and of tradition. Its halls of fame illustrate "the steady trend for sport to become ritually integrated and earnestly or even quasi-sacrally regarded in modern life."[40] These halls preserve the sacred symbols and memorabilia that encourage us to rehearse the contributions of the saints who have moved on. Golf tournaments such as the Masters and the British Open have become annual opportunities for the faithful to return to commemorate the heroic deeds of the past.

Standards established by past heroes become the measures by which modern individuals are judged. Records in sport derive their sanctity from our

> desire to know and fixate the supreme achievements of those
> whom we take to represent us, and this knowledge our

records provide.... [Records] have a definiteness and a finality
to them which a casteless society might need in order to make
evident who is superior and who inferior in native gifts and
promise.[41]

Records function not unlike the sacred writings and the historical accounts
of any religious group, providing a timeless, normative guide by which
later disciples' accomplishments are judged. Also, "like religion, professional sports use past generations as referents for the present and confer
conditional immortality for their elect, through statistics and halls of
fame."[42] Allen Guttmann has suggested, however, that records also are an
indication of

the secularization of society. When qualitative distinctions
fade and lose their force, we turn to quantitative ones....
Once the gods have vanished from Mount Olympus or from
Dante's paradise, we can no longer run to appease them or to
save our souls, but we can set a new record. It is a uniquely
modern form of immortality.[43]

When a record in sport is broken, we are both happy and sad. Not
only has immortality been achieved; immortality also has been stolen from
our midst. Maybe we should place an asterisk next to the new record, just
to ensure that we don't lose sight of the old one and of the one who established it.

Similarly, "Old Timers' Games" have struck me as an enigma. On
the one hand, we fans have the renewed opportunity to pay homage to,
and to rehearse the past accomplishments of, our heroes. The clan gathers
to commemorate and to reassert its lineage. On the other hand, many "old
timers" are just that. They not-so-voluntarily have "been made lower than
the angels" and have taken back a form of mortality that both upsets our
vision of the past and blurs our sense of their successes. The recent development of the "Seniors Tour" in professional golf eventually may suffer
from a similar ambiguity and moral confusion.

Sport thus manifests itself as an American folk religion in various
forms, and these three versions—as myth, value, and ideology; as collective
cultic practice; and as history and tradition—have aided sport as an
American way of life to bestow meaning and cohesiveness upon the lives of
many Americans.

The National Football League Players
Strike as a Test of Folk Religion

If American sport, particularly football, is a folk religion, then it stands to reason that as do other religions, it faces times of trial that test its strength and vitality in American life.

More churchly forms of religion confront times of testing from without, as well as from within, their structures. Tests from without might be times of tribulation or persecution from a variety of sources. These may take the form of political coercion, for example, such as that faced by the Christian church during political revolution or upheaval. Some years ago when I visited Leningrad in what was then the Soviet Union, I remember the sarcastic sense of delight exhibited by our tour guide as she explained how beautiful buildings, which were once Christian churches, are now museums or swimming pools. Churchly religion in the Soviet Union was tested at various times in this century, especially in the form of political oppression.

Churchly religions also face tests from within their own structures and constituencies. Recently, the Lutheran church in America achieved an unprecedented degree of organizational unity, only to have a group of dissenting pastors and parishes withdraw from the denomination. This represents an internal, organizational test. Internal theological or creedal tests also have occurred, as when churches have sought to reestablish doctrinal certainty in the midst of the threat of spreading heretical teaching. Or a more subtle threat from within periodically confronting the Christian church has been the tendency toward accommodation to the cultural milieu. In those cases, the tests have been less visible as they transpired, but their results were significant nevertheless.

In this second part of the essay my argument is that, by analogy, folk religions also may experience times of trial and testing, from without and within. Between August and October 1987, the folk religion of American sport faced such an extended time of testing from within in the form of a strike by its players' union, the NFLPA, or National Football League Players Association.

The strike began on September 22 when the nearly 1600 current members of the NFLPA from the twenty-eight teams in the NFL struck following games of the second week of a sixteen-week, regular season. Twenty-three days later on October 15, the NFLPA ordered its members "back to work" without a contract. The following day, the *New York Times* opined, "In the short run, the owners appeared to be the winners."[44] On October 25, the *New York Times* published a poll conducted by it and CBS News. Of 1,326 people interviewed, 46 percent thought "the owners were more in the right during the four-week strike," whereas only 26 percent said the players were right. Of people interviewed who classified themselves as either "very interested or somewhat interested in pro football," 55 percent favored the owners, and only 30 percent supported the players.[45] From the players' perspective, something had gone wrong. They had called the strike, then returned to play football without a resolution of their grievances, to find that only about one-third of Americans supported their cause, together with people in the media declaring them the losers. From the players' point of view, what had gone wrong? And why?

It seems two issues are involved in exploring this "test" from within the folk religion of American sport. First, although the players' strike was a failure, the folk religion apparently was not discredited. That is, the immediate responses to the strike indicate that the folk religious character of sport not only was not diminished, but actually may have become stronger. Second, although reasons were suggested why the strike had failed, they do not seem to be adequate explanations in themselves. The real reason why the strike failed is because of the strength that the folk religion of sport enjoys in America.

A brief sketch of the historical background of players' organizations in American sports before the 1987 strike in professional football provides a context from which we can understand the strength of the folk religion status of sport in America. During the forty years following World War II, as elsewhere in the West, the United States experienced a time of general economic affluence, widespread consumerism, and the growth of the mass media—especially television. Sport has experienced its versions of these factors, too. In the 1950s, the professional athletes within America's three dominant team-sports—football, baseball, and basketball—all formed players' unions. Those unions began as docile associations, but under the threat of legal compulsion, the league officials and team owners had to take the unions and their members increasingly seriously. All three sports have been threatened with strikes and other forms of job action, with both baseball and football actually being struck prior to 1987.

Football experienced a strike that lasted fifty-seven days in 1982. At its conclusion, one journalist explained, "The owners won because they retained solid control over the game.... NFL players will continue to draw the lowest average salaries in major pro sports.... In sum, the owners preserved their way of life for half a decade."[46] The major issues in 1982 had been economic ones, and the owners were declared the winners in the new contract because of their retaining the economic structure of the game.

Half a decade later on April 20, 1987, the two sides met for the first time to begin the bargaining process in anticipation of a new contract. Both sides were optimistic about the prospects of a settlement; they exchanged their proposals; four months of negotiations began. On August 19, the two sides met for the nineteenth bargaining session, having achieved only limited progress. On August 31 the old contract expired, and on September 8 the union set the September 22 strike date if no agreement should be reached by then.

Without getting into the details of the two sides' main points in the negotiations, one analyst made these observations.

> The players...argue that certain elements of their working conditions are unfairly restrictive, denying them basic rights afforded workers in some other industries.... The union contends that four elements of the current system restrict a player's movement, leaving him shut out of any corner of a competitive marketplace. They are the draft, which annually restocks the 28 teams by an orderly process; the one-way nature of a contract, in that a player is bound by its terms but a team can terminate at any time; and the backbones of the free agency system in place, first-refusal rights and compensation.[47]

Thus the players focused their proposal on issues concerning their rights as workers. Although their proposal had listed seven or eight major issues, this journalist noted three as central—the annual draft of players, the nature of their contract, and the free agency system.

Meanwhile, the owners also proposed a number of items, but repeatedly made the point that one issue was central. On October 11, 1987, for example, the assistant director of the Management Council declared simply, "Free agency still remains the main impediment to a settlement."[48] Four days later, the union acquiesced.

Repeatedly, three reasons were identified to explain the failure of the strike, with the union ordering its members back to work in defeat. These three reasons represent the three major "players" in the dispute—the players, the owners, and the media and public.

First, the players were cited as a reason for the failure of their own strike because of the absence of any underlying unity and purpose within their ranks. On the one hand, the players are a diverse lot, especially in terms of their abilities and attendant salaries. One football fan wrote that the problem facing the NFLPA

> is in the ranks of the players.... This is the heart of the dissension, and the players association should face this very delicate problem: how to attract quality players and at the same time keep a certain parity in salaries. The time for compromise for the players themselves has come.[49]

The letter writer noted the disparity in players' salaries, ranging from $50,000 to over $1,000,000. His "solution" was for players to compromise.

On the other hand, the players faced other forms of dissension, given their various interpretations of their situations. "I started to see a lot of inconsistencies," observed one player who refused to join his teammates in striking. "It's dangerous for people to accept what is told them by a biased source.... Unions had become self-serving entities [who] seldom represent the wishes of all their workers."[50]

That player was one of over 200 who eventually defied their union and played on "scab" teams composed mainly of replacement players for three games during the strike. The union was never able completely to control its "very young" members, who were subject to relatively easy replacement, who lacked a strong sense of institutional memory, and who lacked "bargaining experience."[51] A first possible reason for the failure of the strike thus rested with the union and its members, who were diverse, uncertain, and less than completely committed.

Second, another possible reason for the failure of the strike was the opposite situation represented by the owners and their solidarity. In contrast to nearly 1,600 union members with diverse agendas, the owners of the twenty-eight teams were single-minded and unified. Soon after the players announced their strike, the owners countered with their strategy of bringing in replacement "scab" players to resume the regularly-scheduled games on October 4, an action one reporter called "the most significant act of the strike's first week."[52]

Players and outside observers agreed on the strength of the owners' unified position. Walter Payton, a star player for the Chicago Bears, said that "the National Football League employers are in 'total control' in

America's most famous strike."[53] Similarly, Joel Kaplan, an attorney specializing in management law, said that in disputes between management and union, leverage is the factor that determines who wins. During the replacement player games of October, he noted, the owners were winning because they put on games that counted and because the players lost money.[54]

The owners had solidarity, resources, and expertise—all of which were lacking among the players. The owners' strength constitutes a second possible reason for the failure (from the players' point of view) of the strike.

Third, a less obvious participant was the collective media and public, especially in relation to the ability of the players to communicate adequately their position. A very real problem the union faced was that of communicating its position to a potentially supportive media and public. After the strike was over, only one-third of the public thought that the union position had been right and worthy of their support. The media reduced this point of failure to one of "public relations," that

> throughout the strike the union did a terrible job of getting its ideas across to the press and to the public. Never, for instance, has the union driven home the point that in the decade since the current modified free agency system, ...only one player has changed teams.[55]

Early on, one reporter had noted the poor quality of public relations provided by the players' union, "especially given the potential sympathy [that] the union's grievances could elicit if well understood."[56] Later, the same reporter explained further:

> In dealing with the outside world, the union has been shaky. It rejected offers of help from public relations specialists of more savvy unions and has not used an outside public consultant, deciding that its small staff would go it alone. The results have at times been obvious and self-defeating.[57]

Thus, it is possible that the strike of the NFLPA against the football owners failed because of three factors—the weak, fragmented union; the strong, unified owners; and the inept public relations strategy of the union in dealing with the media and public. As various analysts argued, these were *possible* reasons for the failure of the strike to meet players' expectations. But the real reason is none of these, nor a combination of their factors, although they were certainly possibilities.

Instead, the real reason for the failure of the football strike was the strength of the folk religion represented by sport. Following from the earlier analysis of the ways in which sport manifests itself as a folk religion, I can determine four factors that accounted for the failure of the football strike: fan identification, ritual, mythology, and structure. Together, these four factors combined to energize the folk religion among American football fans.

First, the identification factor is that the public never was convinced that it should see itself in the person of the players on strike. At first, this interpretation of identification does not seem to make much sense. Of course, the public should have preferred to identify with the players who are widely-known heroes in American life. Does anyone know personally the owners in sport who are often portrayed as "heavies" in the popular media?

A number of ironies compose this idea of the strength of identification in folk religion. In American life in the 1980s, labor unions generally did not fare well. Besides that, the very idea of a union representing individual athletes—even in a team sport such as professional football—is a notion that many Americans have not found easy to accept. Probably, the one statistic that loomed largest during the football labor negotiations was the annual "average" salary of the players, $230,000. The union attempted to counter that figure by saying it was really closer to $215,000; that a more adequate statistic was the "median" salary of about $170,000; or that nearly one third of the players made less than $100,000. But the $230,000 figure stuck in many people's minds, via the media. Could anyone really identify with athletes making that kind of money? Was there really any reason for them to strike?

On the other hand, with whom did the public come to identify? Surely, not the owners. But after one week of the replacement, "scab" games, the answer was clear—another point of irony. The public identified with the replacement players. Stories in the popular media emphasized how many of the replacement players were just "regular guys," chasing their own dreams, attempting one last time to fulfill their wish to find a career in professional football. Along with this, when the elite, star players went out on strike, they were probably the ones with whom the public identified with the least, especially in terms of salary. A player with annual earnings of $800,000, for example, stood to lose $50,000 for each of the sixteen games he was on strike. But the public never felt sorry for his losing 3/16 of his salary; instead, he was remembered for earning $650,000 despite being on strike.

In the meantime, the public did miss seeing some of the stars perform on the field or missed watching them on television. But by the second week of the replacement games, nearly one-half of the seats were filled at the stadia anyway. The public was watching the unknown, replacement players. They were watching men play who were really more like themselves than were the regular, star players. Therein lay the real power of identification. The public identified more with "just-average athletes" who more closely embodied a traditional American ideal of individuals seeking to make something of themselves, even when they did not have nearly supernatural abilities. Identification can work in more than one way, and in the case of the strike, the public saw themselves in the role of replacement players, not star players.

Second, the ritualistic factor strikes at the heart of how American sport functions as a folk religion. Attending professional football games or watching them on television on the weekends is a part of the ritualistic gatherings of clans that were noted above. While professional football fans identify with their teams in these ritual gatherings, it is clear that those fans do not identify with specific players as much as we once thought. Instead, fans identify with more anonymous personifications in the form of players wearing uniforms and team colors that they recognize and that represent themselves in some mysterious fashion, regardless of how identifiable the individual players may be to them.

The power of this ritualistic element of the folk religion was demonstrated in Chicago on October 11, 1987, when the Chicago Bears were playing their second game with replacement players. The striking Bears' players called a labor rally for three hours immediately preceding the game, at a site located adjacent to the stadium where the game would occur later. The regular players received a great amount of publicity prior to the game, asking fans to come to the rally, to mingle freely with their heroes, and to receive their autographs. Some fans did come, and after getting their autographs, they went to the game as was their ritualistic wont. Chicago is a strong union city with a "working-man" tradition, but over 32,000 fans performed their weekly ritual regardless of the strike.

The ritualistic strength of sport as folk religion was rarely acknowledged by the media. Americans wish to participate personally or vicariously by means of television in the ritualistic gatherings. Sport teams exert a focal power that acts as a means to that cultic participation. Warren did note that "a football-loving public cares less about bargaining rights and wrongs than about alteration of a Sunday ritual."[58] Even though the regular players were not playing in the games, others were. The games occurred, and that was reason enough for coming together—rather than the absence of the regular players being a reason for staying home or not watching on television.

Third, a mythological factor underlying the failure of the strike is that many of the fans and some of both the media and the players simply could not accept what the union stood for or what it sought to communicate. Instead, fans, media, and even some players believe too strongly in the myths and ideology of sport. In a sense, this explanation of the strength of the mythology of sport is the "other side" of the public relations argument noted above. That is, what might be suggested as a mere failure of public relations may not have been that at all. Rather, people did not accept the union's position because it did not match their personal understanding of what sport generally, and football in particular, means and teaches and helps us to believe. In a column on the strike, George Vecsey noted: "More than any other sport, football is based upon teamwork, continuity, organization—hollow phrases when used too often, but a reality in putting 45 athletes on the field. Management can take familiar uniforms and put them on new players."[59]

Another example of the power of this mythology is an alternative explanation for why the union's position on free agency never captured public attention. "Logically," it seems, it should have appealed to the public, for people really do believe that workers should be able to work where and when they choose. But the management position was that in some mysterious way, free agency would destroy the very structure, the competitive balance within football. In the end, people believed management, not the union, because the myths of continuity and balance and competition are more powerful than is the myth of the right of self-determination. How else can one explain why nearly two-thirds of those surveyed took management's position? At a cognitive level, although perhaps not knowingly, people believe more strongly in the myths that portrayed management's position, than in those of the players.

When those myths overlap with the strength of identification cited above, they become a powerful basis for interpreting the failure of the strike. People did not identify with the players, nor did they accept their myths. Instead, people accepted the ideas of competition, structure, and opportunity for the average person seeking a goal.

Finally, a fourth reason—a structural one—suggests why the strike failed. Professional football is a business, one interrelated with other corporate entities such as the electronic media and advertising. Structurally, the football strike was David against Goliath, and Goliath won. That is, corporate America was on the side of the owners, and the owners had all the advantages in the strike.

The union had hoped that the three television networks would have put pressure on the owners because of lost revenues. If advertisers did not approve of the decreased audience ratings for the televised replacement games, then they would not pay their bills. But Michael Goodwin noted that network officials had analyzed

> that lost revenues could be offset by lowered costs. The reduced costs could come largely through refunds from the league, which has said it would discuss any financial problems the networks encounter because of the strike. "The last I heard, you're still making a profit if you take in more than you spend, regardless of how you do it."[60]

This does raise the further question about how the league could have afforded to refund money to the networks. Warren explained simply, "The teams' huge weekly savings in payroll make the strike a winner."[61] In some detail Michael Janofsky explained that

> The owners appeared to be the winners. Not only were they able to show financial profits from staging games with replacement players—who earn about $4000 a game, compared to an average of about $14,000 a game for regulars—they remained solid in their refusal to give the union what it wanted most, a system of unrestricted free agency.[62]

The hard, structural reality of corporate sport is that the players were naive in believing any clear financial incentives existed for the owners to wish to settle the strike. Structurally, the "deck was stacked" against the players and their union. The folk religion of sport is tied closely to corporate structures that made the failure of a strike likely.

Conclusion

The reality of a modern folk religion in the form of American sport manifests itself in several ways including ideology and belief, cultic observances, and tradition and history. As with churchly religion, so with folk religion is its likelihood of being tested from without and within. One such recent test of the folk religion of sport was the 1987 professional football players' strike.

Whereas popular explanations for the failure of the strike focused variously on the union, the owners, and public relations in the media, the reasons suggested here issue from the strength of folk religion itself. The identification with anonymous and average athletes; the ritual gathering to view football games in person or on television; the mythology surrounding the management position; and the corporate structure of professional football—all are manifestations of the folk religion within which American sport thrives and which suggest that the 1987 football players' strike was doomed to failure. The popular explanations for the strike can be understood only in terms of these "real," more basic reasons suggested by the folk religion of sport.

[1] James Michener, *Sports in America* (New York: Random House, 1976).

[2] Christopher Lasch, *The Culture of Narcissism* (New York: Norton, 1979).

[3] Charles S. Prebish, "'Heavenly Father, Divine Goalie': Sport and Religion," *Antioch Review* 42/3(1984): 306-318.

[4] John W. Loy, Barry D. McPherson, and Gerald Kenyon, *Sport and Social Systems* (Reading MA: Addison-Wesley, 1978).

[5] Michael Novak, *The Joy of Sports* (New York: Basic Books, 1976).

[6] Robert W. Coles, "Football as a 'Surrogate' Religion?," *A Sociological Yearbook of Religion in Britain, #8* (London: SCM Press, 1975) 61-77.

[7] Eric Dunning, "The Sociology of Sport in Europe and the United States," *Sport and Social Theory*, ed. C. Roger Rees and Andrew Miracle (Champaign IL: Human Kinetics, 1986) 29-56.

[8] Philip E. Hammond, "Commentary," *The Religious Situation*, ed. Donald R. Cutler (Boston: Beacon, 1968) 381-88.

[9] James A. Mathisen, "From Civil Religion to Folk Religion: The Case of American Sport," *Sport and Religion*, ed. Shirl J. Hoffman (Champaign IL: Human Kinetics, 1992) 17-33.

[10] Martin E. Marty, "Two Kinds of Civil Religion," *American Civil Religion*, ed. Russell E. Richey and Donald G. Jones (New York: Harper and Row, 1974) 139-57.

[11] Russell E. Richey and Donald G. Jones, "The Civil Religion Debate,"*American Civil Religion*, ed. Russell E. Richey and Donald G. Jones (New York: Harper and Row, 1974) 3-18.

[12] Gail Gehrig, *American Civil Religion: An Assessment* (Storrs CT: Society for the Scientific Study of Religion, 1981).

[13] Robert N. Bellah, "Civil Religion in America," *Daedalus* 96/1 (1967): 1-21.

[14] Marty, "Two Kinds of Civil Religion," 141.

[15] Robert J. Higgs, "Muscular Christianity, Holy Play, and Spiritual Exercises: Confusion about Christ in Sports and Religion," *Arete* 1/1 (1983): 63.

[16] Edwin H. Cady, *The Big Game* (Knoxville: University of Tennessee Press, 1978) 93.

[17] Robert Linder, "Civil Religion in Historical Perspective," *Journal of Church and State* 17/3 (1975): 401.

[18] Robin M. Williams, *American Society: A Sociological Interpretation* (New York: Alfred A. Knopf, 1951) 312.

[19] Anthony F. C. Wallace, *Religion: An Anthropological View* (New York: Random House, 1966) 74-75.

[20] A. Roy Eckardt, *The Surge of Piety in America* (New York: Associates, 1958).

[21] W. Lloyd Warner, *The Family of God* (New Haven: Yale University Press, 1961).

[22] Franklin H. Littell, *From State Church to Pluralism* (Garden City NY: Doubleday, 1962).

[23] Williams, *American Society*.

[24] Martin E. Marty, *The New Shape of American Religion* (New York: Harper and Row, 1959) 32.

[25] Will Herberg, *Protestant—Catholic—Jew* (Garden City NY: Doubleday, 1955).

[26] Will Herberg, *Protestant—Catholic—Jew*, 2nd. ed. (Garden City NY: Doubleday, 1960) 75.

[27] Will Herberg, "America's Civil Religion: What It Is and Whence It Comes," *Modern Age* 17/3 (1973): 228.

[28] Gustav Mensching, "Folk and Universal Religion," *Religion. Culture and Society*, ed. and trans. Louis Schneider, (New York: John Wiley and Sons, 1964) 254.

[29] John F. Wilson, *Public Religion in American Culture* (Philadelphia: Temple University Press, 1979) 135.

[30] Novak, *Joy of Sports*, 20, 34.

[31] Robert Lipsyte, *SportsWorld: An American Dreamland* (New York: Quadrangle, 1975) ix, xiv-xv.

[32] Howard Slusher, *Man, Sport, and Existence* (Philadelphia: Lea and Febiger, 1967) 134.

[33] Harry Edwards, *The Sociology of Sport* (Homewood IL: Dorsey, 1973) 261.

[34] Robert H. Boyle, "Oral Roberts: Small But Oh, My," *Sports Illustrated* 33/22 (November 30, 1970): 64.

[35] Richard Lipsky, *How We Play the Game* (Boston: Beacon Press, 1981) 5.

[36] Slusher, *Man, Sport, and Existence*, 127.

[37] Novak, *Joy of Sports*, 19.

[38] Janet Lever, *Soccer Madness* (Chicago: University of Chicago Press, 1983) 15.

[39] Lipsky, *How We Play the Game*, 39.

[40] Richard D. Mandell, *Sport: A Cultural History* (New York: Columbia University Press, 1984) 230.

[41] Paul Weiss, *Sport: A Philosophic Inquiry* (Carbondale IL: Southern Illinois University Press, 1969) 166, 165.

[42] Michael C. Kearl, "Knowing How to Quit: On the Finitudes of Everyday Life," *Sociological Inquiry* 56/3 (1986): 292.

[43] Allen Guttmann, *From Ritual to Record* (New York: Columbia University Press, 1978) 55.

[44] Michael Janofsky, "N. F. L. Players End Strike but Can't Play Sunday," *New York Times*, October 16, 1987, A34.

[45] Adam Clymer, "Poll Finds Support for Owners," *New York Times*, October 25, 1987, 5:4.

[46] Paul Zimmerman, "The Strike: The Winners, the Losers, and Who Did What to Whom," *Sports Illustrated* 57/23 (November 29, 1982): 19.

[47] Michael Janofsky, "A Deep Division in Labor Dispute," *New York Times*, September 27, 1987, 5:10.

[48] "Strike Talks Recess after No Movement," *Chicago Tribune*, October 11, 1987, 3:4.

[49] Peter J. Rigar, "Marx at the Goal Line," *New York Times*, October 5, 1987, A22.

[50] Jill Lieber, "'I Will Be Ostracized,'" *Sports Illustrated* 67/18 (October 26, 1987): 61.

[51] James Warren, "Will NFL Players Find the Owners' 'Structure' Indestructible?" *Chicago Tribune*, September 27, 1987, 3:7.

[52] Warren, "Will NFL Players Find the Owners' 'Structure' Indestructible?," 3:7.

[53] James Warren, "Labor-management Experts Ponder Players' Tactics," *Chicago Tribune*, October 13, 1987, 4:3.

[54] Warren, "Labor-management Experts Ponder Players' Tactics," 4:3.

[55] Paul Zimmerman, "On the Outside Looking In," *Sports Illustrated* 67/18 (October 26, 1987): 56.

[56] Warren, "Will NFL Players Find the Owners' 'Structure' Indestructible?," 7.

[57] James Warren, "NFL Union Fumbling the Ball in Public Relations," *Chicago Tribune*, October 6, 1987, 4:3.

[58] Warren, "Will NFL Players Find the Owners' 'Structure' Indestructible?," 7.

[59] George Vecsey, "Brand X Football," *New York Times*, September 23, 1987, B9.

[60] Michael Goodwin, "Networks Try Scramble Play," *New York Times*, September 23, 1987, B9.

[61] Warren, "Labor-management Experts Ponder Players' Tactics," 3.

[62] Janofsky, "N. F. L. Players End Strike but Can't Play Sunday," 34.

BASKETBALL

BASKETBALL'S ABBOT
BOB KNIGHT AND THE DRIVE FOR PERFECTION

Lois K. Daly

As a theologian who grew up in Indiana, I should not be surprised that I would find a way to put religion and basketball together. Hoosier hysteria does have a religious tone and fervor to it. This I learned firsthand as my high school team reached the semi-state level of the state tournament during my sophomore year. The team was completely awe struck as it attempted to play in Mackey Arena, the home of the Purdue Boilermakers. There were no miracles that day. Since I grew up with Indiana University basketball, it was clear to me at the time that our defeat was certainly related to playing in the enemy's territory, an enemy that would stop at nothing to crush the forces of the good and virtuous. Surely to play in such a place was a betrayal of the cream and crimson, and an ignominious defeat was just punishment.

The days of such cosmological certainty and divine sanction of wins and losses have passed. Now I recognize strategies and tactics that explain wins and losses, even Indiana wins and losses. Indiana's loss to Richmond during the 1988 NCAA tournament, for example, was clearly the result of Indiana's poor execution. But the way in which basketball suggests itself in religious language and symbol still intrigues me. Given my background, and perhaps I should admit that my parents are both Indiana alumni and my father worked for Indiana University for over forty years, Bob Knight as a subject for study also comes as no surprise. Knight is clearly revered in much of Indiana and elsewhere as a great coach. At the same time, his faults do not go unmentioned or unnoticed there or anywhere.[1] He is especially known for his insistence on a disciplined style of play. Players must play his way or they do not play at all. It is this discipline and its purpose that I wish to explore. I find in it some interesting and close parallels with ancient notions of the spiritual life and the role of discipline in its practice. In this light, Coach Knight may be seen as modern culture's version of the Benedictine abbot.

The connections between sport and religion have drawn the attention of several cultural commentators, sports analysts, and religious studies scholars. Michael Novak, for example, argues that sports flow out of a natural impulse that is radically religious. An element of this impulse is what he calls the longing for perfection.[2] "The hunger for perfection in sports cleaves closely to the driving core of the human spirit. It is the experience of this driving force that has perennially led human beings to break forth in religious languages."[3] One element of religion that Novak associates with sports' drive for perfection is *ascesis*. He explains that ancient Christian monks and hermits borrowed this word for discipline from Greek athletes and used it to describe their own rigorous life. According to Novak, *ascesis* or discipline then signified "the development of character, through patterns of self-denial, repetition, and experiment."[4] This became the method the monks used in striving for perfection.

The connections between sport, discipline, and perfection are also described by the philosopher Paul Weiss. As he explains, athletes are willing to submit to long training periods, little time off, repetitious drills, and the risk of humiliation because sport "offers a superb occasion for enabling young men to be perfected."[5] In short, sport is a means "by which one can become self-complete."[6] This self-completion begins with the acceptance of the body through training and practice. Training, according to Weiss, corrects a "disequilibrium" between mind and body; it begins with very specific moves that make up more complicated acts. In so doing, training makes bodies "habituated in the performance of moves and acts while enabling them to function harmoniously and efficiently."[7]

For Weiss, the athlete's training is directed by a coach who offers examples, advice, drill, criticism, and encouragement. The coach's instruction is usually based on what has been learned from mentors, introducing little innovation. But coaches are more than technicians, according to Weiss, especially coaches of student athletes. In addition to training the mind and body for athletic performance, these coaches also assume "the obligation of enabling young men [and women] to grow into excellence." Continuing to reflect on the role of a coach, Weiss states that "ideally, a coach is a model man, a unified whole in whom character permeates the body, and sensitivity is fired with imagination. He inspires his charges to possess something like his spirit."[8]

The language that Weiss uses is suggestive of Christian theologians who describe the training for perfection involved in the monastic life. Ascetic practices used to train the body and the spirit in the Christian monastic tradition include fasting, austerity, abstention, and mortification.[9] The monk's aim in these practices is union with God, not as absorption into God, but as a union that opens up the human and brings about its perfection. In this way, perfection is the self-mastery of mind and body that comes through self-abandonment. The monk attempts through discipline and training to restore the relationship of body to soul and soul to spirit as willed by God.[10] Toward this end, the monk is committed to a constant, habitual, practice of the "counsels," or the three monastic vows of poverty, chastity, and obedience. The rigor of self-abandonment means that the core of this spiritual life is obedience, obedience to a spiritual father who guides the novice through the process of purification. This process is dominated by the struggle against habitual sins and the acquisition of the virtues through the exercise and repetition demanded by the spiritual father.[11]

The authority of the spiritual father in guiding the neophyte is absolute.[12] Furthermore, as Louis Bouyer notes in his *Introduction to Spirituality*,

> Spiritual fatherhood, according to ancient monastic literature, is exercised primarily in two ways: by the word of counsel which plumbs the depths of hearts and enlightens them as to what they must do—and by the transforming action which the monk, by the sole fact of his presence, carries out and exercises on the life of those who come near him.[13]

The discipline involved in the spiritual life is taught; it is not left up to chance.[14] "The Rule of St. Benedict," the first of the great monastic rules in the Christian West, provides ample illustrations of the discipline of the monastic life and the authority of the abbot, or spiritual father.

According to Benedict's Rule, the abbot determines what and when the monks will eat, when and where they will sleep, and what kind and how much manual labor they will do. All of this is organized around an exhausting prayer schedule. No one in the monastery is to follow his own wishes or to dispute the abbot's word, "for whatever is done without the leave of the spiritual father is to be set down to presumption and pride, and not to the credit of a monk."[15] It is also the duty of the abbot to enforce these rules by admonishing or reprimanding privately, rebuking publicly, punishing corporally, or banishing the offender from the community. Yet the abbot should remember that "he has undertaken the care of weak souls, not the tyranny over the strong." Hence, he should send an older and wiser monk to console and comfort those whom he admonishes, reprimands, or rebukes.[16] The authority of the abbot is clearly absolute, as Benedict explains: "For indeed it is not allowed to the monks to have bodies or wills in their own power. But for all things necessary they must look to the Father of the monastery; nor is it allowable to have anything which the abbot has not given or permitted."[17] At this point, I take it, the parallels between the role and authority of the abbot and Coach Knight begin to be apparent.

Like an abbot, Knight's authority over his team is total. On the court, Knight calls all the shots; there is no room for freedom or creativity. Says Knight, "I decide what a player can and cannot do...I think that teaching basketball is simply trying to get players to utilize the abilities I see in them the way I think is best for the team."[18] From this point of view, there is no difference between control through intimidation and control through respect. Knight simply expects that things will be done his way. Unlike other coaches, year after year Knight insists on one way of doing things. He does not mold his system to the players he has; he molds the players to the system. In recruiting, he looks for players who are willing to say, "Here I am, make me a player. Tell me what has to be done and I will do it."[19]

Off the court, Knight exerts his authority by demanding academic achievement. He demands as much from his players in the classroom as on the basketball court.[20] In fact, his academic demands extend into the summer months as well. Basketball players participate in a non-credit seven week reading and writing program by correspondence.[21] The reason for this attention to academics is not simply athletic eligibility; Knight's aim is to graduate his players with their class, and he comes very close to accomplishing that lofty aim. As Knight has reached more than 750 career victories as a coach, only two of his four-years players have not earned a baccalaureate degree.[22] Knight is known to advocate that the "athletic scholarships given to incoming freshmen should be limited to a number equal to the number of senior athletes who graduate with a degree."[23]

The consequences of challenging Knight's authority on and off the court have been illustrated repeatedly throughout his coaching career.

During the 1984-1985 season, for example, unfulfilled expectations on the court led to the benching of four starters, including All-American Steve Alford, during one Big Ten game and the exclusion of two players, Giomi and Morgan, from another;[24] and in the late 1980s, Knight benched Keith Smart for a couple of games and Ricky Calloway for much of the latter part of the season. Academic problems also surfaced in the late 1980s. Again during 1984-1985, Mike Giomi's academic situation led to his leaving the team[25] and his transfer to North Carolina State. Feinstein's book, *A Season on the Brink*, depicts Andre Harris's academic difficulties during the 1985-1986 season[26] as well as other incidents.

It is clear that Knight perceives his role as coach as a teacher of basketball. As such, he exhibits both of the ways through which the spiritual father exercises his authority. First, Knight speaks the "word which plumbs the depths of hearts and enlightens them as to what they must do." He explains that a teacher has to give a concise, simple, clear presentation of what is expected and to tolerate nothing less. Being tolerant, Knight says, allows the player to become satisfied with his performance rather than growing beyond it.[27] Successful teaching, for Knight, lies in repetition and drill. It also lies in getting his message across in the strongest way he can: through intimidation.

As Joan Mellen pointed out in the *New York Times*, Knight, like all teachers, uses mind games. His method is to attack those who can handle it and speak to others through them.[28] Knight himself admits that not all players can take what he dishes out. But like the Benedictine abbot who has "undertaken the care of weak souls," Knight does not leave his players to console themselves. Instead he sends "older and wiser brothers," his assistant coaches, to comfort and encourage them. Again, Feinstein's book provides ample illustrations of this mode of relating to players.[29]

Knight also exercises his abbot-like authority through his sheer presence, as clearly seen in the Olympic trials. During that time, "Knight spent much of his time perched in a tower in a rare period of silent observation."[30] As one player noted, "The first time, he didn't really say anything, and we were just kind of in awe."[31] That awe led the Olympic hopefuls to demonstrate the abilities that Knight concentrates on, especially tough defense, without his saying a word.

What Knight teaches through his piercing words and his presence is discipline, a discipline that strives to evoke and realize a player's potential, both as a player and as a human being. According to Knight, discipline has four components. It consists of doing what needs to be done, doing it when it has to be done, doing it as well as you can, and doing it that way all the time.[32] This approach applies to offense, defense, class performance, and life. His notion of discipline leads to a sort of self-mastery that parallels the monastic life. It comes in self-abandonment and practice. As Knight explains, "your biggest opponent isn't the other guy. It's human nature."[33] What Knight aims for with this discipline is, in other words, perfection.

There are two keys to Knight's idea of perfection. Neither one of them is winning. Instead, they are execution and playing to one's potential. Execution is very closely tied to his notion of discipline. When asked how to know if someone is playing well without looking at the score, Knight answers: "expect a kid to do the best he can. If he executes something well one time, he knows he can do what you want him to do. If he knows what you want and that he can do it, but for some reason does not execute, then you are getting less than the best out of him."[34] In Knight's book, mistakes are mistakes no matter when they come and what the score is. Mistakes are a failure to execute, a lack of discipline. Up by twenty points or down by one doesn't change things for Knight: "To me," he declares, "not executing matters all the time."[35] As he explains, many coaches are so happy to win that they don't analyze the game and find the mistakes that could cost them a victory the next time.[36] Execution and winning may not be synonymous, but there is a direct relationship between them.

Playing to one's potential is the other key to perfection for Knight. It too is related to discipline, because discipline and accurate execution allow one to play to one's potential. Rather than recruiting classes of blue chip players, Knight goes after players willing to be taught, willing to play the best game they can. As Joan Mellen puts it, "Under the generosity of his vigilance he never asks of a student what he can't give and is furious when one of them tries to do what he's not good at."[37] The ultimate goal, Knight explains, is "to play as well as you can.... Winning and losing doesn't bother me nearly as much as not playing well (whether we win or lose). That is the essence of the whole thing to me—playing well, playing to potential."[38] Furthermore, Knight says, "You could win and still not succeed, not achieve what you should. And you can lose without really failing at all.... I'm sure I'd be easier on myself and on other people if just winning were my ultimate objective."[39]

Like the abbot, Knight uses his authority to instill a discipline that aims for perfection. Unlike the abbot's monks, Knight's players stay under his control (only) for a limited time. But Knight's lessons go with them.

Former players credit him with instilling in them discipline and the determination to excel.[40] According to Pete Newell, one of Knight's mentors, Knight does "the single most important thing in coaching: he turns out educated kids who are ready for society."[41] What he teaches them is hard: "how never to abandon your effort, stick it out to the end, take pride in yourself, believe in your own value."[42] John Feinstein's account of the last sequence of the 1987 championship game, in his article "Back From the Brink," captures the essence of Knight's message when he says, "through all the screaming and yelling, I heard the teaching. And the love."[43]

---

[1] Note that none of the events of 2000, including Knight's dismissal from Indiana University, challenges the analogy drawn in this essay. Indeed, it only becomes more interesting.

[2] Michael Novak, "The Natural Religion," in *Sport Inside Out*, ed. David L. Vanderwerken and Spencer K. Wertz (Fort Worth: Texas Christian University, 1985) 351-52.

[3] Novak, "The Natural Religion," in *Sport Inside Out*, 357.

[4] Novak, "The Natural Religion," in *Sport Inside Out*, 358.

[5] Paul Weiss, *Sport: A Philosophic Inquiry* (Carbondale IL: Southern Illinois Press, 1969) 18-19.

[6] Weiss, *Sport: A Philosophic Inquiry*, 36.

[7] Weiss, *Sport: A Philosophic Inquiry*, 41, 46.

[8] Weiss, *Sport: A Philosophic Inquiry*, 50.

[9] Louis Bouyer, *Introduction to Spirituality*, trans. Mary Perkins Ryan (New York: Desclee Company, 1961) 125.

[10] Bouyer, *Introduction to Spirituality*, 146.

[11] Bouyer, *Introduction to Spirituality*, 243-64.

[12] Bouyer, *Introduction to Spirituality*, 199.

[13] Bouyer, *Introduction to Spirituality*, 210.

[14] Harry M. Buck, *Spiritual Discipline in Hinduism, Buddhism, and the West* (Chambersburg PA: Anima Books, 1981) 7-8.

[15] "Rule of St. Benedict," quoted in *Documents of the Christian Church*, ed. Henry Bettenson (New York: Oxford University Press, 1957) 175.

[16] "Rule of St. Benedict," in *Documents of the Christian Church*, 168.

[17] "Rule of St. Benedict," in *Documents of the Christian Church*, 169.

[18] Quoted in David A. England, "Bobby Knight on Teaching and Coaching," *Scholastic Coach* 52 (December 1982): 59.

[19] England, "Bobby Knight on Teaching and Coaching," 60.

[20] David A. England, "Athletics, Academics, and Ethics," *Phi Delta Kappan* 64 (November 1982): 163.

[21] Elizabeth Kurpius and Mary Rose, "Academics for Athletes at Indiana University" *Phi Delta Kappan* 64 (November 1982): 164.

[22] England, "Athletics," 163.

[23] "Bob Knight," *Current Biography Yearbook 1987*, ed. Charles Moritz (H. W. Wilson, 1987) 317.

[24] Bruce Newman, "In the Heat of the Knight," *Sports Illustrated* 62 (February 11, 1985): 162.

[25] Newman, "In the Heat of the Knight," 164.

[26] John Feinstein, *A Season on the Brink: A Year with Bob Knight and the Indiana Hoosiers* (New York: Macmillan Company, 1986) 221.

[27] England, "Bobby Knight on Teaching and Coaching," 22-24.

[28] Joan Mellen, "At Indiana, A Week in Knight's Classroom," *New York Times*, November 15, 1987, 5:9.

[29] Cf. Feinstein, *Season on the Brink*, 36, 47.

[30] Malcolm Moran, "Knight: The Caller of Every Shot," *New York Times,* July 22, 1984, 5:10.

[31] Quoted in Moran, "Knight: The Caller of Every Shot."

[32] England, "Bobby Knight on Teaching and Coaching," 59.

[33] Frank Deford, "The Rabbit Hunter," *Sports Illustrated* 54 (January 26, 1981): 58.

[34] Quoted in England, "Bobby Knight on Teaching and Coaching," 61.

[35] Quoted in England, "Bobby Knight on Teaching and Coaching," 59.

[36] England, "Bobby Knight on Teaching and Coaching," 61.

[37] Mellen, "At Indiana," 9.

[38] Quoted in England, "Bobby Knight on Teaching and Coaching," 61.

[39] Quoted in Deford, "Rabbit Hunter," 68.

[40] Peter Monaghan, "Indiana's Bob Knight: Hotheaded Tyrant, Misunderstood Genius—or Both?" *Chronicle of Higher Education* 28 (May 23, 1984): 29.

[41] Quoted in Deford, "Rabbit Hunter," 67.

[42] Mellen, "At Indiana," 9.

[43] John Feinstein, "Back From the Brink," *Sport Magazine* 78 (December 1987): 33.

THE FINAL FOUR AS FINAL JUDGMENT
THE CULTURAL SIGNIFICANCE OF THE NCAA BASKETBALL CHAMPIONSHIP

Joseph L. Price

Introduction

During the final week of the 1988 NCAA basketball tournament, Bob Ley of ESPN referred to the pursuit of the NCAA Basketball Championship as the "quest for the Holy Grail," and CBS sports, hyping its exclusive telecast of selected preliminary games and the championship round of play, repeatedly projected its registered logo of the highway sign with the lettering, "The Road to the Final Four." Both of these metaphors suggest that there is a sense of pilgrimage and perhaps ultimacy that attends the pursuit of the National Championship in Collegiate Basketball, NCAA Men's Division I. Certainly, the images of "quest" and "road" reflect the religious fervor that often accompanies the pursuit of the crown by one of the teams and the impassioned support of the team by its faithful followers. Yet the religious metaphors employed by the sportscasters do not expand upon the religious significance of the festival of the "Final Four." At the time of the championship tournament, Skip Bayless, writing in the popular in-flight magazine of American Airlines, brought this issue to popular attention: He wonders how "the Final Four [has] come to be such a religious experience."[1] In contrast to both the metaphors proposed in television journalism and in partial response to Bayless's query, I suggest that a different religious metaphor—that of Final Judgment—more adequately signifies the cultural meaningfulness of the basketball tournament and its championship.

In religious expectations and discussions, questions about Final Judgment focus primarily on those who are judged and secondarily on the character of the judge and the criteria used in reaching the judgment. In itself, Final Judgment is the occasion (usually thought of as occurring after death, the end of the world, or beyond time) when the righteous shall be redeemed and the wicked shall finally have their full punishment meted out. The result of the judgment is that justice and peace will prevail. One prominent biblical image portrays the occasion as the time when sheep will be separated from goats, signifying that the distinctly righteous will be divided from those who are not. Another biblical metaphor depicts Final Judgment as the time when lions and the lambs will lie down together in peace. The literal realization of the latter metaphor again went unrealized in 1988 as the Lions of Loyola Marymount and the Rams of Rhode Island, who are iconographically akin to lambs, were eliminated before they could advance to the Final Four.

For the teams that reach the championship round of play, however, there is no threat of absolute rejection. Already, the inadequate teams—those that failed to win all of their earlier tournament games—have received full punishment by being excluded. They have been given their due merit; the life of their season has been annihilated. The teams that make it to the Final Four are among, one might say, the elect. They have won. They remain chosen after the end of the regular season as they progress to the promised land—whether New Orleans, Kansas City, or Seattle—the site of the tournament's final game in 1988. For those who are among these chosen, the final thing at stake is like the venal concern of Jesus' closest disciples: Who gets to sit in the privileged position at the right hand of the Supreme Judge? For basketball's elect, the favored position is not the one next to God, but that adjacent to American culture's demigod, as the president invites the champion team to visit with him at the White House.

According to religious expectations about the methods for securing final reward, there are two ways to acquire it: by merit and by grace. Similarly, there are two ways that teams begin the process of getting to the Final Four: by merit (winning conference championships or conference tournaments) and by grace (receiving an invitation that does not necessarily recognize teams with the best winning records). Of the sixty-four bids issued to teams for the 1988 NCAA Tournament, thirty were automatic while thirty-four were by invitation. Both grace and works, then, enable the prospect of selection for the Final Four.

Although these initial correlations between the Final Four and Final Judgment play with the correspondence between team mascots and religious images and between tournament procedures and theological concepts, I want to turn attention to the significance of the tournament by exploring some of the values that underlie American concern with the championship. Basically, I will address a series of questions about its significance as an event of judgment, even Final Judgment, for the players, for the winning college or university, for the NCAA, and for American popular culture. My primary concerns are with understanding the character of those who are finally judged, not with *who* might do the judging, whether the NCAA committee that issues at-large bids to non-conference champions or the referees who officiate the games and occasionally determine the outcome by virtue of a controversial call (as was the case with the addition of seconds to the end of the 1987 Kansas game, thereby changing the victor). To provide a context for addressing and assessing these questions, let us first look briefly at the origin of basketball and the history of the championship tournament.

The Roots of Basketball and the Final Four

In his festive collection of essays and musings entitled *The Joy of Sports*, Michael Novak, himself a theologian and a basketball junkie, points out the religious roots of the game of basketball. The game did not have overt religious significance nor an allegorical religious meaning, but it did have a religious "inspiration." Motivated by the Calvinist spirit that endorses competition, the Reverend James Naismith developed the game to provide indoor exercise and to improve its tolerance for the young men at a college for Presbyterian missionaries in Springfield, Massachusetts. Although he designed the game to meet their winter recreational and calisthenic needs, he devised it in such a way that it could be easily understood and minimally equipped, thereby facilitating its dispersion throughout the world by the missionaries. "The idea behind the game was moral, Christian, and hygienic:" Novak avers, "active clean living through vigorous exercise played 'for fun.'"[2] For instance, Naismith originally set out only thirteen rules, one of which, of course, was that physical contact would incur a penalty. Similarly, the rules of the game did not establish exclusive territory for respective teams, and they discouraged the use of force in play. The puritanical influence is apparent not only here in the rules but also in the game's goal, which is above the field of play. It is an ethereal, transcendent halo somehow suspended above the level of this world. Since the ball must enter the goal by the indirect route of an arc, Novak even suggests that the means of scoring is characterized by grace, as exemplified best, perhaps, by the high arc on Keith Smart's baseline jumper that lifted Indiana to a last-second victory in the 1987 championship game.

In contrast to the religiously inspired conception of the sport, the birth of the Final Four was similar to the development of some political campaigns in the sense that it was conceived in the back room of a Chicago hotel in 1938. Plans for the tournament were approved just five months before the start of play; and 5500 fans attended the game between the Western Region champion Oregon and the Eastern representative Ohio State. The first tournament suffered financial losses of more than $2500, a deficit which had to be covered by a loan from the NCAA.

Although the eight-team NCAA championship tournament was not organized until the late thirties, the Helms Athletic Foundation had named a national champion since the turn of the century. Harold Olsen, the architect of the NCAA tournament, urged its adoption to provide contrast to the other post-season tournaments: the NIT, started in 1938; and the small college tournament in Kansas City, an event that would evolve into the NAIA tournament. In addition to providing regional representation, the NCAA tournament was intended to be played at the participant institutions, so that the institutions themselves would attain the greatest benefit. The first championship game was held on the campus of Northwestern University with Oregon beating the club team from Ohio State 46-33; but after its lax organization and financial disaster, the 1940 championship game was moved to Kansas City's municipal auditorium, where the crowd doubled the size of the first year and where a profit of almost $10,000 was recorded. Although the location shifted from participant institutions to civic arenas, the ideal of regional representation practically survived, since eighteen states were represented among the first twenty-two participant institutions in the annual event.

In 1951 the tournament format was expanded from the original eight team format to one which included sixteen teams; in the same year automatic bids were established and issued to conference champions, thus ensuring the geographic diversity of tournament teams. The first Final Four—with the semi-final and final games of the tournament played in a preselected, non-partisan location—was not played until the 1952 championship round in Seattle.[3] Within the past twenty-five years, the tournament size has been extended to thirty-two, then forty-eight, and now sixty-four teams.

The Significance of the Final Four

Since its inauspicious inception in 1938, the Final Four has grown into a festival unrivaled in American amateur athletic competitions.[4] In terms of sporting events that also serve as general cultural celebrations, only the World Series and the Super Bowl, both of which are professional championships, command as great attention and fascination by the American public. In addition to its distinct, amateur status, the NCAA tournament is also unique among the festivals because it is the only major American sporting festival that requires academic affiliation for its participants. According to Bayless, however, it is the amateur character of the Final Four that generates the popularity of the tournament above that of either the World Series or the Super Bowl, whose players are often under multi-year, multi-million dollar contracts.[5]

The cultural arenas in which the Final Four now exerts significant power and attracts incredible attention extend from the economic impact on the NCAA colleges and universities to social action programs for disadvantaged youths. The economic dimensions—both in terms of the financial implosion exerted on the commerce of the host city and in terms of its support for the participant institutions—now produce the most pervasive and profound influence of the championship tournament. Certainly, winning the tournament enhances the public image of the champion institution; but the major institutional benefit for advancing to the Final Four is financial, since all four teams that made it to the final round in 1988 garnered more than a million dollars apiece for their respective institutions.

By no means, however, is the economic significance of the tournament restricted to the teams that make the Final Four. In 1987, for example, the preliminary and final rounds of the NCAA Tournament netted in excess of $43.6 million, with 80 percent of that amount coming from revenues generated by television rights. From the tournament's profit $26 million were distributed to the sixty-four competing institutions, while almost $17.5 million were retained by the NCAA for operating expenses. The success of the 1987 telecast of the Final Four was so great that CBS increased its bid and purchased the rights to telecast the Final Four games in 1988-1990 for $163 million, or more than $18 million per game. With larger revenues the NCAA Executive Committee expanded the NCAA's annual operating budget for 1987-88 by almost 40 percent of the previous year. Half of the budgeted funds were designated for distribution among most of the NCAA Division I institutions and their scholarship programs, while another portion was destined for drug education programs.[6] In these ways the financial rewards of the tournament were extended to the students and athletes throughout the NCAA.

The financial success of the tournament has grown in direct proportion to the increased popularity of the tournament. In 1987 in New Orleans, the Final Four played to record crowds of 64,959 while the preliminary rounds had averaged 16,775 persons per game, making it the most well attended tournament in history. All in all, 666,919 fans saw the teams play in the 1987 NCAA Tournament.[7] Not only were the 1987 arena crowds larger than ever; the television audience for the championship game included more than forty million Americans.

As another indication of the increased popularity of the tournament, the advance demand for tickets has far exceeded their supply in recent years. For the 1988 Final Four festival at Kemper Arena in Kansas City, more than 90,000 requests for tickets were received for the 16,000 seats available. And even before the pairings had been announced for the 1988 tournament, the ticket application forms were published by the NCAA for the following year's championship round in Seattle's Kingdome. Ticket requests, which could not exceed four per application but which totaled more than 194,000, had to be accompanied by full payment, and they could not be honored if they were received *after* April 15, 1988, almost a year before the event. By adding a one dollar handling charge to all ticket applications, the NCAA covered its costs in issuing both tickets and refunds around June 30, 1988. For more than two months, then, the NCAA earned interest on the deposited funds for ticket requests. In turn, the accrued interest was designated to support NCAA outreach or "missionary" programs on drug education and youth activities, such as the Youth Education through Sports and the National Youth Sports Program.[8]

To commemorate the fiftieth anniversary of the NCAA men's basketball tournament, there were a number of public presentations, interactive events, and collector issues that served to recall the history and significance of the Final Four and its final game. The public was invited to participate in the selection of an All Final Four Team through the distribution of weekly ballots published for six weeks during February and March 1988, in *USA Today*. The ballot form also called for participants to select the player of the decade for each of the five decades of the tournament. (One might call this a kind of canonization of miracle workers.) CBS telecast a half-hour special, "Fifty years at the Final Four," just before the first semi-final game of the Final Four. During the week before the championship game, an exhibit at the Kansas City Municipal Auditorium celebrated the golden anniversary with a display of pictures, videos, and memorabilia from the five decades of the tournament. For the more souvenir-oriented fans and collectors, a pictorial history was published, limited editions of commemorative posters were issued, and commemorative medallions featuring the official logo of the fiftieth anniversary Final Four were minted. Somewhat to counterbalance the commercial emphasis on souvenirs, the NCAA also used the occasion of the Final Four to exercise a kind of social concern. For instance, its program for disadvantaged youths—Youth Education through Sport Clinic—was conducted by coaches and players in the Kansas City Municipal Auditorium on the morning of the semi-final matches of the Final Four.[9]

In light of such an array of ways to mark the spectacle of the Final Four, we still must inquire about what it is that generates such excitement for so many persons throughout the country, especially since the audience at the Final Four, including those who attend through the mediation of television and radio, constitutes about one-fourth of the nation's population. One possibility is that it appeals to the American Dream, not one that esteems the survival of the fittest but one that aspires to be representatively democratic, one wherein all have a chance to survive and to thrive. Although the tournament teams are ranked to provide favored seeds in the pairing of games, each team starts with equal footing in the sense that any team that can win six straight games in the tournament will be crowned National Champion. In this way, the underdog myth—a sort of Horatio Algeristic appeal of the poor working hard and getting lucky enough to succeed—also gets played out with the possibilities of a romantic ending. In 1988, the Rhode Island Rams and Richmond Spiders captured the spirit of charm and hope that exemplifies the inexperienced, innocents in quest of the fullness of reward. Similarly, in 1966, the Texas Western (now University of Texas at El Paso) Miners prevailed, defeating the much more historically prominent and successful program at the University of Kentucky, which holds the record for most appearances in the NCAA tournament. That particular clash between the Miners and the Wildcats also unlocked much of the racial prejudice that often characterized sporting spectacles and popular attitudes during the 1960s. Coach Don Haskins of Texas Western, which started five black players in contrast to the all white Kentucky team, received more than 40,000 letters of hate mail in the year following the Miner's upset victory. Following the success of the Miners, however, some of the walls of prejudice began to crumble, for Kentucky's coach Rupp, who had previously prevented blacks from participating in intercollegiate basketball at that university, began to recruit black players.[10]

In addition to this social advance that was occasioned by the Final Four, the tournament has also provided the opportunity for inspired and lucky teams to confirm their seeming destiny. Villanova's uncanny defeat of Georgetown in 1986 and North Carolina State's 1983 stunning upset championship have caused these teams to be labeled teams of destiny: They defied the odds, played from the heart, and came from "nowhere" to claim the final crown. Other kinds of "destined" teams have also received full affirmation in their final judgment, like Marquette's championship in Al McGuire's last game as coach or UCLA's defeat of Kentucky in the final game of Coach John Wooden. In both cases, the final victory provided an occasion for fully rewarding the integrity and efficiency of the coaches and their programs. Their "righteousness" did gain the prize.

Not all expectations and realizations of Final Judgment, however, are affirming. For many players the Final Four serves as a last chance to stand in the limelight, for fewer than 2 percent of all collegiate basketball players are drafted by NBA teams. The NCAA tournament thus represents their final moment for hearing applause for their playing with persistence, skill, and grace that had been so long in the making. For other players who have subsequently succeeded in the NBA, the Final Four has proven to be a time of seemingly ultimate deprivation, of losing the final game. In the 1950s alone, the teams of Jerry West, Elgin Baylor, Oscar Robertson, Wilt Chamberlain, and Bob Pettit—all of whom were to be elected to the NBA's Hall of Fame—suffered final defeat in the Final Four. Likewise, what collegiate basketball fan will forget that Larry Bird's Indiana State team suffered only one defeat all season, to Magic Johnson's inspired Michigan State team in the championship game in the late 1970s?[11]

The Final Judgment of the Final Four

The Final Four as Final Judgment is not a "*Benedictus*" for the Bruins, a "*Gloria*" for the Gophers, a "*Kyrie*" for Kentucky, or a "*Requiem*" for the Redmen. It is not even a cry of "*Dies Irae*" for Depaul's Blue Demons or "*Dies Illa*" for Duke's Blue Devils. (It is interesting that some collegiate institutions portray their demonic mascots not in terms of hot red, but in blue, perhaps making an obtuse academic reference to Dante's icy district of hell?) However, depending upon the Smart flight of the final shot of the Final Four, the judgment might be that of the 1987 "*Hallelujah*" of the Hoosiers.

After citing statistics about the financial significance of the championship tournament and telling stories about its great moments, I suggest that there is a sense in which the Final Four is larger even than the players, the fans, and the season. For the fact that we remember the games, recite their records, and retell their stories indicates some of the primary values of our own culture. In this process *we* encounter a full or final judgment. What we discover, however, is not so much the character of the judge or the criteria of the verdict as it is the deep disclosure—a final judgment—of who we really are. We discover our obsession with souvenirs, with getting some relic that will help us to recreate the moment, to live it again, to experience its otherness, to take us to the realm of possibility, of escape from the routine and regimentation of quotidian affairs.

We also discern our obsession with measuring success in quantitative terms: How large was the crowd? How many homes were tuned in to the telecast? How much money did the game generate for the NCAA itself as well as for its institutions and its causes? What was the financial impact on the host city? Not only do we measure success in such popular and economic ways, we also calculate the game, like life, in terms of time: The game is played against the clock. The Final Four comes at the end of the collegiate basketball season, at the end of winter (which often is imagined as the season of death), and for many of the players at the end of their career. We measure a shot's importance by how much time is left in the game, as with Lorenzo Charles's short buzzer beater to clinch the victory for North Carolina State over Houston in 1983.

The self-disclosure rendered by the Final Four also suggests that we still manifest characteristics of the monotheistic traditions that have formed and informed our heritage. For we yearn to identify with certainty who is at the top, desiring to revere a single team rather than celebrating of an equal group of champions. Although we remember some of the teams that were defeated along the way to the Final Four, we do not honor them as highest champions. Would we be so obsessed with identifying a single champion if the roots of our culture were pluralistically based rather than monotheistically based? Although the question is rhetorical and speculative, it is self-revealing, for it wonders about the ways that monotheistic roots of our culture affect the popular secular expressions and manifestations of contemporary American culture.

The format of the Final Four also reveals our delight in a capitalistic sort of competition. It assumes and plays out the myth of the survival of fittest. Even when teams have been struck down with season-ending injuries to their starters, like Kansas during 1988, the team that has survived has been the one that adapted to the constraints of the situation and overcome potential adversity. In addition, the competitive format of the tournament means that the national champion is determined on the court, not in the popularity polls of press writers who might never have played the game. By having the champion determined in an elimination tournament, we can know with certainty who the champion—the surviving conqueror—is, not necessarily (as the defeated hopefuls and favorites might argue) who the best team is.

Finally, we also sanction our fascination for the tournament with a democratic model of establishing initial equality, that the oppressed or neglected team might make it all the way to the top. The initial equality of the teams is marked by their amateur character and the single elimination format of the tournament. No professional player can rescue or sink a team; and every team faces the equal threat of elimination after a single defeat. Because of its amateur status, the tournament and its championship are not threatened by the personal greed of players seeking salary renegotiation or by the collective action of players striking for increased benefits. It is precisely the amateur character that, according to Skip Bayless, generates the religious fervor of the fans. Why has the Final Four become such a religious event? Bayless suggests: "Because it's divine madness. Perfect imperfection. We've fallen head over Air Jordans for the NCAA's [tournament] because every team *does not* start five first-round draft choices and every game is *not* artfully played and every favorite *does not* have a fair chance to prove its superiority" by making the championship the best two out of three, or four out of seven.[12] The amateur character of the tournament increases our vicarious identification with the players and their performances: By not being in the "other" category of the professional, they more nearly represent us as amateurs, and consequently, they elicit fanaticism from us.

Conclusion

In the end, as with the final score of the championship game, what greater tribute can we pay to the Final Four than to play with it—to dribble it and try to sink a rhetorical (if not analytical) sky hook—while trying to appraise its significance not only for the college basketball fan and it players but also for the culture as a whole?

Now having celebrated the golden anniversary of the NCAA Basketball Championships, we can see how the evolution of the championship series has become so important that we can fairly say that the Final Four is a Final Judgment. By it we judge ourselves, while thinking that the players and coaches themselves are the ones under scrutiny; and it is final, not in the sense of coming at the end of time but in the sense of disclosing more nearly fully who we really are. Perhaps, like the Final Judgment anticipated by millenarian religions, it does not separate the sheep from the goats. But at least it allows the Orangemen and the Hoosiers, the Wildcats and the Sooners, or perhaps some year the Blue Devils and the Crusaders to vie for the preferred place at the right hand, not of God, but of the president.

---

[1] Skip Bayless, "Me, I'd Watch the Pros," *American Way* 21/6 (March 15, 1988): 10.

[2] Michael Novak, *The Joy of Sports: End Zones, Bases, Baskets, Balls, and the Consecration of the American Spirit* (New York: Basic Books, Inc., Publishers, 1976) 101.

[3] "Basketball Play-off Was Launched in a Meeting on a Chicago Rooftop," *NCAA News* 25/7, February 17, 1988, 3.

[4] "Basketball Play-off Was Launched in a Meeting on a Chicago Rooftop," 1, 3.

[5] Bayless, "Me, I'd Watch the Pros," 8.

[6] "Record $79 Million Operating Budget Approved," *NCAA News* 24/29, August 19, 1987, 1-2. Cf. "Tournament Revenue Exceeds Estimate," *NCAA News* 25/26, July 6, 1988, 3.

[7] "A Couple of 'Long-shots' Connect for Berths in Final Four," *NCAA News* 24/13, March 25, 1987, 1.

[8] "Ticket Procedures for '89 Tournament Outlined," *NCAA News* 25/9, March 2, 1988, 1, 3.

[9] "Kansas City Planning Special Salute to Final Four's 50th Anniversary," *NCAA News* 25/8, February 24, 1988, 1, 3.

[10] Robyn Norwood,"Eight Is Enough? UTEP Coach Haskins Almost Runs Out of Players in 27th Season," *Los Angeles Times*, March 18, 1988, III:1, 7.

[11] "Great Players of the 1950s Focused Attention on Final Four," *NCAA News* 25/10, March 9, 1988, 1, 3.

[12] Bayless, "Me, I'd Watch the Pros," 10.

HOCKEY AND WRESTLING

A PUCKISH REFLECTION ON RELIGION IN CANADA

Tom Faulkner

…don't the playoff rites each Spring rouse the only genuine
religious fervor felt by the majority of Canadians? What else
attracts such passionate devotion, adoration, yes, even worship, from so many otherwise unexcitable Canadians? …[It's]
the nearest thing to extant religious fanaticism in the country
today.[1]

Canadian sports writers may be forgiven a measure of hyperbole
during the Stanley Cup Season, but what if there were a nugget of truth in
what Moritsugu was saying? What if being a hockey fan or player is a way
of being religious?

I have set out to raise this apparently frivolous question as a serious student of religion for four reasons. First, I am from time to time
swept away by the experience of being actively engaged in the game of
hockey, primarily as a fan, and I should like to make sense of that "ecstasy"
in a reflective way. I feel the same teasing urge to probe further that drove
Al Purdy to poetic reflection on the game:

I've seen the aching glory of a resurrection
in their eyes
if they score
but crucifixion's agony to lose—the game?[2]

Second, I am intrigued by the close ties that exist between
churches and ice hockey in many parts of Canada, and the explicit claim
made by some church leaders that ice hockey is a suitable means to achieve
the ends sought in Christian education.[3] Third, I find here an opportunity

to make use of the fascinating but generally unapplied sociological model for religion presented by Thomas Luckmann in *The Invisible Religion.*[4] Does it shed light on the human phenomenon of ice hockey? I think that it does. I hasten to add that I think it foolish to regard Luckmann's definition of religion as comprehensive. It is, in fact, what I would call a "first-level" definition only, but it is adequate to my present task.

Finally, I find that raising this apparently frivolous but ultimately serious question about hockey fans and players is a useful way to introduce college students to the study of religion. They commonly arrive in the classroom with the conviction that religion is what happens in churches and synagogues. I find this to be an inadequate starting point, and have found that beginning students become critical of it when invited to apply Luckmann's model to the ice hockey phenomenon in Canada.

Luckmann's powerful argument for understanding religion to be what humans do when they are being human[5] has been criticized by his sometime collaborator Peter Berger for not permitting distinctions between different ways of being human. Berger accepts Luckmann's analysis, but reserves the label "religious" for the modes of self-transcendence (the human quality par excellence) that have to do with the "sacred," as understood by Rudolph Otto and Mircea Eliade.[6] Berger's point is well taken, but I find it a handicap in dealing with beginning students. Most of them resist the conception of the sacred which embraces not only a *mysterium fascinans*, but also a *mysterium tremendum*. Not only do they tend to suppose that religion is done in temples, but they also tend to feel relief that religion has long since progressed beyond the day when religious persons encountered the holy and found it to be "awful."

I am happy to report that students who have been jolted out of the first preconception by an invitation to see hockey play and fandom as a way of being religious soon develop the same yearning that characterizes Peter Berger. They grant that the characteristically human drive for self-transcendence is an essential element in our understanding of the category "religious," but want to know how one is to differentiate between one way of achieving self-transcendence and another. At this point I find students much more open to consideration of the "sacred" as it is generally understood by historians of religion, than they were when they first arrived in the classroom.

I suggest, then, that Luckmann's model of religion is a useful heuristic device in the general study of religion, as well as a helpful tool for reflection upon the experience of Canadian hockey fans and players. Let us test the latter claim by first outlining the pertinent aspects of Luckmann's model, and then using it to say something about how hockey fans and players are religious.

Luckmann's model of religion presupposes the sociology of knowledge described in *The Social Construction of Reality*, jointly authored by him and Peter Berger in 1966.[7] "Reality" is understood to be "…a quality pertaining to phenomena that we recognize as independent of our own volition."[8] Yet it is, they argue, a "social construct," the product of a dialectical and historical progress in which human beings both create their reality and are created by it.[9]

There are many different ways by which this process occurs, by means of which the person finds objective and moral meaning in her experience. But there is one thing which knits it all together—the "symbolic universe," which is "conceived of as the matrix of all socially objectivated and subjectively real meanings. The entire historic society and the entire biography of the individual are seen as events taking place *within* this universe."[10] I like this notion of a "matrix of meaning." It suggests an organic system that is not important in itself, but important insofar as it is the structure within which the person apprehends and acts and develops. The matrix is, like the original Latin, a "womb" whose significance is revealed in the human life that grows within it.

As the ultimate bestower of all meanings, the symbolic universe is the means by which the world or cosmos is created, and by which the individual achieves a biography. Day-to-day experience is integrated within it, and marginal situations (of which death is the most terrifying) are legitimated.[11] Thomas Luckmann returns to this notion of a "symbolic universe" in the *Invisible Religion*,[12] noting that it is by means of a socially-constructed symbolic universe that the individual organism transcends its biological nature, becoming a Self with a biography and a conscience. This process of self-transcendence is, he argues, what makes us human, yet it is also true that that which transcends is religious. Therefore at its most basic level to be human is to be religious.[13]

Two matters are worth remarking in an aside at this point. The first is that although Luckmann is a sociologist, his primary interest in this model of religion is not society (as it is for Durkheim) but the Self. The second is that Luckmann is arguing that the one feature that all religions share in common is the human drive for self-transcendence. I do not infer from this that he regards self-transcendence as the only essential characteristic of any one religion. Luckmann presents what I take to be a "first-level" definition of religion without precluding more complex, and hence more satisfactory, definitions.

Luckmann presses his point by arguing that the world that takes shape as the person lives out his life within a symbolic universe reveals an "inner hierarchy of significance." At the lowest level, one finds the typifications that are so routine as to pose no problem: for example, grass is green. At the next level are typifications that do suggest a need for some reflection: grass requires watering in order to thrive. At a higher level still appear typifications of a much more general nature which not only require reflection but may be problematic: a good farmer cares for his grass. Finally there are typifications at a superordinated level of interpretation that are massively problematic, widely applicable, and far from concrete—the grass belongs to the people, all flesh is grass.[14] Because Luckmann finds a hierarchy of significance moving from a concrete, everyday level of reality to a distinct level of reality in which ultimate significance is located, he feels justified in speaking not simply of the creation of a "world" but of the creation of a "sacred cosmos"[15]—plainly intending to exploit the understanding that the "sacred" is "something more" or "something different," beyond the everyday.

Having described the process of becoming human as "religious," and the world that transcends the everyday as a "sacred cosmos," Luckmann argues that as a human society becomes more complex, there tends to develop a specific institution or institutions whose primary function is to maintain the sacred cosmos.[16] In the absence of a label in Luckmann's text, I propose to call this institution an *ecclesia*, and note that Luckmann assigns to it four characteristics: It is

> characterized by standardization of the sacred cosmos in a well-defined doctrine, differentiation of full-time religious roles, transfer of sanctions enforcing doctrinal and ritual conformity to special agencies and the emergence of organizations of the "ecclesiastic" type.[17]

In short, an *ecclesia* has its own doctrine, its own priesthood, its own judicial system, and is "ecclesiastic." For the sake of clarity I am inclined to invest this term with perhaps more meaning than Luckmann does. Luckmann understands it to refer to the replacement of informal institutional structures realized in lay people and charismatic leaders by more formal structures realized in a priesthood—a fourth characteristic that I believe adds little to the second that he has proposed. I am inclined to stress a notion implicit in Joachim Wach's original use of the term "ecclesiastic" and rooted in the Greek word "*ekkletos*": that is, the notion that the *ecclesia* is a body of people who are "called out," set over against the rest of the world.[18]

The final touch to this sociological model of religion is Luckmann's observation that in a modern, highly complex society, the person has available to her not only one but several symbolic universes, each providing a sacred cosmos sustained by its own *ecclesia*. Typically the person moves from one to the other, donning and abandoning new roles as required:[19] for example, she may move from the business world to the academic world to the sports world to the world of the church. In the face of such a development the person does not have available to her one sacred cosmos which convincingly superordinates all reality. In order to tie together her experience, she must cobble together her own religion, constructing it from material borrowed from her encounter as a sort of consumer with the different sacred cosmoses made available to her by the competing *ecclesiae* of her society. Of course she has no need to do this when she stands within the frame of any given *ecclesia*, but what is she to do when she steps outside that frame? She must construct her own "invisible religion," and the primary context for this distinctively modern enterprise is the nuclear family.[20]

How does Luckmann's model for religion apply to ice hockey? We may begin by arguing that there is indeed a symbolic universe that characterizes hockey. That we may do so is not surprising, given the widely accepted insights into the nature of games in general already suggested by those philosophers who have shown that games characteristically have their own "world," distinct from the rest of human reality.[21]

At the lowest level, hockey is typified by tangible things (skates, ice rinks, a puck) and less tangible but still undisputed qualities. It is incredibly fast (pucks travel at up to 125 miles per hour, lines must be changed every two minutes or less) and rule changes have tended to enhance the game's swiftness. It is colorful, strenuous, and dangerous. These last qualities have been amplified by the technology of television, but even before the camera's eye was able to bring the game close to the spectator, there were features of hockey which served to make the spectator unusually aware of hockey's peculiar qualities. The action is continuous and tends to involve two or three players at a time, not entire teams, thus inviting constant and focused attention. The game of hockey tends to place the spectator physically closer to the action than does any other popular sport, particularly in small municipal or school rinks.

Continuing at this first level of the hockey world we note that, like other games, hockey is characterized by a competitive spirit, by fun, and by graceful physical activity. But when one reflects upon other qualities of the hockey world, one finds that they are problematic in varying degrees.

For example, all games are competitive, but hockey in Canada has tended to go further than most games; winning is valued more highly than is the graceful execution of a play. Players report their frustration with fans who cheer good offensive plays but ignore graceful defensive maneuvers,[22] but the players themselves tend to place scoring ahead of grace of sportsmanship. On one occasion a sportswriter attempted to cheer a defeated Rocket Richard by quoting the founder of the modern Olympics, Baron de Coubertin—"It's not who wins but how you play the game." The Rocket's glum but considered reply was, "That Frenchman sounds like a born loser!"[23]

The speed and continuous action of hockey favor tactics that are really trained reflexes, not thoughtful responses to situations. Doug Harvey, one of the great professional players, was generally regarded by fans as "lazy" precisely because his peculiar style of play was more reflective than reflexive.[24] But there are other consequences of speed and continuous action. Some social scientists have argued convincingly that aggressive action is drastically increased in situations that produce anxiety but permit little or no time for rational consideration before a response is demanded.[25] The hockey world offers solid evidence in support of this hypothesis, for it is characterized by an extraordinarily high degree of aggressive behavior.

Some have suggested that hockey tends to attract violent, aggressive men, particularly from the ranks of lower class society where open aggressivity is valued more than at higher levels of social class. The only careful empirical study that I have encountered which deals with this issue suggests that aggressive behavior is bred within the hockey world, not introduced from outside. Indeed players having a higher socioeconomic status tend to be more aggressive and assaultive than do those from the lower end of the socioeconomic order.[26]

An increasingly problematic typification of the hockey cosmos is its masculinity. Recent changes have created women's hockey leagues at the Canadian college level with formal NHL sanctions, but the sport is still overwhelmingly male. Women make their appearance only as wives of professional players (during period breaks on television or on special cere-monial occasions) or as mothers of adolescent players. Tatum O'Neal may pitch for the "Bad News Bears," but not even superior playing ability could qualify Abby Hoffman as a hockey player in St. Catherine's.[27]

Problematic in a different way is the manner in which hockey sometimes appears to be an individual's sport, and sometimes a team sport. The person who lives out his life within this matrix of meaning commonly understands it to be both. Related to the "team" dimension is the fact that one finds new, unique social bonds developing within the hockey world which ignore or even contradict one's customary social patterns.

I find that in practice it is difficult to distinguish between Luckmann's second and third levels of significance in the world of mean-ing that defines hockey, but there is clearly a hierarchy of some sort here. It is also apparent that there is a cluster of values which give superordinating meaning to the entire hockey cosmos. Among these I should note the widespread conviction that in the hockey cosmos one is Canadian, one is manly (a quality which goes beyond sheer masculinity), and that one is excellent (by which I mean something that has more to do with winning than with the ancient Greek notion of *arete*).

To list these qualities is merely to remind the reader of what he already knows about ice hockey in Canada. But how did these particular features of the game develop? In some measure they are the results of the physical features of the game—of its technology and of its participants. But shaping and sustaining this particular symbolic universe is an *ecclesia*, of which the widely ramifying structure of the National Hockey League is a central but not exclusive component.

First of all, there is a system of doctrine which defines the hockey world. Some of it takes the obvious form of legislated regulations, codified in the NHL. But these formal rules pertain in effect only to the first level of hockey's symbolic universe rule book. There are many other less formal but nonetheless effective sources of doctrine which are available to fans and players, and which relate to higher levels of typification. These include popular books about hockey, the ritual pep talks before and during games, special team rules laid down by coaches and managers, stories and anec-dotes which circulate among players and fans, commentary and interviews in the news media.

Consider for example the typification that, as a competitive sport, hockey places a high premium on winning. Popular sports writer Trent Frayne once wrote a book entitled, *It's Easy: All You Have to Do Is Win*, and introduced it with an account of the Montreal Canadiens refusing to shake hands with the Detroit Red Wings when the Wings won the Stanley Cup in 1945. "The only thing that really matters in professional hockey (or amateur, too, if you really think about it)—is who won—or else, as some-one long ago observed, they wouldn't bother keeping score."[28] Stories like the one about Rocket Richard recounted above make the rounds, and the principal trophy of professional hockey is the Stanley Cup—not awarded for overall excellence, but for most games won in a challenge match at the end of the season. In the dressing room of the Toronto Maple Leafs hangs the motto, "Defeat does not rest lightly on their shoulders."[29] Following the 1976 Stanley Cup series the warmest comment that the announcers could find to say about the hapless Philadelphia Flyers defeated in four games straight was, "It's no shame to lose to a club like this year's Canadiens."

The notion that both the team and the individual are to be prized is reflected in the array of trophies for outstanding achievements by both, and by the custom of naming "three stars" immediately upon the announcement of a team victory. When things are going well, team members being interviewed by the media will single out one or two "spark plugs" who have stimulated a team success, and they in turn will praise a team effort that made their achievement possible. Conversely, a team without a few outstanding individuals is considered dull, while an individual like Greg Neeld who plays to the grandstand instead of with his team is bitterly resented by his mates.[30] The same holds true, I have found, at the level of amateur hockey for boys.

The "team" typification extends beyond the team proper. In any Canadian bar during a televised game, one sees perfect strangers intensely bound together in support of one side—and occasionally willing to assault someone who is cheering too loudly for the other side.[31] Interestingly hockey appears to engage its fans more closely with player action than do other sports where spectator violence is common. In hockey, spectator brawls are most often touched off by player brawls.[32] In any case, solidarity with the team is both a fact and a goal. Friends of Conn Smythe were convinced that he believed that universal support from Toronto fans would in some magical way guarantee a Leaf victory.[33]

The notion that hockey is Canadian is sustained in the television show title, *Hockey Night in Canada*—a twenty-three-year-old institution which today attracts four million viewers to regular NHL games alone, and which remains in the familiar hands of the Hewitt dynasty which began in radio in 1922. It is supported by the government-sponsored Hockey Canada, described as "our game" even by critical writers like Bruce Kidd and Bob Bossin who fear that it is being lost to Canadians, and assumed by the NHL whenever the matter does not jeopardize gate receipts.

In fact, hockey has often been touted as *the* Canadian institution, one that bridges the traditional gulf between English and French in the country.[34] This was more true in the past than in the present. During the 1930s, for example, French Canadian fans rallied fanatically around German Canadian Howie Morenz playing for an English Canadian-owned team that trained and played in English only: the Montreal Canadiens.[35] Those sentiments have altered recently: I watched the Team Canada games in 1972 with both English Canadian and French Canadian audiences, and found the former to be uncritically enthusiastic over Team Canada, while the latter were enthusiastically critical.

One recalls that at the time the Canadiens were in practice a unilingual club, while *francophone* WHA clubs like the Québec Nordiques were ruled ineligible for Team Canada. Since then the Canadiens have acquired their first fluently bilingual coach, Scotty Bowman, who appears regularly in the *francophone* media, but I suspect that there is still a basic trend among French Canadians to see hockey as *canadien* rather than *canadien*/Canadian, let alone Canadian.

The typification that hockey is masculine may be under fire at the rule book level, as women press for their own leagues and, less often, for admission to male leagues. But at the level of informal doctrine, hockey's masculinity is massively and solidly sustained. "Hockey," Gordie Howe declares flatly, "is a man's game."[36] Top professional players trade upon their unambiguously masculine image by endorsing commercial products which marketing experts feel need to be identified with masculinity. I have four nephews who are outstanding amateur hockey players; but my two nieces, who have tried and enjoyed hockey, must accept that they will be figure skaters instead.

Finally we may consider a typification which is implicitly tied to masculinity in hockey: violence and aggressivity, qualities which are virtually equated. I note in particular that the only NHL trophy that bears a woman's name is the Lady Byng—for gentlemanly conduct. Almost synonymous in hockey folklore with Conn Smythe's name is his adage (borrowed, I think, from Leo Dandurand who was fond of it in the 1920s): "If you can't beat them outside in the alley, you can't beat them inside on the ice."[37] One wonders why he bothered to draw a distinction between alley and ice. Bobby Hull has certainly found no need to do so. "Hockey is no sport for cowards, aggression pays off, and not only in games won. The aggressive player not only makes a big contribution to the spectacle, but he is also less liable to be hurt…."[38] Punch Imlach's autobiography bears the self-explanatory title, *Hockey Is a Battle*,[39] and Toe Blake once incurred a $2000 fine for assaulting a referee solely in order to give his Canadiens a concrete demonstration of what the coach meant by calling for aggressive play.[40] But this commitment to violent aggressivity is not confined to professional adult levels alone. Many parents urge their offspring to "hit 'em" in the amateur rinks, often to the despair of less sanguinary coaches. Still it would be difficult to outdo the Peewee coach who addressed his young charges thus:

> If there is any blood on any sweaters it's going to be on their sweaters—not ours…
>
> I want you guys to hit these bums so hard, they will be scared to come back in the rink.[41]

Some have charged that there has been a marked increase in assaultive behavior at hockey matches since World War II,[42] but I doubt that we can muster anything beyond impressionistic evidence for this claim. Surely the record of the famous Ottawa Silver Seven at the turn of the century, and that of the early years of the NHL, bear comparison with post-war bloodbaths on ice.[43] The only assessment that might lay claim to statistical validity is a recent Toronto medical survey which reports that as of 1973 hockey produces more injuries among young Canadians than do baseball, football, and soccer combined. The doctors are convinced that high-sticking habits (nominally illegal) are a major factor in this increase.[44]

That this strong commitment to violence in hockey is in some way peculiar to the Canadian scene is brought home whenever an international match occurs. Europeans charge Canadians with perverting the sport with excessive and even useless body contact, while Canadians take comfort in the fact that the Russians may be good at passing the puck around but "can't take it in the corners."

We may conclude this survey of hockey doctrine by noting that all of the typifications that comprise the matrix of meaning within which Canadians practice and enjoy hockey are understood to stand in some superordinating way to the entire reality of the player or fan. Consider the point made by Bob Pulford, a spokesman for the *ecclesia*: " My story is this: That a Canadian kid who can play this game well, these days, is the luckiest kid in the world. I mean it. There is no limit to how far he can go. The opportunities are tremendous."[45] One finds it legislated directly into the constitution of the Metropolitan Toronto Hockey League that the league aims generally to build "good character and citizenship."[46] It is symbolically implied by the presence of the Hockey Hall of Fame at the geographic center of the Canadian National Exhibition in Toronto. (I leave aside the question whether Toronto is the symbolic center of Canada.)

The second characteristic of an *ecclesia* is differentiation of full-time religious roles. Clearly hockey has come a long way since the first casual matches at Kingston in the mid-nineteenth century. Referees and coaches were made official in the 1880s, and professional hockey made its appearance among Ontario mining towns at the turn of the century.[47] Today there are not only two major professional leagues, but a vast network of professional and amateur leagues, most of them knit together under the aegis of the NHL and embracing almost half a million Canadian males from six years to aging adulthood. It is worth stressing that the direction of this network is firmly in the hands of full-time professionals, and that almost all of the published commentary is provided by professional specialists.

The hockey priesthood is as much given to vestments as any other. I refer not simply to on-ice uniforms, but note the widespread use of jackets and blazers off the ice, each emblazoned with the team's badge and occasionally with the individual's office. Gordie Howe's owner reported to his biographer that he refused to consider himself a genuine Red Wing until he had been issued with his red blazer.[48]

One might quibble that not all coaches and players are full-time, but surely such an objection falls to the ground in the face of the fact that even young amateurs play four to six hours per week in a formal setting, and wear their identifying clothing everywhere. The non-participant may see them as empty signs at best and silly costumes at worst, but those who wear them invest them with tremendous significance.

The development in hockey of an autonomous disciplinary system provides perhaps the most striking evidence of the existence here of a genuine *ecclesia*. Not only are there formal rules which are enforced by three officials in every game, but each team at the professional levels is provided with an informal set of enforcers commonly referred to as "policemen." These individuals are charged with the task of intimidating opposing players, delivering hard checks, and ensuring that the aggressive stance of their own team is maintained. These men are not expected to produce goals, but to regulate the standard of aggressiveness that has come to be associated with Canadian hockey. They are aided and abetted by their coaches, occasionally with verbal encouragement, and sometimes with fines for players who have declined to behave in a satisfactorily aggressive fashion. In 1969, for example, owner Jack Kent Cooke fined each member of the Los Angeles Kings one hundred dollars for *not* disputing a referee's call.[49]

When one considers the full disciplinary system in hockey (officials, "policemen," coaches) one sees that it relates effectively and flexibly to every point of the symbolic universe that makes possible the hockey world. This disciplinary system is also, so far, completely autonomous from the other organs of justice in Canadian society. The first court case involving assault charges in a Canadian NHL game occurred in 1970. Ted Green of the Boston Bruins was charged because of his participation in a brawl during a game. The judge dismissed the case, commenting, "Given the permissiveness of the game, I find it difficult to envisage circumstances whereof a charge of common assault…could easily stand."[50]

During the recent past, several charges of assault have been laid against hockey players and fans in criminal courts in the United States and Canada. So far, all have been dismissed on the grounds that the hockey leagues should discipline their own offenders. An American magistrate has gratuitously suggested that his Canadian colleagues follow his lead on this matter, and the leagues appear to agree with his position. When the members of the WHA Québec Nordiques demanded *en masse* the punishment of a rival team member who had assaulted one of their own, they made it clear that they did not want outside law courts to interfere. When the NHL Board of Governors finally responded to increased public criticism of hockey violence in 1976, the response was a word of caution to each team at the end of the Stanley Cup playoffs, coupled with the assurance that the NHL could deal with any such problems without outside help.

Finally we consider the awareness of hockey fans and players that they are members of an "*ecclesia*," that in some radical sense they are "called out" of the everyday human world. Some hint of this is given in the preceding comments on the disciplinary autonomy of hockey, but still more is provided by the customary behavior of players and fans. Men who play hockey behave in ways that would be unthinkable to them outside of the game: I refer here not only to assaultive behavior but also to affectionate "touching" practices such as hugging and butt-slapping, or superstitious gestures such as wearing the same unlaundered article of clothing for years on end,[51] and tapping the goalie's pads before play starts. Among spectators the clearest demonstration of "ecclesiastic" behavior should scarcely require documentation to Canadians. The most placid, humane person is transformed into a raging, imprecating enthusiast simply by placing her in an arena or before a television set. One might almost say that spectators become, not merely ecclesiastic ("called out of the world") but ecstatic ("standing outside oneself"), were it not for the fact that the furious hockey fan is not "outside" her proper *persona* but firmly centered in it.

I do not think that we need to dwell upon the way in which hockey's symbolic universe serves to integrate the common, everyday experience of players and fans during those times when they are players and fans. Surely it is obvious that participants refer, consciously and otherwise, to symbols, myths, models, customs, rituals, doctrines, etc., that are manifestly part of hockey while they live out their roles as players and fans. But what about the legitimation of crises, of marginal situations? Here I propose to consider three paradigmatic crisis situations: a crippling injury, a death, and a mass riot. In each case they were legitimated within the hockey world under the direction of the hockey *ecclesia*.

On December 12, 1934, during a Leaf game at Boston, one of the Bruin's toughest players, Eddie Shore, became enraged at what he felt were unfair calls by the referee, and delivered a hard check which threw Leaf player Ace Bailey high into the air. Bailey was knocked out, and was feared to be dying, but he recovered consciousness briefly in the dressing room where his first words were, "Put me back in the game! They need me!" Bailey underwent a series of dangerous operations in the days that followed, while other players and sports commentators reported his precarious condition to fans everywhere hour by hour. Two months later it was apparent that Bailey would live, but never skate again, and the Leafs honored him by holding an Ace Bailey benefit night, the feature of which was a match between the Leafs and an All-Star team which included Eddie Shore on its roster.

Fifteen thousand fans attended and, as the two teams lined up in silence at the blue line, Bailey shuffled slowly out to the face-off circle. As he reached it, Eddie Shore broke from his place and skated to join him; the two men shook hands and clapped each other's shoulders, and the crowd broke into wild cheers. Shore, who personally collected more than 900 stitches during his career, played his usual rough game that night.[52]

The NHL did not find it necessary to deal with death on the ice until 1967. Bill Masterson, a twenty-nine-year-old center for the Minnesota North Stars, was given a clean check, but suffered a fatal concussion in falling to the ice. Masterson was not a remarkably distinguished player, but the accident shocked the league. Responding to the crisis sportswriters combined to establish the Bill Masterson Memorial Award for the player who most fitted the description of "unsung hero." They argued (and still do) that his death was not in vain but served as an object lesson in favor of protective headgear in hockey play.[53]

Brawls are a regular feature of hockey matches, but mass riots are rare. The worst occurred on St. Patrick's Day in 1955 after NHL President Clarence Campbell had awarded a season suspension to Rocket Richard for striking linesman Cliff Thompson during a game. When Campbell appeared late at the Montreal Forum to view the next game, he found the Canadiens losing 2-0 and the fans in a murderous mood. Several fans assaulted the league president, and for a few moments it appeared that his life was literally in danger. Happily a police tear gas bomb diverted the crowd from a rush at Campbell, and the forum emptied its fans out on to St. Catherine Street. The police failed completely in their efforts to prevent the mob from destroying store fronts and attacking bystanders, and the disturbance did not finally come to an end until Richard personally broadcast his request that the violence cease. In return he promised his following that the Canadiens would win the Stanley Cup next year.

On the day following the riot one unrepentant sportswriter described the man who had launched the first assault on Campbell as "the real star" of the game. The Canadiens who played to make good Richard's promise during the 1955-1956 season were (deservedly) voted the greatest team of all time by a poll of sportswriters in 1969.[54]

The evidence satisfies me that hockey may be understood in Luckmann's terms as a religion. There is a hockey world defined by a particular symbolic universe sustained by an *ecclesia*, and those who live within that world order their lives according to its meanings and standards. There remains the question, What happens when the individual steps outside the hockey world and seeks to construct his own "invisible religion"? Does he avail himself of any of the meanings made available by hockey?

We should not be surprised to find it so. If Luckmann is correct that the invisible religion is constructed primarily within the framework of the nuclear family, it is worth noting that enormous blocks of family time are hockey time. Not only do adolescent boys spend hours in formal play and practice, but their parents often spend equal amounts of time driving them to and from rinks and watching their games. The televised hockey game is, in some families, the only occasion for all members and generations of the family to gather for the pursuit of common enterprise. Hockey's matrix of meaning is certainly readily available to individuals anxious to cobble together their own invisible religion at home.

Let me suggest eight things that hockey makes available to Canadians engaged in constructing a private self, five of which are attributed to sport in general by psychiatrist Arnold Beisser in his book, *The Madness in Sports: Psychosocial Observations*,[55] but which are present in exemplary fashion in hockey.

First of all, it makes available a space and time in which certain actions may be performed which, though stimulated by our culture, are regarded as illegitimate. Men may embrace each other or indulge in what Al Purdy calls "butt-slapping camaraderie," and all people may indulge in loud, aggressive behavior. Second, it provides biographical continuity. How many other experiences can one enjoy at every stage of one's life? Third, it offers situations in which one may deal with problem situations which are susceptible of fairly clear and therefore satisfying resolution. This is particularly important for the adolescent who is socialized into generally accepted patterns of co-operation and competition, victory and defeat, in the hockey rink; but it is also significant for the adult who may seek without success situations from which she may derive the satisfaction of resolving a problematic issue.

Fourth, we may note that in modern Canadian society the formerly clear line differentiating work from play is being destroyed. Work is increasingly dissociated from its product; play is increasingly organized and disciplined. Canadians who actively play in organized hockey are integrated into a transitional institution where the work/play boundary effectively disappears. Fifth, in a society in which the gender distinctions of masculine and feminine are disappearing, hockey provides unambiguous models of masculinity (and femininity).[56]

I should add at least three other items to the list of ethical and biographical materials provided to Canadians by the hockey world. First, it offers color and effervescence to many whose lives are otherwise unenlivened. There is ample testimony in wartime accounts of the morale-boosting qualities of hockey to justify this claim. Second, hockey may serve as a counter to the alienation that many individuals experience in urbanized settings. One is a little less lonely in Toronto if one may cheer the Leafs. Related to this is the spill-over from hockey that not only reconciles one to one's spatial location but even builds a measure of positive pride in it. Parry Sound is a place to be valued in part because it is Bobby Orr's home town, and the town honors itself when it observes Bobby Orr Day.

Finally, hockey is indeed a "Canadian specific,"[57] the source of a sense that I as a Canadian am better than Europeans, though not so cultured.

There is considerable evidence here to support the view that when one becomes a hockey fan or player, one is doing more than "merely" taking up a game or an entertainment. There is a sense in which one is justified in speaking of hockey as a religion—that is, when one enters the hockey world, there is a tendency to treat its symbolic universe as ultimately meaningful so long as one is within that world. One may even borrow ethical and biographical material from it in order to construct one's own invisible religion. If this is indeed true, then the current debates over the recovery of hockey as a Canadian sport, and/or the moderation of violence in hockey, appear to be of greater significance than they do when hockey is regarded as a mere game. One wonders, for example, if the Attorney-General of Ontario is aware that he is leading an attack on what may literally be a sacred cow. Or, for that matter, we may wonder at the naivete of churches which assume that hockey is an innocent tool which may be safely integrated into their Christian education programs as just one more facet in their effort to provide suitable nurture for adolescents.

My own preference as a fan is for hockey to be a true game, not a religious activity radically autonomous from the rest of reality where ultimate answers to crises are provided by a hockey *ecclesia*. The first-level analysis offered here suggests that hockey is more than a game in Canada: it functions as a religion for many, and does so at the expense of its own playfulness.

[1] Frank Moritsugu, *Toronto Daily Star*, April 17, 1965.

[2] Alfred Purdy, *The Caribou Horses* (Toronto: McClelland & Stewart, 1965) 60.

[3] For example, see the comments by Peter Gordon White in *The Uninvited Church Observer* (February 15, 1969): 14-15.

[4] Thomas Luckmann, *The Invisible Religion: The Problem of Religion in Modern Society* (New York: Macmillan, 1967).

[5] Luckmann, *The Invisible Religion*, 49.

[6] Peter L. Berger, *The Sacred Canopy: Elements of a Sociological Theory of Religion* (Garden City NY: Doubleday Anchor Books, 1967) 176-77, 25, 190.

[7] Peter L. Berger and Thomas Luckmann, *The Social Construction of Reality: A Treatise in the Sociology of Knowledge* (Garden City NY: Doubleday Anchor Books, 1966).

[8] Berger and Luckmann, *The Social Construction of Reality*, 1.

[9] Berger and Luckmann, *The Social Construction of Reality*, 61, 89-90 , 152-53.

[10] Berger and Luckmann, *The Social Construction of Reality*, 96.

[11] Berger and Luckmann, *The Social Construction of Reality*, 96-104.

[12] Luckmann, *The Invisible Religion*, 43-48.

[13] Luckmann, *The Invisible Religion*, 48-49.

[14] Luckmann, *The Invisible Religion*, 58-59.

[15] Luckmann, *The Invisible Religion*, 58-59.

[16] Luckmann, *The Invisible Religion*, 62-63.

[17] Luckmann, *The Invisible Religion*, 66.

[18] In his note 28, Luckmann inaccurately refers the reader to Joachim Wach, *Sociology of Religion* (Chicago: University of Chicago Press, 1945), especially pp. 4, 5, for an account of the "'ecclesiastic' type" of organization. The proper reference is to pp. 141-45.

[19] Luckmann, *The Invisible Religion*, 80-85.

[20] Luckmann, *The Invisible Religion*, 101-106.

[21] See, for example, Johan Huizinga, *Homo Ludens: A Study of the Play Element in Culture* (Boston: Beacon Press, 1950); and Paul Weiss, *Sport: A Philosophic Inquiry* (Carbondale IL: Southern Illinois University Press, 1969).

[22] E.g., Bobby Hull, *Hockey Is My Game* (Don Mills, Ont.: Longmans, Canada, 1967) 96.

[23] Andy O'Brien, *Fire-Wagon Hockey* (Chicago: Follett, 1967) vi.

[24] Frank Selke with Gordon Green, *Behind the Cheering* (Toronto: McClelland and Stewart, 1962) 147.

[25] R. Denker, "Sport and Aggression," in *Sport in the Modern World: Chances and Problems*, ed. Ourmo Grupe (New York: Springer-Verlag, 1973) 382.

[26] Michael D. Smith, "Some Determinants of Assaultive Behavior in Hockey: A Theory and Causal Model." Paper presented at the Third International Symposium on the Sociology of Sport (Waterloo, Canada: August 1971).

[27] Bruce Kidd and John MacFarlane, *The Death of Hockey* (Toronto: New Press, 1972) 5-6.

[28] Trent Frayne, *It's Easy: All You Have To Do Is Win* (Don Mills, Ontario: Longmans Canada Ltd., 1968) introduction.

[29] G. E. Mortimore, *What's Happened to Hockey?* reprinted from *The Globe and Mail* (Toronto: 1963) 6.

[30] Margaret Drury Gane, "Out of His League," *Weekend Magazine* (February 28, 1976): 6.

[31] Hull, *Hockey Is My Game*, 127.

[32] Michael D. Smith, "Precipitants of Crowd Violence in Sport." Paper presented at the First Canadian Congress for the Multi-Disciplinary Study of Sport and Physical Activity (Montreal: October 1973) 10-11.

[33] Frayne, *It's Easy*, 144.

[34] E.g., Lloyd Finley, "Separatism Has No Chance against Peewees." *Toronto Telegram* (February 17, 1969).

[35] Z. Hollander and H. Bock, *The Complete Encyclopedia of Ice Hockey* (Englewood-Cliffs NJ: Prentice Hall, 1970) 152.

[36] Hollander and Bock, *Complete Encyclopedia of Ice Hockey*, 229.

[37] Frayne, *It's Easy*, 143. Cf. Hollander and Bock, *Complete Encyclopedia of Ice Hockey*, 165.

[38] Hull, *Hockey Is My Game*, 74.

[39] Punch Imlach, *Hockey Is a Battle* (Toronto: Macmillan Press, 1969).

[40] Hull, *Hockey Is My Game*, 166.

[41] Quoted by Dick Beddoes, *Globe and Mail,* November 18, 1970.

[42] E.g., Frayne, *It's Easy*, 53.

[43] Henry Roxborough, *The Stanley Cup Story* (Chicago: Follett Publishing Co., 1964) 26-35.

[44] Hospital for Sick Children (Toronto) Cross-Canada survey, reported in *The Catholic Register*, May 8, 1976.

[45] *Daily Star* (Toronto) December 2, 1970.

[46] Quoted by Jim Crear, "Leave the Hockey to the Kids," *Maple Leaf Garden Programme* (n.d.) 48. (Files of the Hockey Hall of Fame, Exhibition Park, Canada).

[47] See Nancy Howell and Maxwell L. Howell, *Sports and Games In Canadian Life: 1700 to the Present* (Toronto: Macmillan, 1969).

[48] Jim Vipond, *Gordie Howe: Number Nine* (Toronto: Ryerson Press, 1968) 32.

[49] Allen Camelli, *Great Moments in Pro Hockey* (New York: Bantam Books, 1971) 53.

[50] *Globe and Mail*, September 4, 1970.

[51] I refer particularly to Punch Imlach's bird-stained and battered fedora, but other examples might be given.

[52] Howard Liss, *Goal! Stanley Cup Playoffs* (New York: Delacorte Press, 1970) 72; Frank Selke with Gordon Green, *Behind the Cheering* (Toronto: McClelland and Stewart, 1972) 118; and Camelli, *Great Moments in Pro Hockey*, 80-83.

[53] Richard Beddoes, Stan Fischler, and Ira Gitler. *Hockey! The Story of the World's Fastest Sport* (New York: Macmillan, 1969) 99; Camelli, *Great Moments in Pro Hockey*, 21-23; and Liss, *Goal!*, 178.

[54] Hollander and Bock, *Complete Encyclopedia of Ice Hockey*, 230; Liss, *Goal!*, 139; Camelli, *Great Moments in Pro Hockey*, 70-72, 39; and Beddoes, *Fischler, Gitler, Hockey!*, 169-72.

[55] Arnold R. Beisser, *The Madness in Sports. Psychosocial Observations on Sports* (New York: Appleton-Century-Crofts, 1967).

[56] I personally should like to see more androgynous models made available to us. I see hockey as a decidedly reactionary, and hopefully atavistic, institution on this score.

[57] Purdy, "Hockey Players," 60.

MYTH AND RITUAL IN PROFESSIONAL WRESTLING

Charles S. Adams

Those who embark upon a discussion of what is known as professional wrestling should probably begin with two books: *Wrestling to Rasslin': Ancient Sport to American Spectacle* by Gerald Morton and George O'Brien,[1] and *Professional Wrestling: Sport and Spectacle*, by Sharon Mazer.[2] These works quite accurately outline the essential dynamics of this activity, clearly establishing professional wrestling's origins in and relationship to sport, its nature as business, and its links to theatrical traditions. Morton and O'Brien end their book with a brief discussion of wresting as ritual, with reference to the work of anthropologist Margaret Mead. My task in this essay is to expand upon that discussion.

I propose to take a little further the question of how to "read" professional wrestling, how to assess the aesthetics of the sport—that is, its shape and how that shape is to be understood and (loosely, at least) appreciated.[3] What I think needs to be expanded upon is the oft argued thesis that in professional wrestling the aesthetic conditions create meaning. Roland Barthes, in his significant essay on wrestling, likens it to theater:

> What the public wants is the image of passion, not passion itself. There is no more a problem of truth in wrestling than in the theater. In both, what is expected is the intelligible representation of moral situations which are usually private. This emptying out of interiority to the benefit of exterior signs, this exhaustion of the content by the form, is the very principle of triumphant classical art.[4]

Indeed, the structures of professional wrestling *are* the meaning in just this way (though I am in the uncomfortable position of placing World Wrestling Federation entrepreneur Vince McMahon and Sophocles in the same paragraph as a result), and those structures are generated by the fundamental mythic and ritual identity of the performance. The elements of professional wrestling that are metaphysical are the most significant aspects of the sport. The physical—the wrestling—is relatively insignificant in and of itself. In the ring (or, as announcers like to call it, the "squared circle"— which itself is a phrase waiting to be deconstructed) the competition between two athletes partakes of Barthes's interiority; furthermore, the real *agon* conflict, or athletic competition, has been washed out of contemporary wrestling where the outcome has been pre-determined by factors other than individual ability. The structure of the institution as a whole makes this quite clear.

Although much of the emphasis in the work (what work there is) on professional wrestling is concerned with its relationship to theatrical tradition (as with Barthes), what does that set of connections tell us about what we call "legitimate" sport? My subject really develops two foci: On the one hand we can see "sport" as theater—indeed, seeing both sport and theater as much the same thing; and on the other hand we can consider sport and theater as having an inherent connection in what we might call an origin in myth and ritual.

At this point the work of the historian of religion Mircea Eliade, whose work on myth and ritual has been applied profitably to football and baseball in other essays in this volume, provides the next proper stop in the construction of a theoretical matrix for understanding professional wrestling. Indeed, wrestling's conversion from "legitimate sport" to "event" has been made for reasons that Eliade would recognize and validate, and ones to which our remaining "legitimate" sports may wish to pay attention. After all, wrestling is older than the other legitimate sports. Perhaps it represents some sort of quite troubling future.

In his work *Cosmos and History: The Myth of the Eternal Return*, Eliade lays out what he calls the "problem" of the study of the myth and ritual of the archaic world:

> ...the metaphysical concepts of the archaic world were not always formulated in theoretical language; but the symbol, the myth, the rite, express, on different planes and through the means proper to them, a complex system of coherent

affirmations about the ultimate reality of things, a system that can be regarded as constituting a metaphysics.[5]

Eliade goes on to argue that these ancient symbols, rituals, and rites can be translated into our language if we can, as he says, "penetrate the authentic meaning of an archaic myth or symbol."[6] He argues that quite often the term that we would use to describe a metaphysical concept in other cultures and times is not present in that reality. However, the activity of ritual may well describe a concept that we could well recognize because symbols and myths are expressive of activities and beliefs that are larger than their surface content. Finally, Eliade argues that the "conscious repetition" of acts or "gestures"—acts and gestures supposedly having their origins in those of the gods—reveals ontology or being itself, connecting humans with the gods in the human's perception of reality. Eliade recognizes his relationship to Jungian thought in all of this, although he is very careful to say that when he speaks of such things as "archetypes" that he is using a pre-Jungian definition of the term that relieves the concept of some of the depth psychology burden that Jung asks it to carry.

What does this "conscious repetition" of acts and gestures have to do with professional wrestling? In most cultures, the sport of wrestling appears in their earliest moments, and it is usually connected even then to ritual. Most certainly, wrestling is present in our culture as well, though it no longer dominates as the sport of cultural choice; but its continued presence makes a case that it still retains ancient meanings. In addition, however, the sport of professional wrestling, in its current configuration, may represent the natural inclination of all sport, as it moves from the primitive origins in battle to pure ritual enactment of those battles. Also, as it becomes more ritually and symbolically pure or removed from its agonistic challenge and distanced from corporeal conflict, the meaning we can attach to it becomes more varied in its possibility, perhaps more disturbing in its implications. As Eliade says, the vocabulary—the symbols—must be inhabited to be understood. In the case of professional wrestling this is not very difficult. What is more difficult is to understand why it works, and if it does work, what its effect in culture might be.

As a case for study, for constructing such a reading, one of the ritual structures on the present scene in professional wrestling today is the World Wrestling Federation (WWF). The WWF is one of what the wrestling cult magazines call the "big two," the other being World Championship Wrestling (WCW), founded by Ted Turner to compete with the WWF for the lucrative television audience that this sport now attracts. The WWF proprietor is Vince McMahon, Jr., who, it is generally agreed, has shown himself to be a brilliant marketer of this sport—almost single-handedly resuscitating it as a national entertainment in the early 1980s. The WWF began as a regional organization, but it has now developed into an international concern through clever use of cable television and advanced marketing techniques—and shares in it can be bought in the stock market. Both the WWF and WCW maintain stables of traveling performers, and they stage wrestling shows throughout the United States and indeed around the world.

The shows are clearly quite lucrative, frequent, and well attended (though on occasion we hear reports suggesting that there may be problems on the horizon with significantly lowered attendance for some events, particularly in the case of the WCW). The shows are supported by television, generally on cable television, but increasingly over the air as well. The WWF and the WCW sponsor a number of programs, creating wrestling events which can be seen virtually every day of the week—and they are not short by television standards, often extending to two hours. In addition, at regular times during the year, both organizations create large pay-per-view events, the most famous of which is the WWF's "Wrestlemania."

The television product is clearly used to market the live arena events and the pay-per-view mega-events. As such, the programs can be viewed as kinds of "info-mercials" in which the entertainment is disguised advertising, and the advertising is for wrestling events and merchandise, with very few other products thrown in. This is not to say that the television programs do not have their own identity and importance. They are presented in a cyclical ritual structure, lasting roughly two months (a time that is shortening as more pay-per-views events are created), and connect the pay-per view events, the major markers of the year. It is in the television shows that story lines are established and in which conclusion is promised. The conclusions are always constructed as moral showdowns and, indeed, more or less resolved. These story lines are supported by a large number of wrestling magazines that are devoted to the sport as a whole. The WWF has its own in-house publications, but there are many others that keep what would seem to be a voracious reading public up to date on the happenings in *all* the federations, of which the WWF is only one.

In early April 1993, the Wrestlemania (from Caesar's palace in Las Vegas, a site that itself suggests classic challenges to religion and the manifestation of all sorts of moral choices) brought to a conclusion a number of stories that had begun roughly three months earlier. What is important to recognize is that in the telling of these stories, very little actual wrestling occurs. What does occur is used to reinforce statements made in the famous wrestling interviews. Major wrestling stars are only rarely allowed to compete with each other, and only when story lines are constructed to allow this to happen in an especially lucrative and dramatic way.

In the early 1993 series of matches, a cycle of story lines revealed fundamental structures at their most sophisticated, and most troubling. If we begin to inhabit the myth and the ritual enactment of the myth, as Eliade suggests we do, then, to echo him, we should ask what kind of "affirmations about the ultimate reality of things" appears? What is the metaphysics? Since the culture enacting this ritual is clearly that of the United States (setting aside the international ambitions of the wrestling organizations for a moment), then our answer should tell us something about ourselves. Although the WWF proprietors might not be altogether aware of how their structures reveal meaning, Eliade would say that if one is in the structure—particularly primitive structures—performing the ritual and enacting the myth, one would know exactly what the structure (or archetypal myth) is about, even if one does not articulate it in the ways a modern academician can understand. I am convinced this is the case in professional wrestling.

In the World Wrestling Federation, the dominant ritual activity is a reflection, perhaps a re-enforcement, of institutional racism in our culture. There are other complex themes that are addressed (sexism, jingoism, homophobia, for example), but the particular "affirmation" of institutional racism dominated the story lines of early 1993. The main story, then, began with the appearance in the WWF of a new wrestler, Yokozuna, advertised as a 505-pound Japanese sumo champion (actually, his "name" is the term for the highest rank in sumo). He was managed by Mr. Fuji, a former wrestler himself. Mr. Fuji was very nearly unique in professional wrestling in the sense that his character had always been that of an evil one, a dark force, or as the magazines often refer to it, a "rulebreaker" or "heel." Although the "wrestler" who had taken on the character of Yokozuna is actually from Samoa, ironically an American territory, it is crucial in the racial story line that he and his "manager" be Japanese.

Yokozuna began a reign of terror in the WWF, flattening every foe in his path. He wore sumo garb in the ring, and he was preceded by Mr. Fuji and two flower girls. Mr. Fuji carried and waved a large Japanese flag. In interviews, Mr. Fuji did virtually all the talking, as Yokozuna apparently knew no English. Responding to this terror, was Jim "Hacksaw" Duggan, who in a series of passionate speeches decried Yokozuna's appearance in the WWF and cited Yokozuna's contempt for Americans as requiring response. Duggan was known for his character as an all-American redneck who carried an American flag into the ring along with a section of two-by-four. To be brief, Duggan challenged Yokozuna to a match, vowing that he would at least knock Yokozuna off his feet for the first time ever; although this feat had been done already, it had been conveniently forgotten. The match took place, and Duggan succeeded, but in his joy he turned his back on Yokozuna. In a "sneak attack," which was thoroughly compared to Pearl Harbor in all the rhetoric that followed, Yokozuna blinded Duggan with ritual salt, which in sumo events is used for purification. With this profanation of the cleansing agent, Yokozuna proceeded to squash Duggan repeatedly underneath his massive bulk. Duggan was removed from the arena on a stretcher and supposedly sent into retirement. But that sort of premature delegation to retirement only sets up additional story lines for heroic return.

Yokozuna's dispatch of Duggan set up a world title match at the pay-per-view "Wrestlemania," which Yokozuna had previously qualified for by winning the previous big pay-per-view event, "The Royal Rumble." The reigning champion in early 1993, Bret "The Hitman" Hart, had been through many incarnations, but most recently he had been constituted as a good guy, a smaller man who won by the "excellence of execution" and "science," the latter an important wrestling term.[7] In the big "Wrestlemania" match on an early April Sunday in 1993, Yokozuna, benefited from a dastardly act by Mr. Fuji, who again threw ritual salt in the eyes of his opponent. (As a subtext, the use of sumo salt in WWF matches raises an interesting confrontation of ritual wrestling traditions.) To the consternation of a huge audience, Yokozuna gained the title from "the Hitman." He held it for two minutes as Mr. Fuji, gloating about his achievements began to taunt former WWF champion Hulk Hogan, the dominant personality in professional wrestling in the 1980s. Unwisely, Yokozuna offered to put the title up again on the spot. Hulk Hogan had fought a match earlier in the day in a triumphant return to the WWF following a "retirement" passed off as due to age and injury but really generated by accusations of cocaine and steroid abuse. Without Hulk Hogan's contributions to the ratings, ticket sales and marketing efforts had been in serious trouble. The Hulkster, as he was known to his fans, acquired the title in a matter of seconds, and left the ring to his theme song (the major wrestlers all have theme music), with the repeated refrain "I am a real American."

Clearly this confrontation was racist, or at least xenophobic, in its fundamental structure. The morality play that was performed in this enactment of the ritual appeals to belief structures that are apparently very powerful for its audience, which, I think, understands it or experiences it in terms consonant with Eliade's understanding. The other matches on the Wrestlemania bill, and others in the WWF played this out as well. Another featured match pitted "Razor Ramon" against Bob Backlund: Ramon, a huge man, was supposedly Cuban, although his "real" name is Scott Hall and he is a midwestern farm boy. Backlund was a former champion, an all-American Minnesotan. For this match, Ramon was portrayed as evil, and he spoke of himself as "oozing machismo," clearly a racist characterization. Another well known wrestler in the WWF at that time was Kamala the Ugandan Giant. He had been a "bad guy" until shortly before the spring Wrestlemania in 1993—that is, until he was rescued from his handlers by the Reverend Slick (a caricature of an African-American evangelical type), who became his new manager. For his WWF role, Kamala could not speak, except for uttering incoherent noises; he went barefoot, and he wore a loincloth. In preparation for the "Wrestlemania" card, Slick supposedly had been teaching him to say "I am a man," in a sad echo of Jesse Jackson. However, Kamala did not make the line-up for participants in "Wrestlemania '93."

The racist attitudes are evident throughout the WWF structure and among its participants. Other stereotypical wrestlers reinforce similar racist attitudes: Tatanka, presented as the "native American" wrestler, was given a shot at a minor title—the Intercontinental belt. He was a "good guy" whose character was structured with all of the attributes of the "good" Indian. Or Irwin R. Shyster, known as IRS, whose appearance was that of a glasses-wearing accountant, suggested a Jewish character. He was a terrible villain, threatening his victims with audits. The "good-guy" Latino wrestler was known as El Matador and wore a bull-fighter outfit: He lost often. Building on cultural stereotypes, nearly all the wrestlers establish a clear ethnic or racial identity at some point. Although the stereotypes were often recognized as such, the attitudes portrayed by the stereotypical characters were always in the process of being reinforced by the WWF events.

Several kinds of story lines, other than the racist one that can be identified in WWF, are regularly present, and at times they become quite powerful. They usually involve comic book figures like the Undertaker, who has miraculously become a hero—though he is a death figure, or the Giant Gonzales a nearly eight-foot-tall wrestler—a mutant of sort—who for the April 1993 Wrestlemania card, entered the WWF structure as a "bad guy." He and the Undertaker fought in an inconclusive battle of the titans. Most of the story lines that are not built around national or ethnic identity revolve around friendship and betrayal, and the morality plays that these narratives play out are as interesting as those of race I use as my primary example here.

The WWF may be successful because of its ability ritually to tap into the darker "myths" of American society. Yet the organization tries to pass itself off as progressive as well, when that makes good business sense; at the time of all the events I have mentioned the WWF also participated significantly in the Somalian relief fund of the Red Cross. This effort also has a ritual—in this case specifically legitimizing—element in it, one we can see throughout elements of our society which may look marginal in many respects.

The point is that the play's the thing. Taking the WWF "Wrestlemania" as a sample "sporting" event, we can conclude that often the "meaning" of the event is communicated through the story line that gets ritually enacted; and the story line often reflects the underlying values and problems of society more than it manifests the particular athletic prowess of a participating individual or team. In this play of professional wrestling, where we know that the outcome is now predetermined, where exteriority—or elements outside the "play," outside the individual partici- pant's determination—dominate any possible internal structures, we can see how far away we are from making cultural progress on social problems such as racism. As the WWF attempts to make money through its ritual enactment of cultural verities, cynically exploiting whatever is there, our culture's underlying racism is both revealed and reinforced and even depended upon. One feels certain that if the culture wished to express more positive elements, that these would be exploited too. I indicated ear- lier that one significant question an analysis of professional wrestling might generate is what it tells us about other sports. I propose a simple answer whose potential meaning I have already indicated: Wrestling may simply be at a more advanced stage in the process of codifying the ritual or mythic element in sports than our other forms—though if we look closely we might see signs of similar developments in other sporting endeavors.

[1] Gerald W. Morton and George M. O'Brien, *Wrestling to Rasslin': Ancient Sport to American Spectacle* (Bowling Green: Bowling Green State University Popular Press, 1985).

[2] Sharon Mazer, *Professional Wrestling: Sport and Spectacle* (Jackson: University Press of Mississippi, 1998).

[3] We must continue to call it sport because the traditions of sport generate the aesthetic frame of wrestling in most respects—though by law professional wrestling is not classified as sport in most places any longer, and has a technical/legal status as "sports entertainment."

[4] Roland Barthes, "The World of Wrestling," in *A Barthes Reader*, edited by Susan Sontag (New York: Hill and Wang, 1982) 22.

[5] Mircea Eliade, *Cosmos and History: The Myth of the Eternal Return* (New York: Harper, 1959) 3.

[6] Eliade, *Cosmos and History*, 3.

[7] Hart is himself the subject of an interesting documentary entitled *Hitman Hart: Wrestling with Shadows*, broadcast on the A & E cable network in December 1998. The film is interesting as straight documentary, but in the world of wrestling one has to be careful and consider how seriously to accept its "reality." In an article entitled "Pinning Reality to the Mat," *Chronicle of Higher Education,* September 24, 1999, B9, Peter Plagens has questioned whether the film is not itself a hoax, similar to, but more complex than those of the wrestling it is about.

CONCLUSION

AN AMERICAN APOTHEOSIS
SPORTS AS POPULAR RELIGION

Joseph L. Price

Religious Dimensions of Sports

Each year, on a Sunday toward the end of January, more than half the American population, and perhaps as much as one-tenth of the entire world's, rivets its attention on a single, remote event. By then, the Super Bowl has dominated public attention for weeks, and viewers tune in to face their televisions like an electronic *qiblah*. In 1985, the Super Bowl commanded such power that the public celebration of Ronald Reagan's inauguration was shifted from the constitutionally required day for the swearing in of elected presidents, January 20, a Sunday, to the following day, a frigid Monday in Washington, DC. Meanwhile, that Sunday in Palo Alto, California, Joe Montana and his crew of San Francisco 49ers commanded full national attention as they beat the Miami Dolphins. The football championship has not only come to take precedence over national political rituals: economic exchanges and entertainment performances have also become dominated by the event. Fans, in fact, spend more money on the Super Bowl—making a pilgrimage to the game; attending parties bedecked with official Super Bowl paraphernalia; placing bets and entering office pools—than Americans spend on traditional religious practices and institutions throughout the entire month.[1]

The religious impact of sports, however, extends beyond the popular fascination with this most prominent national sporting event. Every week during intercollegiate sports seasons, fans orient their schedules toward their team's game, devote their attention to plays and players, and put on masks (painting their faces and bodies, dyeing their hair, and wearing color-coordinated jerseys, jackets, and sweatshirts) to increase their identification with their team. The religious significance of their activity is described succinctly by American philosopher George Santayana, who thought of religion as "another world to live in." Yet Santayana "could not have anticipated how, for many millions of [Americans]…, what he meant by 'religion' would one day be displaced in the most immediate, existential, and emotional sense by organized spectator sports."[2] For tens of millions of devoted fans throughout the country, sports constitute a popular form of religion by shaping their world and sustaining their ways of engaging it. Indeed, for many, sports are elevated to a kind of divine status, in what I would call an American apotheosis.

Sports Illustrated journalist Frank Deford was among the first to identify the kind of religious power that sports exert on modern Americans. Deford suggests that if Marx had lived at the end of the twentieth century in the United States rather than in Victorian England, he would have declared that sports is the opiate of the people, anesthetizing them to the class struggles and focusing their hopes on events that project fulfillment through a vicarious form of participation and through an often delayed form of gratification.[3] This poignant critique of sports and culture also indicts the demise of traditional religion's influence at the end of twentieth century. Other critics have drawn this conclusion more explicitly: "The decline of religion as a source of significant meaning in modern industrialized societies," Joyce Carol Oates avers, "has been extravagantly compensated by the rise of popular culture in general, of which the billion-dollar sports mania is the most visible manifestation."[4]

The fusion of sports and religion is neither eccentric nor particular to modern America. Throughout history, and across multiple cultures in the modern world, mythic and ritual significance has often been recognized in a number of sports events and play activities. In ancient Greece, the Olympic games were only one set of games performed in honor of the gods—for their entertainment—since the gods were thought to be too serious to engage in the recreational play and physical exercise, which they nonetheless enjoyed. In Central America, Mayans played ball games officiated by priests, on courts attached to temples, and with victory perhaps demanding the sacrifice of the team captain. Among the tribes and nations of pre-Columbian Native Americans in North America, the game of lacrosse bore religious weight in its ritual enactment of conflict and combat between contestant tribes, and perhaps in the use of its rackets to forecast or foresee future events. For the Oglala Sioux, the seventh sacred rite of Tapa Wanka Yap, or "the throwing of the ball," combined spiritual and sporting dimensions. In Japan, sumo wrestling tournaments still utilize the Shinto purification rituals of throwing salt, and the space for the matches and the hierarchy of wrestlers reflect certain Shinto values. The physical and mental control demanded by karate and other Asian martial arts can be understood as a spiritual discipline. Eugen Herrigel also discusses Asian traditions and discipline in his well-received *Zen and the Art of Archery*, in which archery is called a sport but is also recognized as a disciplined form of spiritual exercise: the archer seeks to become unified with the bow and the target, precisely by not focusing on the athletic aspects of shooting an arrow. Finally, especially in South America and Europe, the game of soccer promotes a sense of national identity that is rightly considered religious.[5]

In America, sports have been identified as a form of civil religion by Michael Novak, as a form of folk religion by sociologist James Mathisen, and as a form of cultural religion by Catherine Albanese.[6] However, several other scholars—trained in literary critical procedures or historical methods, rather than in religious studies or theology—have challenged whether sports could constitute a religion, which they insist, is characterized by transcendental, sacramental, and uplifting social elements. Sociologist Harry Edwards holds back from calling sports a popular form of religion, suggesting instead that it is "essentially a secular, *quasi-religious* institution. It does not, however, constitute an alternative to or substitute for formal sacred religious involvement."[7] Other scholars who have focused on the similarities between particular sports and religious life concur with Edwards. In his analysis of collegiate football, Edwin Cady examines the ways in which college games provide a cultural spectacle for intensifying and celebrating rivalries. Yet Cady contends that the "Big Game" is not in itself fundamentally religious, since it is not, as he perceives it, essentially sacramental. Nevertheless, he allows that the "Big Game" might feel sacramental in approximately the same way that good art does, and he identifies the "Big Game" as being "the most vitally folklorist event in our culture."[8] On different grounds, Joan Chandler refuses to classify sport as religion since both priests and believers, on the one hand, and fans and players, on the other hand, would probably not identify the objects of their devotion as addressing or meeting the same needs.[9] Voicing yet another set of concerns, Robert J. Higgs contends that "sports are like religion in many ways just as they are like war in some ways, but they are not equatable with either."[10]

Despite these reservations and protests against classifying sports as religion, it seems reasonable to do so. Even though sports does not have all characteristics of a religion, neither does any particular religious tradition, because such comprehensive definitions of "religion" are simply ideal norms against which actual religions are measured. Likewise, athough Charles Lippy, in his recent study of popular religiosity in America, hesitates to call sports a religion, he does identify a crucial factor for considering sports as a form of popular religion: the media. The incredible growth of spectator sports, he observes, has corresponded to, if not emerged out of, the expansion of media coverage of sports events.[11] Less than three decades ago, for instance, the only sports events that would be televised during weekdays or prime time were the World Series and the Olympics. Triple-header coverage of football games was restricted to the college bowl game day on New Year's. Nowadays, most fall Sundays let couch coaches and quarterbacks view three full NFL games, while channel flipping to at least two others. With cable systems providing increased coverage of college sports, it is possible to view five football games on most Saturdays in season, and to see scores of basketball games throughout the weeks of winter and spring.

As sports coverage of Sunday events began to increase in the mid-1970s, journalist Frank Deford observed that "the churches have ceded Sunday to sports.... Sport owns Sunday now, and religion is content to leave a few minutes before the big games."[12] Not only do the overwhelming majority of Americans identify themselves as sports fans, as mentioned above, but "sport, in its spectatorial and participatory forms, permeates our technological society to the extent that few are left untouched by it."[13] The public's attraction to broadcast sports events represents more than merely the pursuit of entertainment, for "sports affect people, and their lives, far more deeply and for a longer time than mere diversion would."[14]

Among the first scholars to consider the popular religious dimensions of sports in America are sociologist Harry Edwards and theologian Michael Novak, both of whom identify several characteristics common to sports and religion. According to Edwards, these characteristics reflect ideas and images related to deity, authority, tradition, beliefs, faithful followers, ritual sites, and material elements. Superstar athletes correspond to religions' gods and deceased players serve as saints; the coaches and executives who sit on boards and commissions and make and interpret the rules are like religious patriarchs and high councils; the reporters and broadcasters who chronicle sports events and tabulate their statistics are like the scribes of religious traditions; sports trophies and memorabilia are like religious icons; the formally stated beliefs that are commonly accepted about a sport are like religious dogmas; sports stadiums and arenas are like houses of worship; and halls of fame, both the facilities for different sports (e.g., the Baseball Hall of Fame at Cooperstown, New York, and Pro Football's Hall of Fame at Canton, Ohio) as well as the most local of sports "shrines"—trophy cases—are religious shrines. Finally, he identifies the faithful or devoted fans of sports with the true believers of a religious tradition.[15] With these perceptive points, Edwards prompts further reflections on how aspects of sports indeed correspond to elements of religions.

Most of Edwards's connections are drawn from a comparison of sports with theistic, scriptural religious traditions. In particular, his association of superstar athletes with gods calls the accuracy of his comparison into question, because the sports heroes are living, physical, visible actors, while the gods, for all their presence and potency, remain invisible and non-material.[16] Yet historian of religion Charles Prebish supports Edwards in his assessment that sports heroes function as gods. "The child's worship of [baseball great] Ted Williams," Prebish offers, "is no less real than his or her reverential adoration of Christ, and to some, Williams's accomplishments and capabilities in baseball were unquestionably godly."[17]

The reverence and respect accorded to sports heroes and events are not restricted to children or to fans unfamiliar with characteristics of religion. On a Saturday afternoon in late November 1993, more than 7000 professors of religious studies convened at a hotel in Washington, DC for the annual meetings of the two largest professional societies in religious studies. Midway through the afternoon's sessions, a televised event claimed the attention—yea, devotion—of many of the professors. Initially, observers might have thought that the Notre Dame-Boston College football game was quite unlike the religious rituals that the professors studied. But as time wound down in the game, more than a hundred scholars spontaneously gathered around a lobby television set to watch the final kick, and, during the time out called before the snap and placement, several of them fell to their knees in front of the television set or at the edges of their sofas while others sat with hands clasped as though in prayer. When the winning kick went through the goal posts, the players on the field and fans in stands leapt into each other's open embraces and cried with tears of ecstasy, and the scholarly supporters of Boston College turned their faces upward, thrust their arms upright, and shouted and whooped with joy in front of the hotel television. Their posture, volume, and spirit resembled a display of spirit-filled believers shouting, "Hallelujah!" As theologian Michael Novak notes, the joy of victory in an athletic contest often prompts such a religious response, for winning games generates a feeling that "the gods are on one's side, as though one is Fate's darling, as if the powers of being course through one's veins and radiate from one's action—powers stronger than non-being, powers over ill fortune, powers over death," which is sampled in defeat. But victory, Novak asserts, "is abundant life."[18]

In contrast to the jubilation of the Boston College followers, dejected fans of the Fighting Irish reacted with rituals of mourning, first expressing shock that such a "tragedy" (as some of them put it) could occur, then denying that the upset could be real, by proposing scenarios and plays that could have altered the outcome, and finally acknowledging the loss and its pain. "To lose," Novak also notes, "symbolizes death, and it certainly feels like dying; but it is not death." Such a symbolic rehearsal of death, Novak relates, is characteristic of the Christian sacraments of baptism and eucharist, wherein the communicants symbolically experience death and rebirth.[19]

The religious sensibility of sports involves more than the supplanting of divine roles by sports superheroes, or the substitution of religious rites and doctrines with corresponding sports rituals and rules. For the religious sensibility of sports derives from their basic spiritual dimensions and from the public's potential engagement with them. Addressing fundamental questions about the nature of religion and its exemplification in sports, theologian Michael Novak, like Edwards, draws up a list of corresponding facets between sports and religion. But unlike Edwards, Novak does not restrict the foundation for his comparison to a theistic perspective. In contrast to the somewhat tentative identification of sport with religion that Edwards finally affirms, Novak is forthright, even if ambiguous: "Sports *is*, somehow, a religion." Throughout *The Joy of Sports*, Novak celebrates the spiritual dimensions and impact of sports, revels in various acts of sporting competition and in the admiration of sports heroes, and, particularly in his chapter "The Natural Religion," specifies the fundamental correspondence between sports and religion—that they are "organized and structured." Like religions, which "place us in the presence of powers greater than ourselves, and seek to reconcile us to them," sports help participants to confront the uncertainties of "Fate" by playing out contingencies in games, and by recognizing the role that chance plays in the outcome of contests.

Religions regularly help persons to confront their anxieties and dreads about failure, aging, betrayal, and guilt, while competitive sports consistently engage participants in situations that "embody these in every combat." Because both athletes and believers espouse a self-imposed discipline of their physical bodies to their wills, they develop "character through patterns of self-denial, repetition, and experiment."[20]

Novak also identifies sports with religion by remarking that both establish high standards of expectation, demand discipline, and strive toward perfection. Such pursuit of excellence creates and cultivates a climate of reverence—in religious traditions, manifest in devotion to saints; in sports activities, evident in celebration of heroes. In addition, Novak notes, religions normally create a sense of belonging by focusing initially on the bonding of local communities. This sense of affiliation becomes a paradigm for the germination and nurture of larger commitments—from local to national, from earthly to universal. Sports similarly generate a sense of identity with "the home team" and the loyalty that such a self-understanding entails. One of the means for generating this group identity is through rituals that are common to both religions and sports: even as religions use chants and songs and certain gestures, so too do sports bond teammates and fans together by using cheers ("Two bits, four bits, six bits, a dollar: All for our team, stand up and holler") and songs ("Take Me Out to the Ball Game," which features the call to "root, root, root for the home team," during the seventh inning stretch, or the school "fight song" at football games) and bodily movement (clapping, giving "high fives," slapping each other on the back, and so on). With each of these forms of acting and interacting, fans and players unite as a single body.

The Spirituality of Sports

Underlying these common facets of religion and sports is the experience of *flow*, which Mihaly Csikszentmihalyi defines as "the state in which people are so involved in an activity that nothing else seems to matter; the experience itself is so enjoyable that people will do it even at great cost, for the sheer sake of doing it." Applying his insights on the psychology of optimal experience to persons' participation and performance in sports and games, Csikszentmihalyi recognizes that such opportunities go beyond the boundaries and expectations of ordinary experience. Temporarily set apart from ordinary folks during sports contests and performances, players and spectators cease to act in terms of common sense, and concentrate instead on the peculiar reality of the game.

Such flow activities have as their primary function the provision of enjoyable experiences…. Because of the way [that sports] are constructed, they help participants and spectators achieve an ordered state of mind that is highly enjoyable.[21]

"The peculiar reality of the game," as Csikszentmihalyi refers to it, constitutes the core of the spiritual power and religious significance of sports, and develops out of their ritual aspects—the game's time, space, rules, and purposes. In ritual and in play, Johan Huizinga noted, performance space is set aside, demarcated as the "field of play" wherein a certain set of rules apply. During play or ritual, performance takes shape in a time of its own, certainly surrounded or engulfed by the chronometric measure of ordinary time but set off in such a way that the duration of the game conforms to a different standard of temporal computation, as in the play of baseball with its "innings" or in tennis with its sets and matches. Even the games that utilize a clock, such as football and basketball, run the clock and stop it at appointed times, measuring game time according to a different set of rules than those that govern the calculation of ordinary time. Finally, special rules within the designated space and time for play, such as rules regulating tackling (allowed in football but impermissible in ordinary relations) and taunting (forbidden in basketball, but not in ordinary affairs), create a microcosm, an area and time within whose confines an order is established.[22]

Like Huizinga, historian of religions Mircea Eliade recognizes the worldmaking functions of ritual, although he takes a somewhat different perspective regarding their purpose. Eliade applies the concepts of ritual space and time to his analysis of humans as *homo religiosus*: for him, the categories of time and space provide the orientation for cosmicization, or the development of a worldview, construing and maintaining one's way of being in the world. All such acts of cosmicization are fundamentally religious because the establishment of order in a new world—even one such as that of a game—replicates the cosmogonic act of the gods in the creation of the world. Sacred time, like play time, is discontinuous with ordinary time. It is reversible and replicable, a different realm of time in which one might forget ordinary time.[23] Like priests performing and laypersons attending religious rites, athletes and spectators lose track of ordinary time when the game is good—when the intensity of play fully engages the participants. It is a realm of time that is satisfying in itself, because the actions that take place within it are meaningful within the time frame itself, although they may express meaning beyond the block of sacred time or may provide release from the strictures of ordinary time.

Obviously, sports do not constitute a religion in the same sense that Christianity and Islam, Buddhism and Taoism are religions. But sports are "a form of religion," as Novak simply puts it, because they provide "organized institutions, disciplines, and liturgies" and because they "teach religious qualities of heart and soul. In particular, they recreate symbols of cosmic struggle, in which human survival and moral courage are not assured."[24] Through their symbols and rituals, sports provide occasions for experiencing a sense of ultimacy and for prompting personal transformation.

The kinds of personal and social transformations that sports proffer do not depend upon winning a game or achieving a personal best performance in a contest, although both may certainly generate religious experiences. Instead, the transformative potential of sports themselves extends to all participants, whether or not competition is undertaken. The transformative potential of sports involves, as Charles Prebish puts it, "redemption as well as rebirth into a new type of reality, separated from ordinary reality by its sense of being permeated with ultimacy and holiness, with beauty and freedom."[25] The ultimacy or holiness of the religious experience derives from its location, not in a remote realm of transcendence, but in a sense of alterity generated by the freedom and beauty of the sports activity itself.

When considering the significance of sports as religion, one can distinguish between the sport's spiritual presence and power for athletes, and fans' allegiance to teams and heroes. In established religious traditions, it is not uncommon for priests and laypersons to enjoy various levels of engagement and enrichment in their religious exercise; so too with sports, wherein athletes experience dimensions of selfhood and the quest for perfect performance in ways strikingly different from the experiences of fans.

In her examination of the spiritual experiences of athletes in competition, even where that competition is simply a struggle with oneself to achieve a "personal best" performance, Carolyn Thomas draws inspiration from Jean-Paul Sartre's assertion in *Being and Nothingness* that a person's goal is "to attain himself [or herself] as a certain being, precisely the being, which is in question to his [or her] being." For athletes, Thomas claims, "sport is a lived experience that, despite teammates or fans, is ultimately a solitary quest that reflects highly individual, personal, and subjective intents." Serious athletes, she asserts, "often unknowingly...enter the world of sports in search of self, in search of the reality of a given moment, in search of truth."[26] To engage the most profound level of truth requires that one become introspective and meditative, opening oneself to the Other that resides at the innermost dimension of self. In this sense, then, sports constitute an essential, spiritual pursuit—seeking truth and self-awareness.

> When performers voluntarily enter sport and commit their whole beings to the sport experience, they transcend, or go beyond, outside distractions to a fusion of subject and object that allows them to know both the sport and self in an authentic, profound, special, and very individual way. It is this kind of "knowing" that has the potential to provide a source of meaning, a sense of purpose, and a basis for self-understanding.[27]

Although an athlete might articulate this self-understanding following a performance, he or she might not be conscious of this knowing dimension during the performance itself. In fact, the opposite is probably the case, according to Phil Jackson, coach of the Chicago Bulls, son of Pentecostal ministers, and student of Zen Buddhism. The secret for playing basketball well, he says, is "*not* thinking": a Buddhist sense of being aware of what everyone on the court is doing and responding to, interacting with, and directing the flow of the game, precisely by *not* thinking.[28] The self-awareness that, upon reflection, leads to an articulation of self-understanding and disclosure of truth is the experience of flow.

A casual observer, of course, would be unlikely to perceive the pursuit of self-awareness and truth in a Division I intercollegiate contest, because of corruption, attempts by some players and coaches to win at all costs, booster clubs that provide illegitimate support for certain players and teams, and the like. "Often portrayed in terms of greed, egocentricity, and immorality, these [Division I] forms of sport...that focus on competitive ends...seem a far cry from a historic dependence on religion." But even in such contexts, Thomas concludes, sport "provides a place where people can dominate fear and passion; a place where adventure and purpose and commitment can remove a sense of dread that may otherwise prevail."[29]

The spiritual experience of athletes in their performance of sport is not only the introspective pursuit of personal, foundational truths, but also includes their appreciation of simplicity and harmony in team play, and their quest for a perfectly synchronized performance. This quest for perfection arises out of the fundamental human dissatisfaction and uneasiness that constitute the human condition, but "sports nourish this drive [toward perfection] as well as any other institution in our society."[30] Even when the pursuit of a perfect performance in sports becomes corrupted or distorted—when it moves toward selfish goals rather than the joy and disclosive possibilities of play itself—it still manifests the fundamental human desire for fulfillment. The willingness to subject personal preferences to the good of the team constitutes the basic religious aspect of team sports. "Even for those who don't consider themselves 'spiritual' in a conventional sense, [the process of] creating a successful team—whether it's an NBA champion or a record-setting sales force—is essentially a spiritual act," asserts Phil Jackson. "It requires the individuals involved to surrender their self-interest for the greater good so that the whole adds up to more than the sum of its parts."[31]

Devotion to Sports

In contrast to an athlete's experience of spiritual harmony in team play, fans manifest the religious power of sports in their expressions of allegiance and respect. A most explicit recent example of this devotion was the "religious overtone," as Phil Jackson put it, of the press coverage when Michael Jordan contemplated returning to the Bulls following his eighteen-month retirement. "Perhaps it was just a reflection of the spiritual malaise in the culture and the deep yearning for a mythic hero who would set us free," Jackson mused. "Whatever the reason, during his hiatus from the team, Michael had somehow been transformed in the public mind from a great athlete to a sports deity." In yearning for the possibility of his return—expecting almost an eschatological second coming of sorts—some of the most fervent fans made their way to the United Center, where the Bulls play their home games, and knelt and prayed at the foot of Jordan's statue—a shrine to his transcending the court, his being "Air Jordan."[32]

Certainly, sports fans exhibit a kind of devotion that often is described in terms of religious dedication or intensity. They express their fervor not only in the religious rituals of supplication for success, but also in the negative expressions of prayer for others' destruction or failure. In the Puerto Rican town of San Germán, Jackson recalls, "the fans hated the Gallitos [Jackson's team] so much that they lit candles the night before we arrived and prayed for our death."[33] The most extreme form of this attitude is surely that of the Colombian soccer fans who assassinated Andres Escobar for having accidentally scored a goal against his own team in the 1994 World Cup competition. Most fans, of course, do not resort to death threats and murder but they express their dedication and devotion by the size of wagers on favorite teams, the extent to which they will go—the sacrifices that they will make—in order to make a pilgrimage to an important game, and the ludic masking that they often assume in order to establish full identity with their favorite team or its mascot.

One of the most vivid displays of a fan's devotion to a sport occurs in *Bull Durham*, the popular, romantic baseball movie. The opening sequence behind the credits features sepia tones of photographs from the collection of Annie Savoy, whose wall gallery serves as a sort of shrine to bygone baseball superheroes and their seemingly cosmic feats. The soundtrack features a blues singer wailing "Yes, yes, yes" (a secular rendition of "Amen," which translates "so be it") to a mournful gospel melody. Then we hear Annie deliver her confession:

> I believe in the Church of Baseball. I've tried all of the major religions and most of the minor ones. I've worshipped Buddha, Allah, Brahma, Vishnu, Síva, trees, mushrooms, and Isadora Duncan.
>
> I know things. For instance, there are 108 beads in a Catholic rosary and there are 108 stitches in a baseball. When I learned that I gave Jesus a chance. But it just didn't work between us. The Lord laid too much guilt on me.
>
> I prefer metaphysics to theology. You see, there's no guilt in baseball, and it's never boring....
>
> I've tried 'em all, I really have. And the only church that truly feeds the soul day in and day out is the Church of Baseball.[34]

Annie's experience of awe and sustenance in baseball is not merely aligned with her annual romantic liaison with one of the Durham Bulls. Her enduring love is for baseball, the game itself, and the way that it makes sense out of life.

What Annie seems to sense in her devotion to baseball is that somehow the game of baseball dramatizes a myth, a set of contingent relations or a display of possible outcomes in ways that make life meaningful. Scholars have also proposed that baseball enacts elements of a myth whose meaning often corresponds to its athletes' and fans' hopes. For example, A. Bartlett Giamatti, former commissioner of Major League Baseball, suggests that baseball's space and rules correspond in many respects to the ancient omphalos myth, which reflects upon the creation and ordering of the world from the center of the earth, often a cosmic mountain.[35]

In addition to personal acts of fan devotion such as Annie Savoy's, the group behavior of fans also has religious import. According to a *Sports Illustrated* survey in the 1970s, three-fourths of Americans identified themselves as sports fans.[36] In 1990, the Indiana State High School tournament's championship game hosted 41,046 fans, a national record, in the Hoosier Dome at Indianapolis. "Hoosier Hysteria"—Indiana's obsessive love of basketball, especially at the high school level—has been called the state's religion; "and indeed it is the church and the team," Barry Temkin observes, "that stand as the two most important institutions in many a town—and not necessarily in that order."[37]

The expressions of devotion by fans are not restricted to fervent individuals; they also extend to communities that often establish their identity by supporting their local team and celebrating its heroes. One of the memorable scenes in the popular basketball film *Hoosiers* reflects such devotion by an entire community, as the headlights on a caravan of cars light the town's pilgrimage to an "away game" on a Friday night. In Kentucky, too, the reverence, hope, and community bonding associated with high school basketball can be seen in the fact that the Metcalf County High School gymnasium, for instance, seats more fans than the population of Edmonton, the town where it is located. A similar phenomenon has been chronicled by H. G. Bissinger in *Friday Night Lights*, an analysis of a season in the life of the Permian Panthers (Odessa, Texas), and of the community's dreams for justification and validation in terms of the success of the high school football team. In Kentucky, part of a community's dream is that the local high school stars might become immortal by playing for the vaunted University of Kentucky Wildcats. When at the start of his junior year of high school Metcalf County star point guard J. P. Blevins signed a letter of intent to attend Kentucky, the gymnasium was filled as the entire community celebrated his accomplishment, not merely as a rite of passage for a budding star's achievement but as an enduring validation of their own way of life and their love of Kentucky Wildcats basketball.[38]

Challenges for Sports and Faith

There are at least three points of continuing concern for those who wrestle with comparing the religious creed with the code of the sports cult. The first issue is a theological one. Although religions do not necessarily involve the worship of "God" or "gods," they do orient their followers toward an ultimate force or pantheon of powers, whether personalized as "gods" or whether identified in abstracted ways, for example Buddhism's path of enlightenment or Shinto's abiding sense of family and tradition. One of the primary challenges for religious studies scholars who undertake theological analysis of sports is to identify within sports a source of ultimate powers for evoking and inspiring radical transformation among participants and faithful spectators.

The second issue emerges out of ethical concerns about the inculcation and transmission of values. Not all of the values are negative, as some might want to claim in light of ongoing exposés about athletes' corruption, their appreciation and practice of violence, the cultivation of bodily deformation as a way to achieve success (as with the use of anabolic steroids), and the use of cheating in order to win at any cost. James Mathisen, among others, challenges the naive notion that sports, in and of themselves, promote the building of admirable character.[39] It should be noted, however, that not all religions adopt and encourage humanistic, pacifistic, and compassionate values; so the critique of sports on the grounds that they promote violence, bodily abuse, and an aggressive competitive spirit does not, of itself, separate sports from established religious traditions.

In any case, many celebrate the beneficent aspects of sports, in contrast to these more negative portrayals of the potential evils in store for sports devotees. Michael Novak, for instance, writes: "Sports are our chief civilizing agent. Sports are our most universal art form. Sports tutor us in the basic lived experiences of the humanist tradition."[40] Thus, a challenge for scholars who pursue a religious studies critique of sports is to identify and classify the values in sports that motivate action of players and interaction with and among faithful fans.

Finally, some theological critics have been reticent to consider sports as religion since they recognize that many traditionally pious persons are also avid sports participants and fans. "Is it possible to maintain multilateral religious affiliations? Can the proponent of sport religion also retain standing within his or her traditional religious affiliation?" Prebish asks. "Ostensibly no!" he responds, reasoning that anyone who identifies sports as his or her religion would be "referring to a *consistent pursuit* that is also the *most important pursuit* and a *religious pursuit*. If this individual were to then state that he or she is also a Jew or a Protestant or a Catholic or whatever," Prebish concludes, "he or she would be referring to *cultural heritage only*, to the complex series of factors that are essentially ethnic and locational rather than religious."[41] This conflict arises most frequently out of monotheistic concerns, since in monotheistic traditions true believers can adhere to only one form of faith. However, if we recognize, with historians of religion like Mircea Eliade, that it is possible for persons to be simultaneously religious in apparently competing ways, then a new respect for pluralism might arise, and we could consider ways to appreciate the rhythmic or antagonistic forces for allegiance among devoted fans who are also faithful followers of an established religious tradition.

In short, although difficulties exist in trying to specify exactly the nature and extent of sports as religion, sports do exhibit many of the characteristics of established religious traditions. Most importantly, they exercise a power for shaping and engaging the world for millions of devoted fans throughout America; they enable participants to explore levels of selfhood that otherwise remain inaccessible; they establish means for bonding in communal relations with other devotees; they model ways to deal with contingencies and fate while playing by the rules; and they provide the prospect for experiencing victory and thus sampling, at least in an anticipatory way, "abundant life." In America, quite simply, sports constitute a form of popular religion.

[1] See Joseph L. Price, "The Super Bowl as Religious Festival," *Christian Century*, February 22, 1984, 190-91. Statistics about the extent of gambling on the Super Bowl appear in Bill Christine, "The Big Gamble," *Los Angeles Times*, February 3, 1999, D1, D6.

[2] Joyce Carol Oates, "Lives of the Latter-Day Saints," *Times Literary Supplement*, July 12, 1996, 9. According to Ninian Smart, "the heart of the modern study of religion is the analysis and comparison of worldviews," which include the "history and nature of the beliefs and symbols which form a deep part of the structure of human consciousness and society." *Worldviews: Crosscultural Explorations of Human Beliefs* (New York: Charles Scribner's Sons, 1983) 3, 2.

[3] Frank Deford, "Religion in Sport," *Sports Illustrated* (April 19, 1976): 91. Although Deford himself does not draw the analogy out in quite the way that I have laid it out, his remark sparked several subsequent interpretations in the manner that I have suggested.

[4] Oates, "Lives of the Latter-Day Saints," 9.

[5] For an excellent introduction to the religious functions of the Greek Olympiad, see Judith Swaddling, *The Ancient Olympics* (Austin: University of Texas, 1984). For an explanation of the Mesoamerican game of ball, see S. Jeffrey K. Wilkerson, "And Then They Were Sacrificed: The Ritual Ballgame of Northeastern

Mesoamerica through Time and Space," in Vernon L. Scarborough and David R. Wilcox, eds., *The Mesoamerican Ballgame* (Tucson: University of Arizona Press, 1991) 45-71. For information about the religious significance of lacrosse, see Stewart Culin, *Games of the North American Indians* (New York: Dover, 1975 [republication of the *Twenty-fourth Annual Report of the Bureau of American Ethnology to the Smithsonian Institution, 1902-1903*]) 563 ff. For an exploration of the religious origins of the rite of throwing the ball, see *Black Elk Speaks. The Sacred Pipe: Black Elk's Account of the Seven Rites of the Oglala Sioux*, recorded and edited by Joseph Epes Brown (New York: Penguin Books, 1971) 127-38. For an examination of the spiritual challenge of archery, see Eugen Herrigel, *Zen in the Art of Archery*, trans. R. F. C. Hull, with an introduction by D. T. Suzuki (New York: Vintage Books, 1971). For a discussion of the spiritual dimensions of the martial arts, see, for example, Peter Payne, *Martial Arts: The Spiritual Dimension* (New York: Crossroad, 1981). For an imaginative, literary exploration of the connections between discipline, spirituality, and one of the martial arts, see Harry Crews, *Karate Is a Thing of the Spirit* (New York: William Morrow, and Company, 1971). For an analysis of Brazilian soccer as a civil religion, see "Sports *in* Society: *Futebol* as National Drama," in Gregory Baum and John Coleman, eds., *Sport*, "Concilium: Religion for the Eighties" (Edinburgh: T & T Clark, 1989) 57-68.

[6] Michael Novak, *The Joy of Sports: End Zones, Bases, Baskets, Balls, and the Consecration of the American Spirit* (New York: Basic Books, 1976) 18-34; James A. Mathisen, "From Civil Religion to Folk Religion: The Case of American Sport Sport," in *Sport and Religion*, ed. Shirl J. Hoffman (Champaign IL: Human Kinetics Books, 1992) 17-33, especially 21-24; Catherine Albanese, *America: Religions and Religion* (Belmont CA: Wadsworth, 1981) 322.

[7] Harry Edwards, *Sociology of Sport* (Homewood IL Dorsey Press, 1973) 90, emphasis added.

[8] Edwin Cady, *The Big Game: College Sports and American Life* (Knoxville: University of Tennessee Press, 1978) 78.

[9] Joan Chandlers "Sport Is Not a Religion," in Hoffman, *Sport and Religion*, 55.

[10] Robert J. Higgs, "Muscular Christianity, Holy Play, and Spiritual Exercises: Confusion about Christ in Sports and Religion," *Arete* 1:1 [1983], 63. Since publishing his essay in the initial issue of *Arete*, the journal sponsored by the Sports Literature Association, Higgs has published a more expansive study of the convergence of sports, religion, the military, and education: *God in the Stadium: Sports and Religion in America* (Lexington: University Press of Kentucky, 1995). Rather than focusing on issues pertaining to the exercise or perception of sports as religion, however, the work studies the development of "muscular Christianity" or "Sportianity" in America.

[11] Charles H. Lippy, *Being Religious, American Style: A History of Popular Religiosity in the United States* (Westport CT: Praeger Publishers, 1994) 228.

[12] Frank Deford, "Religion in Sport," *Sports Illustrated* (April 19, 1976): 92, 102.

[13] Carolyn Thomas, "Sports," in Peter Van Ness, *Spirituality and the Secular Quest* (New York: Crossroad Press, 1996) 506.

[14] Novak, *Joy of Sports*, 26.

[15] Edwards, *Sociology of Sport,* 261-62. Cf. M. C. Kearl: "Like religion, professional sports use past generations as referents for the present and confer conditional immortality for their elect through statistics and halls of fame" (quoted in Mathisen, "From Civil Religion to Folk Religion," 24.) Then Mathisen comments: "In our desire to fix in time the achievements of those we look back upon as our representatives for time immemorial, we attribute a sense of sanctity to them and their accomplishments.... When a record is broken in sport, we are both happy and sad. Not only has immortality been achieved, but previous immortality proves to have been conditional and so has been stolen from our midst. Maybe we should place an asterisk next to the new record, just to ensure that we do not lose sight of the former one and of the hero who established it."

For a specific connection of superstar Michael Jordan with a kind of deific projection, see Jim Naughton, *Taking to the Air: The Rise of Michael Jordan* (New York: Warner Books, 1992) 134. Naughton reminds us of the warning of former sportswriter Red Smith against the "godding up of ballplayers," and

Naughton also suggests that, with Jordan's air quality, he embodies the nearest thing to transcendence that we are likely to see.

[16]Cf. Oates, "Lives of the Latter-Day Saints," 9: "For the 'sports fan' the team or idolized athlete provides a kind of externalized soul: there to be celebrated or reviled but, as the God of the ages apparently was not, *there* in full public view."

[17]Charles S. Prebish, *Religion and Sport: The Meeting of Sacred and Profane* (Westport CT: Greenwood Press, 1993) 64.

[18]Novak, *Joy of Sports*, 47-48.

[19]Novak, *Joy of Sports*, 21.

[20]Novak, *Joy of Sports*, xi (emphasis added), 29-30.

[21]Mihaly Csikszentmihalyi, *Flow: The Psychology of Optimal Experience* (New York: Harper & Row, 1990) 4, 72.

[22]Johan Huizinga, *Homo Ludens: A Study of the Play-Element in Culture* (Boston: Beacon Press, 1955) 1-27. In an effort to connect modern sports to its origins in play and ritual, then, Allen Guttmann has written three distinct volumes that always implicitly, and occasionally explicitly, comment on the religious significance of American sporting events, especially for the fans. Guttmann's earliest work, *From Ritual to Record: The Nature of Modern Sports*, includes the trenchant observation that "one of the strangest turns in the long, devious route that leads from primitive ritual to the World Series and the *Fussballweltmeisterschaft* is the proclivity of modern sports to become a secular kind of faith." (New York: Columbia University Press, 1978) 25. See also Allen Guttmann, *Sports Spectators* (New York: Columbia University Press, 1986), and Allen Guttmann, *A Whole New Ballgame: An Interpretation of American Sports* (Chapel Hill: University of North Carolina Press, 1988), especially chaps. 2, 5, and 6, in which Guttmann treats "The Sacred and the Secular" in Native American games, "The National Game" (implying a national identity—and perhaps civil religion—associated with baseball), and "Muscular Christianity."

[23]Mircea Eliade, *The Sacred and the Profane*, trans. Willard R. Trask (New York: Harcourt, Brace, and Co., 1959), chaps. 1-2, especially pp. 30-34.

[24]Novak, *Joy of Sports*, 31, 21.

[25]Novak, *Joy of Sports*, 70.

[26]Thomas, "Sports," 498-99.

[27]Ibid., 509-510.

[28]Phil Jackson and Hugh Delehanty, *Sacred Hoops: Spiritual Lessons of a Hardwood Warrior* (New York: Hyperion, 1995) 115.

[29]Thomas, "Sports," 502, 508.

[30]Novak, *Joy of Sports*, 27.

[31]Jackson, *Sacred Hoops*, 5, 11-12.

[32]Jackson, *Sacred Hoops*, 16-17.

[33]Jackson, *Sacred Hoops*, 70-71.

[34]Ron Shelton, *Bull Durham* (Los Angeles: Orion Home Video, 1989).

[35]A. Bartlett Giamatti, *Take Time for Paradise: Americans and Their Games* (New York: Summit Books, 1989) 86ff. For an alternate application of the omphalos myth to baseball, see my essay in this volume, "The Pitcher's Mound as Cosmic Mountain." An interpretation of football as reflecting distinct American myths can be found in my brief essay "The Super Bowl as Religious Festival," also collected in this volume. Myths, although they are more ambiguously suggested, underlie basketball, according to Phil Jackson, *Sacred Hoops*, 7.

[36]Cited in Prebish, *Religion and Sport*, xiii.

[37]Barry Temkin, "Indiana's 'Impossible Dream' May Soon Be No More," [originally published in the *Chicago Tribune*] reprinted in the *Denver Post*, February 11, 1996, C3.

[38]Mark Woods, "Basketball prodigy a Kentucky blueblood," [originally published in the *Louisville Courier-Journal*] reprinted in the *Denver Post*, February 2, 1997, C11. Cf. H. C. Bissinger, *Friday Night Lights: A Town, a Team, and a Dream* (Reading MA: Addison-Wesley Publishing Company, 1990).

[39]Mathisen, "From Civil Religion to Folk Religion," 22.

[40]Novak, *Joy of Sports*, 27. In another essay in his collection, he promotes the potential good in sports even more hopefully: Novak testifies: "What I have learned from sports is respect for authenticity and individuality (each player learning his own true instincts, capacities, style); for courage and perseverance and stamina; for the ability to enter into defeat in order to suck dry its power to destroy; for harmony of body and spirit.... In sports, law was born and also liberty, and the nexus of their interrelation. In sports, honesty and excellence are caught, captured, nourished, held in trust for the generations" ("The Metaphysics of Sports," 43).

[41] Prebish, *Religion and Sport*, 72.

INDEX

D

E

F